CAREER LIMITING MOVES
Interviews, Rejoinders, Essays, Reviews

CAREER LIMITING MOVES

INTERVIEWS, REJOINDERS, ESSAYS, REVIEWS

ZACHARIAH WELLS

BIBLIOASIS
WINDSOR, ONTARIO

FIRST EDITION

Library and Archives Canada Cataloguing in Publication

Wells, Zachariah, 1976-
[Essays. Selections]
  Career limiting moves : interviews, rejoinders, essays, reviews / Zachariah Wells.

Issued in print and electronic formats.
ISBN 978-1-927428-35-1 (pbk.).-- ISBN 978-1-927428-36-8 (epub)

  1. Canadian poetry (English)--20th century--History and criticism. I. Title.

PS8155.W34 2013   C811'.5409   C2013-903209-6
                                             C2013-903210-X

Edited by Dan Wells
Copy-edited by Allana Amlin
Typeset by Chris Andrechek
Cover Designed by Kate Hargreaves

 Canada Council
for the Arts
Conseil des Arts
du Canada
 ONTARIO ARTS COUNCIL
CONSEIL DES ARTS DE L'ONTARIO
50 YEARS OF ONTARIO GOVERNMENT SUPPORT OF THE ARTS
50 ANS DE SOUTIEN DU GOUVERNEMENT DE L'ONTARIO AUX ARTS

 Canadian
Heritage
Patrimoine
canadien

Biblioasis acknowledges the ongoing financial support of the Government of Canada through the Canada Council for the Arts, Canadian Heritage, the Canada Book Fund; and the Government of Ontario through the Ontario Arts Council.

PRINTED AND BOUND IN CANADA

Contents

INTERVIEW

In memory of Andrew Bruce Wells,
who made me love a good fight.

INTRODUCTION

THIS IS WHERE I'M SUPPOSED to tell you how bad things are in the world of contemporary poetry and what I'm doing to correct our wayward course. This is where I'm supposed to strop my knives and grind my axes. This is where I should be promulgating my aesthetic platform and denigrating anyone with the bad taste to diverge from it. Right? Well, was I ever possessed of such puerile intentions, I'm glad to say I've long outgrown them. Besides the fact that I'm leery of totalizing syntheses—which tell us far more about a critic than about what she's criticizing—I am more than a little surprised to be writing this at all. If you told me ten years ago that I'd be publishing a book about poets and poetry, I'd have snorted.

Ten years ago, I had dropped out of grad school and but a scattered few of my poems had graced the pages of marginal magazines. (Does anyone else remember *The Amethyst Review*?) Working as an airline cargo agent in Resolute Bay, Nunavut, I found myself about as far as you can get from a literary scene without leaving the planet's atmosphere. My obscurity caused me no unease, nor was I cut off from the outside world; I had a dial-up internet connection, an IBM ThinkPad and all manner of time on my hands. One day, I came across the website Bookninja.com, thanks to a link from Goodreports.net, a site I frequented.

Identifying myself only by my initials, I started weighing in on Bookninja's lively discussion boards. Whatever I was blathering on about caught the eye of George Murray, one of the site's adminis-trators, and we started having a bit of back-channel palaver. At his request, I sent George some of my poems. George then introduced me to Paul Vermeersch, who asked me for a poetry manuscript, which he accepted in short order and published the following year as *Unsettled*, my first trade collection. George, an editor for *Maisonneuve*, gave me an online poetry column, which we called "The Zed Factor."

Carmine Starnino also liked the cut of my cyber jib. Carmine and I had met briefly once or twice in Montreal, where I'd attended Concordia University for a couple of terms and where I spent my weeks off from the Resolute job. But now he started giving me space in *Books in Canada* for longer review-essays. He and George also co-published "Strawman Dialectics," a position paper I wrote before I'd done much of anything by way of reviews, but the ethos of which I still stand behind, having now reviewed well over 150 titles. That essay has pride of place in this book because good arguments have much more value than the feelings of individual artists—and because bad arguments from authority need to be challenged.

So, if you're one of those people who wishes I'd never turned my hand to criticism, now you know who to blame. But my persistent pursuit of this venal pastime is on me. Turns out I like it. Reviewing, you see, constitutes a formal and disciplined manifestation of my favourite indoor sport: arguing. I grew up in a political household and extended family, in which one member was more likely to call another member a moron for their views on the prohibition of hard drugs than to say "I love you" or "good night." Dinner guests would leave our house shaking their heads, convinced that we hated each other, but for us Wellses, an intemperate set-to possessed no greater personal significance than a hug. (We've never been much on hug-ging.) It could get ugly. I remember my mom's sister, visiting from Ottawa with her mild-mannered RCAF General husband, defend-ing, over supper, Bush Jr.'s invasion of Iraq. There wasn't much left of her once my dad and I got through ridiculing her reasons—they were ridiculous—and she clearly found the experience much less amusing than we did.

We didn't set out to hurt my aunt's feelings, but by bringing up the topic, she might as well have cried, "Release the hounds!" And so it goes with publishing. You put your work out into the world and someone, sometime is bound to say something nasty about it. If you're lucky. Most publications draw neither praise nor fire. While I've been decried as snarky by a few who'd prefer us all to sing Kumbaya and save the sniping for private convos, and while I've had everything from my psychological well-being to my motives to my manly bits questioned, my actual motivation comes from nothing so much as a yen for a good scrum. I'm with Angela Carter, who said that a day without an argument is like an egg without salt. (I prefer pepper, myself.) If, on occasion—and if you appraise what follows honestly, you have to admit that I have been by no measure relentless—my arguments have been more forceful, it's either because I'm up against a consensus or because I think that what I'm arguing against, like poor Aunt Ruth's stance on Iraq or Jan Zwicky's take on reviewing, is particularly contemptible— but still likely to be found credible by a dismayingly large cohort of readers. I see no point in gainsaying arguments that would only find traction among the insane and idiotic.

Irritation, alas, is no fuel for long-term endeavour, especially one as poorly paid, time intensive and generally thankless as this one. There are no Canada Council grants or Griffin Prizes for critics. Yea, ire might catalyze an explosion now and again, and I won't deny that the odd piece in this book I wrote "just for badness," as the Newfoundland expression for self-delighting mischief has it, but you will find far more love than anger in these pages and I stand with Nietzsche in insisting that even my naysaying has been a yea-saying; not a blow but an embrace.

If I would have snorted at the idea of this book ten years back, it's because poetry was then, as now, my chief concern and greatest love. In university, I came to see literary criticism as parasitic and trivial, formulaic and uncreative—antithetical to the act of writing poetry itself. Given time away from school and a fresh approach, my view morphed. Criticism, I now see, is not only a gesture of appreciation, but also a process of self-instruction. Writing reviews and essays has led me to read not only more deeply than I might otherwise, but also beyond the pale of my comfort zone: to interrogate my own assumptions about poetry. Inevitably, such venturing has informed, improved and expanded how I write my own poems. Criticism, more than a means of enshrining, flattering and reaffirming my views, has proven a way of cultivating and enriching them.

However malleable it may be though, we can never escape our own subjectivity, and the pieces collected here no doubt betray my biases, inborn and acquired. Any critic's work stands as a kind of alternative autobiography and as a statement of their own values. So it should be. So it has been with the critics whose work has informed my own. I've included two interviews as a reminder to take the rest of the prose for what it is: the product of my personality and of my knowledge as applied diligently to a given text at a given time.

While my writing has managed to alienate a few fragile egos and righteous souls over the years, I mean the title of this book more as joke than lament. Reviewing books has been, if anything, a counterintuitive way for an anti-social lout like me to make friends and attract admirers. Editors have offered me more reviewing work than I can or care to accept and several years ago I started getting unsolicited invitations from publishers—three, besides Biblioasis—to submit a book of essays and reviews. Such a level of interest stuns even me, one of those rare people who enjoys a good sit-down with a collection of occasional criticism. Were it not for busyness and inertia, I might have published a version of this volume three or four years ago. More time in the barrel has not only made the book longer but, I think, far stronger than it might have been. You are, of course, free to disagree.

Zachariah Wells
Halifax, September 6, 2013

REJOINDERS

STRAWMAN DIALECTICS
A Negative Review of Jan Zwicky's Negative Review of
Negative Reviewing

IN A SPECIAL ISSUE of *The Malahat Review* (#144, Fall 2003) devoted to reviewing, philosopher-poet Jan Zwicky takes to task reviewers who take authors to task. She makes many points, most of them dull, in the course of positing several arguments, all tendentious, often specious and occasionally sentimental. But because Dr. Zwicky is a highly regarded figure in our literary world, I fear that her essay will be given more attention and credit than it would merit if delivered by a lesser-known writer.[1] I will therefore endeavour to refute her position point by point.

But before I get to the dropped threads and loose ends of Dr. Zwicky's essay, I would like to shine a light through a gaping rent in its weft. This *abîme* is the fictional character, Negative Reviewer (let's call him Negs for short), who is the antagonist of her story, terrorizing—to death in the case of poor John Keats—the sensitive artists who are her tale's beleaguered heroes. The problem with Negs is that he is a whole cloth invention and bears scant resemblance to any actual flesh-and-blood reviewer. Negs proceeds like a semi-conscious juggernaut; he is a "hit-person"; he "trashes stuff"; he makes "power grab[s]"; he "trust[s] immediate impulse[s] to reject"; he attacks and lays waste like a barbarian in a Roman bath. He is emotionally retarded and possibly sociopathic. He is a caricature, a composite perhaps of the

---

1 Indeed, some nine years after its initial publication, it was reanimated—unrevised—online by Canadian Women in the Literary Arts, whereupon it went viral.

more vitriolic sides of Solway, Sarah, Starnino, Houlihan, Henighan, Metcalf, Marchand, et al. Unfortunately, Zwicky does not deign to name names in her piece—presumably because this would be "mean-spirited," and would reveal her essay actually to be what it claims to repudiate—so all we're left is poor, silly little Negs with his impoverished soul, myopic vision and narrow mind, stuttering over and over his stunted critical credos. He plays strawman student in this quaint dialectic to Zwicky's sagely ignorant Socrates.

My first objection is perhaps a quibble, but I think it's symptomatic of Zwicky's duplicitous rhetorical strategy. She begins her essay with Byron's supposed lament that "the critics killed Keats." This is an odd quotation to use in an essay of this bent because the poem from which it is pulled is in fact critical of Keats, whom Byron once snarkily called a "pissabed" of no real talent and a "tadpole of the Lakes." For those unfamiliar with it, Byron's satirical quatrain from "John Keats" reads in full:

> Who killed John Keats?
> "I," says the Quarterly,
> So savage and Tartarly;
> "'Twas one of my feats."

This could, perhaps, with an Olympic leap of imagination, be interpreted as damning of the reviewers and not a lampoon of Keats. But why, then, would Byron ask his publisher to suppress it, if not because it was in bad taste to make fun of a dead man? Byron also wrote of Keats's fate in *Don Juan*:

> 'Tis strange the mind, that very fiery particle,
> Should let itself be snuff'd out by an article.

'Tis then rather ironic that Zwicky waxes Byronic. It would seem she should have taken greater care in selecting both champions and villains to tilt for her cause[2]; her knight errant would

---

2   One almost wonders if Zwicky is unaware of Shelley's "Adonais."

rather be sleeping with his sister and her villain is a fabulous phantom.

But let's pretend that Negs' unidimensionality, and the inappropriateness of Byron as defender of the artist's right to be left unmolested, don't fatally compromise Zwicky's thesis. Do the rest of her points hold up under scrutiny?

Zwicky prefaces her disquisition with an Augustinian confession: she too, when she was young and foolish, was a Negs, and how she now regrets and repents the horrible things she once said. She makes "this confession not to try to put the past behind [her], but to make it clear that [she] know[s], from the inside, where the arguments for negative reviewing come from, and that in [her] analysis of the issues [she's] talking as much to [herself] as to others." In other words, she is addressing us sinners as a sinner herself, from ground-level, and not as some impeccable saint on high.[3] The fundamental flaw with this line of thought, as I see it, is that Zwicky falls prey to a common fallacy: she generalizes from a particular. From her intimate knowledge of her particular condition, she extrapolates a universal law, in assuming that her reasons for negative reviewing are the same as everyone else's. Already, she is on epistemological *terra infirma*—but at least she has tipped us off to the fact that she has a history of arguing in bad faith.

She goes on to say that "*the idea that we have a duty to be negative ...* assumes the existence of a canon or at least a standard of excellence." But this is itself an assumption, is it not? Might one not just as easily, and more plausibly, posit that the idea of this duty is the manifestation of a yen for, of a striving towards, such a standard of excellence? An impossible task, surely, but human excellence stems from the pursuit of ideals. Is this not

---

3 We have all done foolish things in our youth which may give us cause for regret. I, for instance, got so drunk when I was fifteen that I had to be hospitalized. How we deal with these mistakes after committing them is a true index of character, of an individual's mettle. If I were to follow Zwicky's line of reasoning after my unfortunate mishap with drink, I should never have touched alcohol again, and gone throughout the land preaching to others the virtues of temperance. This would, however, be an extreme reaction to a stupid mistake.

what distinguishes us from other animals, for better and for worse? Is this not what makes us the singularly fascinating and terrible creatures that we are? Is our *duty* not to be as characteristically human as we can be and not, as Nietzsche famously phrased it, all-too-human? Yes, the suggestion that the canon needs "a cohort of hit-persons … to maintain its authority" *is* "worse than silly," and does not bear examination. But in her essay, this statement is made only by Zwicky, ventriloquized through the mealy mouth of her witless strawman Negs. Perhaps someone somewhere has made such a silly statement at some time, but she fails to establish this with any authority, asking us instead to take her word for it.

Next, Zwicky cautions us to make sure that if we do have the temerity to make a critical judgment, that it "stand the test of time." This is a patent absurdity.[4] As well to say to the artist: before you publish your work, make sure that it will last for perpetuity. Otherwise, you know, don't bother. But Zwicky's caveat is even sillier than this, for the vast majority of criticism, unlike the art and would-be art it considers, makes no bid for immortality. Christian Wiman says that "aiming at eternity with critical prose is like praying to a potato. You may very well get God's attention, but only because He likes a good laugh." The enterprise is, by nature, ephemeral; its arguments are for today and contingent on the circumscribed conditions of the here-and-now.

Not only that, but exceptions to the rule—that rare criticism we still read long after its original publication—often seem downright wrong in retrospect. Consider Ben Jonson's opinion that Donne, "for not keeping of accent, deserved hanging." Or Samuel Johnson on Milton's *Lycidas*:

> In this poem there is no nature, for there is no truth; there is no art, for there is nothing new. Its form is that of a pastoral, easy, vulgar, and therefore disgusting: whatever images it can supply are long ago

---

4 And it raises the inconvenient question: should not positive evaluations also have to meet this exacting standard? If not, why not? Fulsome praise is far more likely than harsh judgment to look silly in the future.

exhausted; and its inherent improbability always forces dissatisfaction on the mind.

How about Randall Jarrell on Auden:

> Auden's desire to get away from the negativism typical of so much modernist poetry has managed to make the worst sections of his latest lyrics not much more than well-meaning gush. These sentimental parodies are far more dangerous than any gross ones could possibly be. If we have wicked things to say, and say them badly, not even the Girl Guides are injured; but if we say badly what is "spiritual and valuable," we not only spoil it, but help to replace or discredit the already expressed good that we wish to preserve.

Which seems awfully *à propos* in the present context. Zwicky might as well have mouthed the famous dictum of one of her favourite philosophers, Wittgenstein: "What we cannot speak about we must pass over in silence." What we cannot speak about, in Zwicky's argument, is poetry we dislike. And a sort of selective silence on the topic is exactly what she recommends, as we shall see.

But before we get to Dr. Zwicky's prescription, we must navigate a rather treacherous divagation she steers into the waters of free speech. She argues that "opinions about theses and arguments are qualitatively different from opinions about artistic achievement"; that one cannot make analogies between reviewing and political debate. Although she discourses at great length on this topic (she herself uses the word "prolix" to describe this passage), she never quite explains why such analogies are untenable, or even why this comparison is relevant to her own thesis and argument, which become vague and extremely tendentious at this point. If anything, public policy *must* be discussed alongside art in this country, where next to no art goes unsupported by one form of government subsidy or another.[5] In our Canadian

---

5   Bert Archer makes this point eloquently in the same issue of *The Malahat Review*.

context, then, the reviewer can be a sort of ombudsman on the lookout for rash *gaspillage* of taxpayer's cash. Better a Negs in this role than some semi-literate zealot from the political right, such as spring up from time to time, denouncing funding for the arts on the basis of Purdy's "The Blue-Footed Booby" or Molly Starlight's *Where Did My Ass Go?*

Speaking of waste, Zwicky says that negative reviews "kill trees."[6] If we're going to get all eco-anxious about publishing, how many more trees are felled by the proliferation of dull, unaccomplished, unsold and unread fiction and verse? Far more, I'd venture to say, than by a few column inches of review space. Should the reviewer not assault such gross and unjustifiable depletion of natural resources? Zwicky's terminology throughout her essay brings to mind another trenchant political analogy: the abortion debate. By insisting on the term "negative reviewer," where a more neutral and less judgmental term like "skeptical reviewer" could—and in my view should—be employed, she is doing the same thing that *soi-disant* Pro-Life activists do when they call Pro-Choicers "murderers." She fails, in other words, to imagine a philosophical system in which a certain kind of review is an ethical choice and not a crime against humanity.[7] The term "negative reviewer" is in and of itself a condemnatory distortion of an aesthetic and ethical sensibility—in other words, exactly what Zwicky claims to dislike.

Zwicky's argument goes from makeshift to gimcrack when she compares negative reviewing to telling a friend that she's fat. This is absurd. Art is something done intentionally and publicly, whereas very few people opt to be overweight on purpose or as a public

---

6 Whereas positive reviews, presumably, are all printed on handmade, unbleached, recycled, post-consumer, ancient forest-friendly sheets, delivered to their readers by horse-drawn wagon.

7 Zwicky dragged her argument to its nadir of cringe-inducing absurdity in 2012 when, in *The National Post*, she likened negative reviewing to rape: "In sexual encounters, our culture condones sadistic behaviour only between consenting adults. I see no reason to think that our standards should be different for critics and the critiqued."

act. And there is no obligation—in fact, it should be avoided in most cases—for the reviewer to have a personal relationship with the author whose work—not person—is under review. If a *doctor* tells you to lose some weight, the appropriate response isn't tears but the treadmill.

If we do tell our friends they're fat, Zwicky remonstrates, we should at least do so using the first person singular, in order to "focalize the reviewer" and eliminate any "illusion of authority." This is one of the only points on which I agree with her, but really, it's a stylistic preference[8] and not terribly significant. Zwicky does not give the anonymous reader—as much of a strawman as poor Negs, in her imagination—much credit for critical judgment, and gives the almighty reviewer entirely too much for her ability to sway the public. It is manifestly clear that a statement made by a reviewer is a subjective opinion, and as such open to debate, whether she says "I think" or "it is."

Zwicky says that the harshest judgment a critic can pass on a work is silence, and that we should "keep our mouths shut" about books we don't like. Very true. As Oscar Wilde wrote in *The Picture of Dorian Gray*: "There is only one thing in the world worse than being talked about, and that is not being talked about." But if you regard this vow of silence within the framework of Zwicky's argument, you start to realize that it rubs against the grain of earlier statements she has made. Think back on her admonition that we make sure what we say stands the test of time. If we ignore certain books altogether, how can we possibly know if our opinions, or the works to which they pertain, have lasting merit? Time cannot judge silence, nor can anyone marshal arguments against it. Is it not the height of egotism to *not* review a book because one doesn't

---

8   An editor I work with once told me to eschew first person. When I told her that I objected to that rule on principle, it was explained to me that the rule is in place to prevent people from indulging in the anecdotal strain of book review that is so prevalent, linking irrelevant details of the reviewer's personal life with the book under review. This narcissistic chattiness seems to me a greater problem than any "illusion of authority"; at least the non-person might help an ill-disciplined reviewer to focus on the task at hand.

like it, to deprive it of exposure and let it slip into obscurity without comment? Does one not owe it to one's art to give everything that aspires towards it a fair shake?

To me, this kind of advice reveals Jan Zwicky's programme for what it really is: sublimated passive aggression. This is not, I believe, an intentionally vicious strategy. Rather, the opposite: it signals an insufficient critical consciousness of the agenda she advances, which is fundamentally anti-intellectual (an odd position for a philosopher to put herself in) and footed on the wobbly post of subjective feelings. Not that emotions should play no role in criticism, but if they're not complemented by razor-sharp thinking, what you get is, to revisit Jarrell's phrase, well-meaning gush.[9]

In the final section of her essay, we get Dr. Zwicky's prescription for healthy reviewing, which involves "listening" and "appreciating," as opposed to "speaking" and "judging." She tells us that the responsible reviewer will be a sort of "literary naturalist"—a precious metaphor which she proceeds to beat to an unseemly death, analogizing meanwhile what she earlier said should be kept discrete (i.e. politics and art)—and advances Hass, Heaney and Dragland as avatars of this desirable style. And I can't fault her choices. Heaney's prose, in particular, occupies a place of honour on my lit-crit shelf. But heaven help me should I be so dogmatic as to assert that his is the only valid mode, or even the best. What I find most pernicious about Zwicky's thesis is its impulse towards homogeneity, towards orthodoxy, towards the erasure of personality and sanctification of a narrow band of approved critical

---

9   Besides ethical and aesthetic considerations, there is a practical dilemma posed by Zwicky's editorial insistence that critics review only books about which they are enthusiastic: How can one possibly know one's response to a book before reading it? If an editor sends a book to a reviewer and the reviewer hates the book, what is to be done? Have the reviewer mail the book back to the editor? Have the publisher send a review copy of another book to another reviewer (who may or may not be favourably disposed towards it)? Have the book go unreviewed because one person happens to dislike it? Does the reviewer forego her fee because she could not produce a sufficiently appreciative piece of prose? Must she lie in order to get paid? Clearly, such a policy opens a Pandora's Box of vexing problems.

manoeuvres: *thou shalt not* is the tone of the piece, however humble it pretends to be. Yes, I love Heaney's criticism, but I also love William Logan's. One is avuncular, the other irascible, but I love them both for the same basic reason: each critic's prose is an emanation of a vital personality.

All of us in our lives require a certain amount of praise, but also a modicum of tough love if we are to develop into well-formed beings. Art, in this regard, is no different from the species that makes it. Zwicky insists, quoting Rilke, that we must evaluate art with love, not criticism. Unfortunately, Rilke misses the point that criticism and love are not mutually exclusive.[10] Or perhaps Zwicky misses the point that not every precious word published in a book amounts to art.

The fundamental problem with Jan Zwicky's essay is that she traffics in untenable dualisms and thereby knots herself into hopeless self-contradictions. The "negative reviewer" she presents is a figment, without whom her argument implodes. The opposite of love, as Elie Wiesel has said, "is not hate, it's indifference." Or, as Jarrell puts it in concluding his above-quoted essay on Auden, "analyses, even unkind analyses of faults, are one way of showing appreciation." While condemning knee-jerk reflexes to reject, Zwicky indulges in her own. Her wistfully romantic position constitutes gross negligence on the part of a philosopher and artist: a willful refusal to see all sides of an issue or, at best, a failure to imagine the world from a perspective other than her own. So much great art, what we now label classics, got hammered out on the anvil of the *agon*, or public contest, with little or no regard for the feelings of the individual artist. So many great works were found wanting, only to resurface triumphantly in a later age; the contempt in which they were held becomes an integral narrative element of their histories and in some cases a spur to creation. Without the critical and commercial "failure" of *Moby Dick*, Melville would never have written *Bartleby the Scrivener*.

---

10   Ironically, Stan Dragland, writing in the same issue of *The Malahat Review*, does not miss this point. "Love," he says, "embraces disagreement."

Being an artist in the public sphere involves consent to, or at least risk of, crucifixion. In some countries, this is no metaphor. Our poets, however, are well enough supported—mentored and nurtured to within an inch of their lives!—that they should be able to take the odd verbal drubbing and trudge on—if they are real artists and not coddled children. With no dissenting opinions, there is no dialectic; culture and art stagnate; we fail to mature and we are left prey to the merciless philistine forces of an agora whose powers of persuasion make nasty book reviewers look like so many slow lorises. Critics—whether their evaluations are positive, negative or, as is most often the case, both and neither—constitute a fierce and loyal rearguard against darkness. May they do so always.

Too Many Michaels
A Review of a Review of a Review and the State of Reviewing in Canada

Dear Internet,

I am writing to you in response to Jonathan Ball's letter to *Geist*,[11] which proffers a review of Michael Hayward's review of Michael Winter's novel *The Architects Are Here*. I have not read Hayward's review, and do not know Hayward or his work. However, I feel nonetheless perfectly equipped to say that I feel this review of a review is typical of the poor quality of complaints about book reviewing in Canadian words. What I tender, then, is a review of a review of a review.

The original review of a review contains thirty sentences. I will comment briefly on some of these sentences in some kind of order.

1. The opening sentence says that Jonathan Ball is writing a response to Michael Hayward's review of Michael Winter's novel *The Architects Are Here*. So far, so good, but I think Mr. Ball would have done well to avoid the repetition of the word Michael. Too many characters with the same name can be confusing. See *Wuthering Heights* or just about any Russian novel.

2. The second sentence informs us that Mr. Ball doesn't really know what he's talking about. This bodes ill for what follows.

11   Jonathan Ball's letter can be read here: http://lemonhound.com/2009/01/16/dear-geist-jonathan-ball-takes-up-the-question-of-reviewing/.

3. The third sentence merely announces the obvious. There is here another gratuitous and entirely avoidable repetition of the word "review." This is bad form, as any workshop leader will tell you.

4. The fourth sentence tells us that the original review contains ten sentences. This factoid imparts nothing of substance about the review itself, nothing at least that can't be gleaned by a quick count of the periods [n.b.: this is an example of how one can avoid excessive repetition of a word] in Hayward's review. Since there is a link to Hayward's review, anyone who wishes to can do so with ease. (I haven't bothered to confirm the accuracy of Mr. Ball's count, since I have no interest in Mr. Hayward's review, nor in the novel about which it is written, since the location in space of architects is not a topic, frankly, that jingles my bells.)

5. The fifth sentence is little better than throat-clearing. If Mr. Ball is going to comment on each of the sentences, he should really just get down to it, *n'est ce pas?*

6. The sixth sentence is not commentary, but summary. Moreover it is summary padded by extraneous quotation that could have been compressed by the use of paraphrase. Furthermore, it contains an incredible improbability, viz. "notes the other books in which English has appeared." Since English has in fact appeared in every book ever written in English, every book ever translated into English and any book in another language that quotes something spoken or written in English, I find it extremely implausible that, as Mr. Ball says, Hayward "notes the other books in which English has appeared." Only one fifth of the way in, Mr. Ball has already stretched credulity beyond the breaking point.

7. The seventh sentence shunts attention away from the review of the review and towards the author of the review of the review,

notably towards his belief that shunting attention away from a novel and towards its author is "an intellectually bankrupt move, yet one still common in the 21st century." Leaving aside the gratuitous use of the dubious temporal label "21st century" (presumably, Mr. Ball is referring to the Common Era) and its reference to the putative life and times of a supposed messiah/divinity, it must be noted that this is an intellectually bankrupt move and already was so late in what is, in the Western World and other benighted nations burdened with the belief that an almighty incorporeal divinity one day planted his seed in the uterus of a virgin, commonly referred to as the 20th Century CE.

8. The eighth sentence informs us of an obvious fact (obvious, at least, if you've read Hayward's review, which, I reiterate, I have not): that Hayward says that recurring characters exist in fiction.

9. The ninth sentence belabours the point made in the eighth sentence and, again, proves nothing about nothing.

10. The tenth sentence (ten of thirty, remember) reminds us that we're already forty percent through Mr. Hayward's review, which anyone who passed grade six mathematics could tell you.

11. The eleventh and twelfth sentences get us to the midway point of Hayward's review, and yet nothing of interest (to me, anyway, but as I said, this is a topic I find rather dull, so perhaps it's best to seek another opinion) concerning that review has been written yet.

12. I will not mention the thirteenth sentence, as I believe this to be bad luck.

13. [Intentionally Left Blank]

14. In the fourteenth sentence, Mr. Ball complains that Mr. Hayward gives no examples of Mr. Winter's "fine writing." Since Mr. Ball has already stated, repeatedly, that Mr. Hayward's review only contains ten—count 'em, ten!—sentences, I can't begin to fathom where he expects Mr. Hayward to deposit the kind of extensive quotation which demonstrations of fine writing require. This is a *novel* Mr. Hayward is talking about (I assume, not having read it or Mr. Hayward's review), not a freakin' haiku.

15. In the fifteenth sentence, Mr. Ball poses a rhetorical question, the answer to which he takes to be given. This is an example of the rhetorical fallacy of logic known as "begging the question." (Not to be confused with the linguistic fallacy of using the phrase "begging the question" when one means to say that the question begs to be asked.) The actual answer to Mr. Ball's question is not "no," as he assumes, but "sometimes."

16. But to say "sometimes" would certainly beggar the rhetorical force of his next sentence, which draws its strength from an unexamined assumption, amongst people who assume that their BA makes them smart, that "readability and narrative speed or suspense" are not literary values.

17. The seventeenth sentence—already seven longer than Hayward's and yet not notably more substantive (I'm guessing)—ignores the fact that Michael Winter himself often makes public statements to the effect that "[Gabriel] English is based on Winter himself." Of course, he doesn't say it quite like that, since he is Michael Winter and referring to oneself by one's own last name is very odd practice, even for a Newfoundlander—albeit a "mainlander" from the "mainland" of England (hence, perhaps, the choice of surname for Winter's fictional alter ego). This is another testament to Mr. Ball not knowing what he is talking about. For instance, Mr. Ball seems to think that a continent

(viz. North America) can have a "fascination for 'true stories.'" One hardly need be a geographer to know that a continent, being an inert land mass, can have a fascination for nothing. This is an example of what is commonly known in critical terminology as an anthropomorphic fallacy. Another example is when Mr. Ball says that fiction has a "secret heart." This is not so much an anthropomorphic fallacy as an anatomical absurdity, since no animal possesses any such organ as a secret heart.

18. The nineteenth sentence claims, in essence, that the point contested in the eighteenth sentence—look it up—"is beside the point and has nothing to do with the novel as it stands." This is redundant. Also, the word "again" is used incorrectly by Mr. Ball, since he did not in fact make this argument beforehand.

19. In the 20ᵗʰ sentence, Mr. Ball makes another argument based on nothing better than his poorly digested education in postmodern literary theory.

20. In the 21ˢᵗ sentence, Mr. Ball assumes that Mr. Hayward is "reproducing [an] assumption." It is by no means clear that this is the case; we have only Mr. Ball's word for it. Also, Mr. Ball's authoritative-sounding statement that the "values of literary realism" are "defunct" is without basis in fact. While one could argue that the subjective free-agent values of literary realism ceded ground to the more empirical, deterministic values of literary naturalism in the late 19ᵗʰ Century (Common Era; see above), it would appear from the number of realist novels being published every year, in this country (viz. Canada) and elsewhere, that the values of literary realism are far from defunct. That Mr. Ball wishes they were so does not change this fact.

21. In the 22ⁿᵈ sentence, Mr. Ball again complains about Mr. Hayward's failure to provide quotations, this time in defense of Mr. Hayward's complaint of an "overabundance of "clutter""

in Mr. Winter's novel. Presumably, Mr. Winter's book, being a novel, is long. Just how Mr. Ball expects Mr. Hayward, in a short review—ten sentences, recall!—to provide quoted examples of longueurs is beyond me. Also, it should be considered that the intentional introduction of "clutter" into a text is stylistically infelicitous.

22. In the 23rd sentence—thirteen more than the original review!—Mr. Ball finally gets to the final sentence of Mr. Hayward's review. This proves Mr. Ball's superiority. Since Mr. Hayward could only dedicate ten measly sentences *to an entire novel*, whereas Mr. Ball has dedicated twenty-three to a measly ten-sentence review, Mr. Ball is clearly the superior critic and his blog a publication infinitely more sophisticated than *Geist* magazine. But wait, there's more to come!

23. In the 24th sentence, Mr. Ball makes a sweeping statement, without citing a single concrete example by way of corroboration. He is also guilty of the fallacious assumption that there are such things as "actual literary qualities," when no such critter has ever been observed on this planet (or on any other, to the best of my knowledge). It would be very helpful to know what Mr. Ball thinks these qualities are. Furthermore, Mr. Ball makes reference to "what fiction is." As far as I know, this is not a settled question; again, if Mr. Ball is going to say that Mr. Hayward doesn't know what it is, it would be very helpful to know what Mr. Ball thinks it is. Other than the obvious, that is: not fact. One thing is certain: fiction, as such, can't "do" anything. Fiction is something made by a human. Humans do things. Like write novels. Which are fiction. Which pretty much just sit there until someone picks them up and reads them. Or decides not to read them. As I have. (It occurs to me now that Mr. Ball's "review of a review" might in fact be a cleverly disguised work of fiction. If this is so, I offer Mr. Ball my hearty congratulations, for he has constructed a truly ingenious artifice.)

24. What sentence are we on again? Oh yes, the 25th. In which Mr. Ball repeats that he has not read Mr. Winter's book, thereby reminding *Geist* why he is ill-qualified to review Mr. Hayward's review.

25. In the 26th sentence, Mr. Ball gives Mr. Hayward—who presumably did read Mr. Winter's book, and bully for him—"the benefit of the doubt and assume[s] that [Mr. Hayward] is correct in his value judgements" [sic]. Isn't this just a little bit rich?

26. In the 27th sentence, Mr. Ball says "only three out of ten sentences has anything of interest to say about the novel." Assuming that Mr. Ball is correct in this assessment (and I can hardly do otherwise, having read neither Mr. Hayward's review, nor the book on which it is based), if Mr. Hayward were a baseball player and his sentences were at bats, Mr. Hayward would be batting .300. In Major League Baseball, this is good enough to earn you millions of dollars a year. Not too shab. The 27th sentence is sadly marred grammatically (as are several others in Mr. Ball's review-of-a-review; I'd cite them all, but that would mean rereading it, and frankly I'm not so inclined), in that the phrase "these claims" has no apparent referent. If Mr. Ball meant that "the claims made in *these sentences* are unsupported as written," he should have said so.

27. In the 28th sentence, Mr. Ball makes an absurd statement that flatly contradicts the content of the preceding 27 sentences.

28. In the 29th sentence, Mr. Ball makes another such statement.

29. In the ultimate sentence of Mr. Ball's review-of-a-review, he makes another sweeping generalization, based on no stated evidence. Even if Mr. Ball is right about the deficiencies of Mr. Hayward's review, in the absence of concrete evidence in support of his claims, Mr. Ball is guilty of the logical fallacy of generalizing from a particular (although it could be argued in this instance that the fallacy in

question is actually an over-inclusive premise—i.e. that reviewing in Canada sucks—but this is to split hairs). Further, Mr. Ball commits the cardinal sin of introducing new material in his conclusion when he refers to "ideological claims" made by Mr. Hayward. Now, I haven't read Mr. Hayward's review, as I might have mentioned, so it could well be that there are "ideological claims" festering within it like so many Mensheviks. But I kind of doubt it, since Mr. Ball's point-by-point plot summary of Mr. Hayward's review seems to say nothing about such "ideological claims." Also, this last sentence of Mr. Ball's contains a split infinitive; only language mavens will insist that this is an error in English grammar— in fact, it is a hangover from Latin, in which the solecism actually does impede sense—but it nonetheless mars what should be a strong concluding statement. That statement is further marred by Mr. Ball's reference to "dying literary values." Presumably, these are the values of literary realism referred to earlier in Mr. Ball's review-of-a-review. Unfortunately, in that previous sentence, Mr. Ball said those values were defunct. Defunct is synonymous with dead (see E.E. Cummings' poem "Buffalo Bill"). Something cannot be both dead and dying. So which will it be, huh?

I mean to pick on Mr. Ball in this instance. And I am certainly suggesting that his review-of-a-review is poorly written and otherwise incompetent.[12] Fortunately, I don't think this has much to do with what reviewing of reviews in Canada has become.

Sincerely,

Zachariah Wells

January 18, 2009

---

12 Ball, for his part, was a great sport about it. He posted a link to my piece, calling it "mean-spirited but brilliant," and subsequently interviewed me on his blog. This kind of response is exactly how things should go in matters of such small consequence, but not everyone takes a joke as well as Mr. Ball, alas.

Reviewing with André

WHEN CANADIAN NOTES & QUERIES' *contributing editor Zachariah Wells read André Alexis' critical essay "The Long Decline" in a recent issue of* The Walrus, *he had a nagging feeling of* déjà vu. *A couple of days later, he realized why ...*

February 1, 2010

Dear Mr. Alexis,

Thank you very much for submitting your essay, "The Long Decline," to *Canadian Notes & Queries*. We are by no means averse to critical prose that casts a harsh light on the work of *CNQ* editors, as yours does, and we certainly sympathize with your frustration in the face of the inarguable and, it would seem, ineluctable decline of book coverage in Canada's major dailies (although our Senior Editor, John Metcalf, might demur, since he was already saying, thirty years ago, that "our newspaper reviews are not unusually illiterate"). We also, as I'm sure you know, appreciate pugnacity in the criticism that we publish and your piece is imbued with that quality from beginning to end. That said, I'm afraid we can't accept your essay, at least not in its present shape.

Because your work shows a fighting spirit we like and because critics willing to be blunt are thin on the ground, our editorial board thought that instead of sending you a form rejection letter, we'd provide you with a critique of your essay, in the sincere hope that if it's not useful to you in revising this piece, it at least helps you sharpen any future critical undertakings.

Some of the problems with your essay are architectural and others adhere more to the details. I'll start with the big picture concerns.

STRUCTURE

I hope it doesn't seem condescending to trot out a bit of standard-issue undergraduate advice: before you start writing, you should figure out what your thesis is and plot an outline of your essay, ensuring that all major points and sub-points of each paragraph are pertinent to that thesis. It's clear that you haven't done this by your second paragraph, in which you ask, "Where to start?" The muddle you're in becomes apparent again later, when you write: "How we reached this pass is difficult to articulate. Or, rather, there are so many interesting narratives, it's difficult to settle on any single one." But the demands of the critical essay are such that, before submitting a draft to an editor, the critic, as a minimum requirement, needs to have figured out what narrative it is he's trying to articulate. The most disappointing aspect of your essay is that it fails to do this, repeatedly.

At the outset, it seems that you are intent on excoriating the tattered hide of newspaper review sections. But you've barely got started on this essay about editorial and publishing problems when you abruptly change topics, lamenting how "woefully incompetent" reviewers are "these days." You make a token gesture back to the disappearance of reviews from "our dying newspapers," but this is a non-sequitur in your new topic; is the problem not enough reviews, or is the problem too many badly written ones? Some combination thereof, presumably, but you don't spend enough time developing your arguments for the reader to know what exactly you're getting at.

Another non-sequitur in this paragraph is the assertion that Canada has failed "to produce a single literary critic of any worth, at least since the death of Northrop Frye." Besides the fact that this is objectively incorrect (since, for example, Peterborough's own Hugh Kenner, a critic with a substantial international reputation who is widely credited with restoring Ezra Pound's literary credibility and whose book *The Pound Era* is a critical classic, was still alive and writing for a good decade after Frye's death; if by "produced," you mean that we haven't had a new critical voice of that stature emerge, I would remind you that Frye has only been dead for eighteen years, so we can't possibly know what critics the country will produce in the post-Frygian era), by including this statement in a paragraph about the incompetence of reviewers, you elide the manifest differences between someone who writes a review for a newspaper or periodical and a scholarly critic. Such distinctions between practitioners and genres must be made if a reader is to have a proper idea of what it is you are writing about.

From there, we have another awkward transition to a long, rambling paragraph about British critic James Wood—whose relevance to an essay about Canadian newspapers/reviewing/criticism you don't make clear—and from there, somehow back to "our reviews," which begets another non-sequential shift to a paragraph about how John Metcalf—who to the best of my knowledge has never been an employee of a newspaper—is to blame "for this state of affairs." By this point, you've taken so many quicksilver twists that the reader must be forgiven for wondering precisely *what* state of affairs it is you're decrying.

Next, we move on—again with no connective tissue to speak of—to a third topic: Northrop Frye and Margaret Atwood, whose "academic" approach, we learn, was the burr under Metcalf's saddle. If you were writing an essay about John Metcalf's criticism, this might not be a bad place to start. Indeed, the seven paragraphs of this section are easily the most cohesive of your essay—although even here, you tend to wander, saying in one breath that Metcalf is at fault and then later saying that it's not so much him as the people "who have been influenced by him," which seems to me a bit like blaming Christ for the sins of St. Paul. Were this section focused on and fleshed out, I have every reason to believe—well, to hope at least—that you'd be able, with editorial assistance, to produce a piece of criticism we could publish.

However, your need to tie in this relatively extended take on Metcalf to the Problem with Today's Reviewing—the former, given the structure of your essay, amounts to a lengthy digression—sabotages any such hopes. Before you can say anything of real substance about Metcalf's criticism, you are making another abruptly clumsy segue—"So, one could legitimately say that Metcalf has turned a generation of reviewers away from 'academic' evaluations of literature"—back to your original complaint: that Canadian book reviewing has been going downhill for twenty years.

Finally, for reasons that are again far from clear, you end your piece on Canadian review culture by talking about James Wood. It is perhaps apposite that a series of ill-connected pensées should be capped by one last non-sequitur—but it is nevertheless unfortunate.

I have spent so much time on the structure of your piece because I believe that this major flaw of your essay is the chief begetter of its manifest infelicities. Your failure to plan and plot your structure, your negligence when it comes to measuring twice before you cut, has led to a house in which, to borrow from poet Alan Dugan, "nothing is plumb, level or square." In such a house, one must force things into place, stretching, bending and cutting in a graceless, Procrustean manner to make everything fit.

LACK OF QUOTATIONS TO SUBSTANTIATE ARGUMENTS

Because you have tried to cram so many things into one essay, you have left yourself little space in which to quote. There are no quotations of any length; the longest you use is no more than a few words. This is a significant lacuna in an essay that is almost 3500 words long, and it calls into serious question the authority of your arguments.

One of the only things you do quote is a remark by Philip Marchand to the effect that

> ... anyone who does not appreciate the greatness of Tolstoy is "deficient in taste, period." A dubious opinion, given that Henry James, who has as great a claim to "taste" as Marchand, disliked *War and Peace,* and the late-career Tolstoy felt that his own early work was too verbose ... Marchand's statement is about himself, his belief in *War and Peace*'s greatness. He offers no defence of his opinion, believing that none is required.

This four-word quotation, for which you provide no context, comes from the autobiographical essay "Confessions of a Book Reviewer," which serves as the introduction to Marchand's book *Ripostes*—not from a review or a work of criticism. Marchand's essay, I would add, is considerably more nuanced than you seem willing to admit. He even confesses to the sorts of doubts you say earlier that reviewers never admit to:

> Every critic must sometimes suspect, upon feeling baffled by a book, that there are other, more acute readers who actually have understood the author's intentions—understood them, and relished the results. *They* are not baffled. But meanwhile, intelligence has failed you, the critic. In a few cases, it may have failed so badly that your remarks will serve to amuse posterity.

He also says that *Cat's Eye*—a novel written by a poet, which you say he's against—is a good book, if not a major one. Marchand is not talking about something so picayune as *liking* Tolstoy (and let the record show that he has elsewhere sided with James and Tolstoy so far as to prefer *Anna Karenina* to *War and Peace*, to which he does not actually refer explicitly in his essay, by the bye). He's saying that Tolstoy is a major writer who cannot be ignored; unfortunately,

Henry James isn't around to consult, but it's hard to imagine him disagreeing, since he, after all, couldn't ignore Tolstoy either.

This isn't about pleasure at all, but about perspective. He's saying that it makes no sense to put Atwood next to Tolstoy and determine that Atwood is in the same league. By providing a sound bite and by failing to contextualize that bite, you misrepresent what he is saying. Rather than engage with his argument, you opportunistically poach a pull-quote so that he might serve as your tackling dummy.

Your failure to use quotations is particularly troublesome in an essay that argues against criticism as mere opinion. Of Metcalf, you complain: "He takes sentences or paragraphs that he considers examples of brilliant writing and then does the written equivalent of pointing and saying, 'There, you see?'" This is a fair criticism, if true, but not only do you provide no examples of this pointing, you fail to avoid it yourself. Metcalf's approach, as portrayed by you, at least gives a reader some basis on which to agree or argue with him. As Marchand puts it in the same essay from which his maligned Tolstoy remark was untimely ripped (after juxtaposing two paragraphs and saying, in precise terms, what he likes in one and dislikes in the other): "The reader may feel free, at this point, to make his or her own judgements about the writer's critical tastes."

In consistently failing to provide examples, you go one worse than Metcalf and co. Consider, for example, your claim that Metcalf "tends to like finicky prose, and he particularly likes English versions of finicky prose. His own sentences, those he quotes as examples of 'good writing,' are often overwritten and, at times, awkward in their frank desire to be good." One expects at this point to see at the very least an example of such an overwrought, pre-pubescently awkward sentence, but one's expectations are frustrated.

It is truly unfortunate that you didn't quote anything here because the "finickiness" of a sentence is something that can actually be quantified, using such mathematical tools as the Gunning Fog Index or the Flesch-Kincaid Grade Level Readability Test. This is precisely the sort of analysis that Marchand does provide in his comparison of sentences by Michael Ondaatje and Russell Smith. The latter, it should be noted, is a writer whose fiction has been edited and published by Metcalf, and yet Marchand's example of what he sees as a characteristic Smith sentence is *demonstrably* unfinicky in its diction and syntax. The least you could have done was provide an equally concrete example of what you deem to be "finicky prose."

Rather than pointing, you gesture vaguely in the general direction of something and sniff, "Need I say more?" Your essay pays lip service to the idea that mere opinion is bad, but its manoeuvres betray another message: *their* opinions are bad, but *mine* are good—so good I don't even need to defend them. You actually make this explicit when you say, "On the evidence, I think Metcalf and I have similar sensibilities. But those who have been influenced by him—Ryan Bigge, for instance—are not on the same level [ed: as Metcalf and by extension as Alexis] and don't possess the same credibility, though they allow themselves to make the same kinds of pronouncements."

Ah, so credibility justifies opinion. And how does one go about amassing this capital you call credibility? Or is it bestowed upon one by divine fiat like a birthmark, discernible only to those similarly endowed? The assumption of one's rectitude and others' wrongosity is of course at the heart of most debates and there is nothing inherently wrong with it as a starting point, but it is disingenuous to pretend that one is against opinion as such—in an opinion piece.

POT AND KETTLE-ISMS

This is far from the only example of failing to practise what you preach. In the same essay in which you decry "personal attacks and collegiate vitriol," as well as certain critics' practise of "insulting" their targets, you write disdainfully of "a short, pompous man with thick, dark-rimmed glasses (a self-styled 'critic')." Just because, unlike Starnino and Bigge, you don't name the person you're belittling doesn't mean that you aren't being an asshole. It just means you're less brave than they are in dishing out your disses. Either that, or this bespectacled little man's a character you've invented.

In an essay that begins "Toronto is the city in which I have been disabused of any number of notions, where I have lost a certain innocence," you later proclaim: "This is neither criticism nor reviewing but autobiography. Marchand is telling me something about himself. Starnino is telling me about his sensibility and how much he believes in his beliefs. Bigge is settling a personal vendetta with McLaren." (By the way, while I am familiar with the details of Bigge vs. McLaren, it is not safe to assume that all your readers will be, so if you're going to cite the conflict, you really need to explain it.) Throughout your piece, which you admit is prompted by your "idealism," you tell us of your preferences, your sensibilities, your beliefs. You tell us that Stan Persky is "one of [your] favourite Canadian reviewers," but you say absolutely nothing about why he is, never mind—pardon the repetition—quoting something from one of his putatively wonderful reviews.

BROADSTROKE GENERALIZATIONS

By sidestepping the specific, you wander into the wilds of the general. A few cases in point, besides the aforementioned dismissal of all post-Frygian critics.

You argue that the '80s era *Globe* Books was "an inspiring venue for Canadian intellectual life." In defense of this thesis, you mention Persky (again, without reference to what made him a worthy critic) and nothing else. One can only assume you're working from memory and can't actually recall any other contributors. You do mention Jay Scott, but then admit that he didn't write for the Books section; what you don't seem to be aware of is that this makes him an irrelevant addition to your essay, unless you think the fact that he quoted Barthes renders him sufficiently bookish to merit a nod.

As noted above, you say that "Canadian literary reviewers are so woefully incompetent, it makes you wonder if there's something in our culture that poisons critics in their cradles." A reader can only assume that you believe that there is not a single book reviewer in a country of over thirty million who is even competent at his or her job. This in spite of earlier saying that *Globe* Books Editor Martin Levin "still manages to dig up capable reviewers now and then." Is a capable reviewer not a competent one?

By promoting Metcalf as the prime mover of all incompetent and vicious critics, you do exactly what you say Metcalf is guilty of: you paint yourself into a corner. You concede that it is "rhetorical to blame any single person for the current state of critical affairs." Personally, another "r" adjective comes to mind to describe such a perversely hyperbolic statement—Metcalf himself would be more than a little surprised to learn of how widespread his pernicious influence has been—but in spite of your *caveat lector*, you proceed to make the case against Metcalf anyway.

Because the case is, by your own admission, dubious, the "facts" you corral to bolster it do not hold up under scrutiny. You say that Solway, Starnino, Marchand and Bigge are followers of Metcalf, as evidenced by the fact that Metcalf has "edited or published" them. While it's true that Metcalf has edited collections of prose by Solway, Starnino and Marchand, it should be noted that Solway is only a couple of years younger than Metcalf and was engaged in sorties against the literary establishment long before he made contact with him. Further, one could with some accuracy claim that Starnino learned a thing or two from Solway, who actually *was* a mentor to the younger critic, but the *Montreal Gazette* had far more to do with giving Starnino his start as a reviewer than Metcalf did—much as Marchand, as you'll know from having read "Confessions of a Book Reviewer," cut his critical teeth in the pages of the *Toronto Star*. All three of these writers have indeed published books edited by Metcalf, but the vast majority of the content in those books had been previously published by people other than Metcalf.

It is certainly reasonable to posit that all four of these men share a certain outlook or sensibility, but it is a Reed Richardsesque stretch to call Solway, Marchand and Starnino Metcalf's "children," as you do. With Ryan Bigge, the case is weaker yet—no better than speculation, really. The only piece of evidence I know of linking Bigge to Metcalf is Bigge's publication of a review of a book by Andrew Pyper in *Canadian Notes & Queries*. While Metcalf has long been on *CNQ*'s masthead, he is not, nor has he ever been, the Reviews Editor. That job, at the time of Bigge's review, belonged to Michael Darling, who also once commissioned me to write a review for *CNQ*. I subsequently joined *CNQ* as an editor and replaced Michael as Reviews Editor when he stepped down in 2006. I have served in that capacity for approximately four years, during which time I have had very limited exchanges with John Metcalf, who has never once told me what to have reviewed, nor whom I should hire to write for *CNQ*. I therefore think it entirely probable that Ryan Bigge has never had so much as a conversation with Metcalf,[13] never mind the paranoid notion that Bigge is some kind of Metcalf acolyte.

If the Metcalf, Marchand, Starnino or Bigge of your essay appeared in a novel, say, the author of that novel might justly be charged with creating cardboard characters. It strikes me as a singular failure of imagination on your part—a failure made willful by the suppression of facts—that you can only see, or choose only to portray, one dimension of these rather complex individuals. You speak of "the shallow, self-aggrandizing rhetoric that now passes for criticism." Do you really want to go there? In *this* essay? Do you really believe that all Carmine Starnino does is insult poets? Or was this another rhetorical flourish? You leave an informed reader in the position of having to decide if you're being ignorant or dishonest and neither option, needless to say, redounds to your credit. Is Bigge's review of Leah McLaren's book actually representative of his normal reviewing approach? Is this someone who reviews for the sole purpose of avenging hurts

---

13   Bigge later confirmed this suspicion in an email to me.

suffered? Is he allowed no mulligans on your course? I've already pointed out nuances in Marchand's writing that you've missed/glossed over. Do I really need to remind you that Metcalf—whom you paint as an occasionally amusing curmudgeon with good taste but bad judgment—was appointed to the Order of Canada for his contributions to culture in this country, most notably for his role as mentor and editor to dozens of writers? Don't take my word for it; how about Alice Munro's: "I have the feeling he is the one person who can tell what's fake, what's shoddy, what's an evasion, maybe even mark the place where a loss of faith hit you … It won't matter what compliments you've been getting from other quarters." You should be familiar with those words, as they appear on the jacket of *The Aesthetic Underground*, a book to which you refer. This isn't to say that Metcalf is or should be beyond criticism. He isn't. But he has earned a great deal more respect than you seem willing to grant him. And here's the thing: your failure to give him his due does no harm to Metcalf, but rather to your own argument against him; assaults this feeble invariably wind up with the assailant more badly wounded than the intended target.

LIMITED KNOWLEDGE OF THE FIELD

All of these leaps, stretches, elisions, omissions and errors of fact accumulate to convince this reader that you have a very limited knowledge of the field you are writing about. That James Wood's name is "the one" you hear mentioned is a rather dismal indictment of the literary company you keep. In conversations I have with other writers, names like David Orr, Helen Vendler, Harold Bloom, Tom Paulin, Marjorie Perloff, Michael Hoffmann, Ange Mlinko, James Fenton, the recently deceased Thomas Disch, Seamus Heaney, Paul Muldoon, Clive James, Stephen Burt, Edna Longley—to name randomly a few off the top of my head—come up routinely. One can certainly argue about the relative merits of each writer's criticism, but they are by no means low-profile figures; several of them are practically celebrities, at least as well known as Wood, if not better.

They are, it is true, primarily critics and/or reviewers of poetry; that they occur to me is reflective of my own primary interests and reading habits. It could be that the fiction field is comparatively barren—my own knowledge of it is too limited to agree or disagree with such a statement, though even I can at least summon the name of Sven Birkerts without undue strain—but if so, you would have done better to restrict the scope of your essay to fiction reviewing or fiction criticism, instead of using the broader "literary" rubric. Since you have invited Solway and Starnino into your essay, however, it is clear that you did not intend to focus exclusively on fiction reviewing. At any rate, if you hope to salvage anything from this essay, I urge you to acquaint yourself with the writing of today's prominent literary critics. If nothing else, it should provide you many hours of pleasure and stimulation.

I hope you can see, Mr. Alexis, why *CNQ* can't accept your submission. If nothing else, it is an affront to the array of talented reviewers whose work has graced our pages in recent issues, but which seems to have flown over your radar, set as it is to scan the ground immediately in front of you. I suggest you sample some of our back issues before submitting to us again. Read, for example, Anita Lahey's mettlesome re-appraisal of Gwendolyn MacEwen; James Pollock's bracing overview of the oeuvre-to-date of Jeffery Donaldson; Carmine Starnino's generously spirited assessment of Karen Solie's achievements (a far cry from the insults you suggest is all he's capable of dispensing). I don't mean to say, either, that *CNQ* is the only venue for thought-provoking literary reviews. While the newspaper situation is sad indeed, there are a few smaller-circulation publications dedicated to criticism that is substantial in terms not only of column inches but also in rigour and erudition. Some of these are print magazines, such as *Arc* and *The New Quarterly*. Others are Internet-based. Speaking of which, I'm puzzled, if not altogether surprised, that you neglected to tell readers that the reviews of Stan Persky, for example, can still be read online at *Dooney's Cafe*. Clearly, he's moved on from *The Globe and Mail*. Would that you followed his lead.

I'll detain you no longer, sir. If you decide to rework the material in your essay, you are more than welcome to resubmit the results to us. If, however, you decide to seek another market for the piece as is, I'm sure you'll have little trouble finding one. As you say, editorial standards in this country are, by and large, depressingly low.

Best regards,

Zachariah Wells

WE ARE MORE OR LESS
(With No Apologies to Shane Koyczan)[14]

Define Canada?
You might say the home of McSorley
Or Ron Hextall
Who inspired innovative use of the hockey stick as lethal weapon
But we're more than just aggravated assault
And salt-of-the earth goons
In wheat-growing and steel-making towns

Some say what defines us is our excessive consumption of over-
proof beer
And our friendly-to-a-fault willingness to give strangers' directions
Even if it's just "Ya can't get there from here"
Or some other bum steer
We are so friendly to strangers
We greet them at the YVR airport—with Tasers!

We are vegans and seal-clubbers
We are seamen and land-lubbers
We are loggers and tree-huggers
We are dipsomaniacs and abstemious tea-chuggers

---

14   Koyczan delivered his poem "We Are More" at the opening ceremonies of the Vancouver Olympics. It can be heard here: http://www.youtube.com/watch?v=Pq_xddkO064.

We are a land of such equal opportunity
That not only our politicians, but our serial killers too
Can be hog farmers or Air Force brass
(That they are drawn still from the ranks of white men
Is a matter of some concern, but we're working on that, let me
    assure you)

We are constantly taking it up the ass
From our neighbour, for which we say not only thank you
But please sir, could I have some more?
Because we are more
We are the global economy's friendliest whore
We are vast tracts of pristine land
We are pipelines, tailings and tar sand
We are exporting asbestos to India
Our number one motto's "Buddy, get it inta ya!"

We are raping our fish stocks and when we reap our forests
We replace 'em with fast-growing stands of future bum paper
We're melting, we're melting
And all the while we're belting out smug odes
As we keep putting the rubber to the road

We campaign from the left and govern from the right
We turn off the light and take back the night
We are getting tough on crime
And we're doing it on your dime
Think art grants expensive, how 'bout hard time?

We are universal healthcare—if you're in the right province
We are kernels of truth and nuggets of nonsense
We are paying recompense in monthly installments
We are a ragged patchwork of problematic diversity
We are in debt to our eyeballs for going to university

We just can't decide
We were perpetrators of genocide
But we don't call it that and we feel really bad about the whole
    thing
We have interned innocent citizens and taken their belongings
On a dérangé le peuple Acadien
Comme tout le monde, on dit merci et de rien
Mais une fois à la maison, on donne un coup de pied à notre chien

We are one Jew too many
We are not two solitudes, but as long as the knackered nag still
    knickers, might as well flog 'er
We are a game of Don Valley Parkway frogger
We are a pedophilic diocese
We are increasingly obese
We are plus-sized and disingenuously self-deprecating
We are eating where we are defecating
We are doing your dirty work, as long as it pays
We are not the sum total of our feel-good clichés
But you need more than an upbeat demeanour to sweep garbage
    away

Saying "we are more" is just one more trite meme
We are still trying to forge what we mean
And what this means is
We made our bed
But we must change the sheets if we want to make it clean

WHY I AM NOT A PEOPLE'S POET

AS THE TITLE OF MY TALK[15] implies, what follows is not an academic discussion so much as a personal statement. While I am the holder of bachelor's and master's degrees, I am no scholar—except perhaps in the most dilettantish sense of the word—nor have I ever been employed as a teacher. I have, rather, paid my way in the world primarily by means of what most people with my level of education would consider "underemployment"—i.e. in workplaces where most of my co-workers are considerably less educated than I am and where my formal education, while occasionally of indirect use, is of no particular benefit to the performance of my duties and might even be deemed a liability by some.

It's a minor irony that my job, serving the *public* as a railroad service attendant, has prevented me from attending in person today, though the train I'm working on is probably rolling through Sackville right about...now. It's a credit to the organizers of this conference that they have, appropriately, made it open to people like me, unaffiliated members of a broader public than is normally represented at academic colloquia. It comes as no surprise to me that it should be so at Mount Allison, which has distinguished itself over the years as a first-rate *teaching* institution.

*

15   This talk was prepared for the Public Poetics conference at Mount Allison University. Because I couldn't attend, I sent in an audio recording instead.

In an interview published on *Maisonneuve* magazine's website three years ago, poet and English professor Alessandro Porco asked me about what he called my "populist propensity." It was a fair question, given the subjects, stances and diction of much of my work, but I have had a rather ... vexed relationship with populism as a stance and, moreover, with the groups of Canadian poets who proudly espouse it. A big part of the problem for me is that my membership in what we problematically call the "working class" is non-hereditary, voluntary, and not quite full-time.

Because I was a smallish child, I was placed in the front row of class pictures in the early grades of school. In those pictures my pants are conspicuously knee-patched and I could easily be taken for the Poorest Kid in Class. My ragamuffinesque attire, however, reflected not the picturesque pennilessness of my parents, but an ethical decision to favour free hand-me-downs over the new, designer clothes sported by my classmates—most of whose parents probably had more cause for status anxiety than my father, a deputy minister of PEI's provincial government, and my mother, an Ontario doctor's daughter who worked as a high-level federal civil servant before moving to the Island. In fact, faced with the notorious inadequacies of my home province's public education system and a dearth of extracurricular activities, I did as a teenager what few, if any, of my peers would even have thought of trying, much less have been financially able to achieve: I left PEI to attend a private school in Ottawa—the same private school where my father had been head boy thirty-seven years previously.

I helped pay for that privilege by working full-time in the summer, starting when I was fourteen, serving ice cream to the public. When I went to university, I stayed out of student debt by handling cargo and baggage for an airline on Baffin Island. In the summers following my second and third years, in fact, I toiled every day from May through August, sixty to ninety hours a week, with only four or five days off after the first twelve weeks. In each of those seventeen-week binges, I logged over a thousand compensated hours—about as many as half a year's worth of full-time employment.

So I know what hard work is, but that work has always been undertaken in support of intellectual and artistic pursuits. Since graduating from the University of King's College in 1999, I have continued working "semi-skilled" blue-collar jobs—after leaving First Air in 2003, I started work with Via Rail in 2004. The days have been long, but the weeks short and the pay decent. This path has therefore afforded me the leisure to pursue my writerly vocation alongside my wage-earning work—a balance that teachers and full-time freelancers know is very hard to strike.

Because the breadwinning I've done has not only underwritten, but has also informed my writing, I have been tabbed by some of my fellow writers as a blue-collar poet, but I have never, *pace* Todd Swift in a response to my review of his anthology *Modern Canadian Poets*, "fancied myself a man of the people." Not only is my own position too obviously equivocal to allow me such a delusional arrogation, but my experience tells me also that "the people" are themselves too much of a mixed bag for any single person to reasonably claim representative status.

*

Which hasn't stopped me from being pigeonholed, of course. Six years ago, I was invited by James Deahl and Jeff Seffinga to be one of three judges for the Acorn-Plantos People's Poetry Award. Tentatively, I agreed, pending more information. When I learned that I and the two other judges would only see twenty of the submitted titles—a longlist vetted by the prize's administrative committee—and that the shortlist and winner would also be determined by the committee, I declined to participate.

Mr. Seffinga told me that "the informality of the award is paramount," that it might reflect the spontaneity of the original prize given to Milton Acorn—but this byzantine backroom gerrymandering was the opposite, it seemed to me, of informal. It was also opaque, since the prize committee, Seffinga told me, does "not publish the names of entries, authors, or judges." I wrote a longish email back to him, outlining my reasons for saying no, but never received a reply.

The whole business smelled Bolshie. In his email, Seffinga proved that besides bureaucratic convolution and secrecy, the committee also shared the Soviet flare for historical revisionism. Acorn, he told me, had been "presented with a hastily struck medallion proclaiming him 'the Peoples Poet' [sic] by an informal group of his peers at a blues bar on Spadina Ave in Toronto." Anyone who has read Richard Lemm's scrupulous biography of Acorn, however, knows that "[t]he actual name of the award was 'The Canadian Poets' Award.'" The prize was—and continues in its more formal latter day incarnation to be—one given to a poet by his peers—as, ironically, Seffinga had acknowledged—and not by any collectivity so nebulous as "the people." By renaming the prize, that rather important reality has, effectively, been sentimentally elided.

I have a lot of time for such spontaneous demonstrations of love and anger as The Canadian Poets' Award. The very year I was approached for jury duty by Deahl and Seffinga, I had spearheaded a similar prize for Goran Simić when the Canada Council, for reasons bureaucratic, deemed his book *From Sarajevo, with Sorrow* ineligible for the Governor General's Award. Following an email fundraising drive, I presented Goran with a cheque and a hand-turned wooden bowl at Fellini's Shoe, a now-defunct Cabbagetown restaurant co-owned by the poet. A couple of people suggested to me that the prize be made an annual affair, but I demurred, having seen the paving stones cooked in the kiln of good intentions often enough to know that the prize would become a brittle, friable thing if formalized, as Acorn's award has been.

People's Poetry is populist in much the same way that The People's Republic of Korea is: for the people, whether they like it or not. Or, unlike a totalitarian regime, whether the people are even aware of it. If we take as given the truism that poetry is read almost exclusively by poets, then "people's poetry" must only be read by people's poets. I have encountered little evidence to the contrary wandering the aisles of Via Rail's coach cars, and the scattered few non-specialist poetry readers I've met over the years have had rather more eclectic tastes than the advocates of accessibility-above-all assume.

For all the rhetoric and political leanings of organizations and individuals associated with it, People's Poetry is more Astroturf than grassroots, and, like most every poetic school and movement, defines itself largely in revanchist terms of its opposition to other poetries. Which is a much safer bet than planting your flag on the ice floe of actual popular taste. As Kierkegaard said, "If a man adopts public opinion today and is hissed tomorrow, he is hissed by the public."

*

I first discovered the oxymoronic nature of People's Poetry several years prior to my exchange with Seffinga. As a young writer in the late '90s, I bought a copy of *Poetry Markets for Canadians* to help find outlets for my then half-baked poems. Two possibilities I came across were *The People's Poetry Letter* and Mekler & Deahl's annual Sandburg-Livesay anthology. They seemed likely venues for someone writing plainspoken, civic-minded poems about his blue-collar job and hardscrabble surroundings, as I was at the time. And so they were. I won the absurdly alliterative "People's Poetry Political Poem Prize" in 1999 for a soliloquy in the voice of a melting iceberg, and a poem of mine about belly-loading a 727 was chosen by Ray Souster for the 2000 edition of the Sandburg-Livesay anthology.

In a later number of *The People's Poetry Letter*, I read an editorial by Ted Plantos in which he railed against the "academic charlatans" of "Can-litter." In particular, he singled out such "puffed up icons" as Atwood, Ondaatje and Cohen. At the time, I was employed as a cargo handler in Iqaluit, but had recently wrapped up an Honours BA in English and was about to start an MA at Concordia University. With one foot on the tarmac and the other inside the door of the ivory tower, it seemed to me that Plantos properly understood neither world.

I wrote him an 800-word letter to the editor, in which I pointed out that the CanLit seminar I'd recently taken at Dalhousie included not just his reviled icons—whose greatest sin, ironically, seemed to be their popularity—but also such People's Poetry idols as Acorn, Purdy and Livesay. I concluded by saying that

> If the People's Poetry movement is not careful, it runs the risk of becoming just as cliquish, of catering to as select and incestuous a coterie, as the academic elite of which you are so critical. I don't see the usefulness of labels and distinctions. Poetry, good, bad or mediocre, is *necessarily* people's poetry, even if not explicitly so.

I can't recall exactly what Plantos wrote to me in return, but suffice to say that my critique was … not appreciated. What I didn't realize at the time was that People's Poetry already was an insular tribe. The only other modification I'd make to my statement today, with a decade-plus of writing, criticism and book reviewing behind me, would be to delete "good, bad or mediocre." For all the proliferation of styles, schools and movements, poetry cannot properly be said to have a spectrum of quality.

Poetry is a property of things—"the language of being," Robert Bringhurst has called it—and not a genre. There is not a place in it for the genuine, as Marianne Moore famously wrote, because it *is* the genuine. A piece of writing either is poetry or it isn't. Saying things like this, I suppose, betrays me as an "elitist." If this means being more interested in execution than intentions, then it's a label I can live with, at least more comfortably than "populist," which has the significant disadvantage of being presumptuous and condescending.

*

It is also remarkably sentimental.

In Western Canada, parallel to the predominantly Ontario-based People's Poetry movement, Tom Wayman has been the prime mover behind what he has called "industrial writing." In the introduction to his *Selected Poems* in 1993, Wayman wrote that "Overall, my intention is that the complexities revealed by my poems should be the complications of our everyday existence, rather than newly-created difficulties or mysteries generated by tricks of language or poetic form. Clarity, honesty, accuracy of statement have been my goals." Wayman writes positively of the "centrality of daily work" in his poetry and positions his writing as a mature alternative to the childish fantasies that predominate elsewhere. "A grown person," he says, "who constantly evades having to cope with reality, who lives in a world of dreams however beautiful, we consider immature if not mentally ill. The contemporary industrial writing provides maturity and a healthy balance to literature."

Never mind if you find such work prosaic and didactically facile, as I did the vast majority of the poems in Wayman's 1981 anthology *Going for Coffee: Poetry on the Job*[16]; such objections must be symptomatic of your literary childishness. Never mind what causes you pleasure; Wayman knows what's good for you. It's hard to tell whether his positioning is merely naive, or is rather a cagey bit of niche-carving on the part of a highly educated chemist's son who has sown hay in the fields of academe from the seeds of a few blue-collar jobs worked as a young adult.

More probably the latter, as Wayman occasionally betrays an awareness of the equivocal position he occupies. But even when he owns his privilege, he doesn't seem to understand its ramifications. I saw the self-styled "Squire of Appledore" read at the Vancouver Writers' Festival in 2007, where he gave a hammy rendition of a poem about all the money he has made plying his poetic and academic trades. I say "hammy" because he read the poem as though

---

16   The only notable exception being several poems by Peter Trower, of whom I knew nothing at the time.

his gob was actually stuffed with cash. In this simplistic treatise on capitalism, Wayman was playing for easy laughs, pandering to the well-heeled crowd's liberal sensibilities. This is populist poetry at its unabashed abysmal worst, intellectually dishonest and aesthetically crude, pitching its palpable designs to the back rows of the audience. What Wayman probably didn't realize is that a good many members of the crowd that night thought he came off as an idiotic clown.

*

In "The Public and the Poet," a Norton lecture delivered at Harvard in 1955, Edwin Muir spoke of such flagrant attempts to appeal and the antithetical relationship they have with poetry. "The supreme expression of imagination is in poetry," said Muir,

> ... and so like philosophy and science it has a responsibility to itself: the responsibility to preserve a true image of life. If the image is true, poetry fulfills its end. Anything that distorts the image, any tendency to oversimplify or soften it so that it may be more acceptable to a greater number of people, falsifies it, degrades those for whom it is intended, and cannot set us free. This means that the first allegiance of any poet is to imaginative truth, and that if he is to serve mankind, that is the only way in which he can do it.

Muir does *not* say that the poet, in the absence of a bona fide public, should "turn inward into the complex problems of poetry, or be concerned with poetry as a problem." What he suggests instead has been a touchstone for my practice as a writer in the public realm. "In the end," Muir says,

> ... a poet must create his audience, and to do that he must turn outward. Even if he is conscious of having no audience, he must imagine one ... The poet need not think of the public—its vastness and impersonality would daunt anyone; he should reflect instead that in

no other age than ours … has a poet had to deal with it. He has to see past it, or through it, to the men and women, with their individual lives, who in some strange way and without their choice are part of it, and yet hidden by it.

Put another way, audience for the poet is a problem similar to character for the novelist: it must be conjured from thin air and yet it must be credibly substantial in its volatile, often self-contradictory, inconsistencies. The failure of People's Poetry and of the "industrial writing" championed by Wayman is, primarily, a failure of imagination. Their thinking is binary and they do not see past or through "the people" to the individual lives of authentic folk, in all their vice, virtue and perversity. The "people" they claim to represent, but in whose critical intelligence and aesthetic sensitivity they plainly have no faith, are a mob of faceless, bloodless mannequins.

In this, they make a similar error to economists who base their calculations upon the assumption that people, conceived as "econs," will always act rationally in their own self-interest, despite everything we know to the contrary about actual human behaviour. Which is why the Acorn-Plantos People's Poetry Award procedures must be so tightly constrained, I suppose. Otherwise, the jurors, being people, might just make a wildly inappropriate choice.

Soaked in a Heart of Sapphire, Delicate as an Origami Bird

At its best the jury award citation is a rather unfortunate sub-genre of para-literary prose, consisting often of boilerplate (to the point that the same citations were actually recycled verbatim for different books in consecutive years [2003–2004] for the Danuta Gleed award) and abstract purple gushes of hyperbole. Because of this, I was glad to see when my book *Track & Trace* was shortlisted for the Atlantic Poetry Prize that the anonymous jury remained silent, letting their choices speak for themselves.

It would seem, reading the six citations for this year's[17] Gerald Lampert Award shortlist, that rather than being group composi-tions, they are the product of three different jurors, each responsi-ble for two books. The citations for James Langer and Robert Earl Stewart are solid, creditable pieces of prose, dealing with specific, concrete elements of the books and demonstrating reasonable adjec-tival restraint. There are a couple of "awk" moments in the Soraya Peerbaye and Kate Hall citations, but nothing terribly awful.

Two of the Lampert citations, however, transcend the genre's intrinsic mediocrity, making the leap to incredibad writing. Here's what "the jury" had to say about Marcus McCann's *Soft Where*:

> *Soft Where* by Marcus McCann is a hard-hitting cutting edge poetic expose of a world filled with experimentation and valour. This stun-ning book explores the possibilities of bringing image to life, written in the language of the people and soaked in a heart of sapphire. The

---

17   2010.

> jury was intoxicated by this book, and feels this young writer should
> be encouraged in every and all ways—to the full extent of poetic
> promise. The language in *Soft Where* is as stark and meaningful as the
> images which express a lifestyle hard-lived and yet as delicate as an
> origami bird.

This is a brilliant bit of anti-genius. It starts off alright, but goes
downhill in a hurry when the writer uses two stale compound adjec-
tives. Okay, so this is some kind of journalistic take on something?
On what? On a world of corruption and depravity? Graft and bug-
gery? Nope. Of "a world filled with experimentation and valour."
Phew. Good thing there are hard-working young poets out there
digging up all that experimentation and valour for us to see in the
clear light of day. Next, we have the cliché of a "stunning book"—
the effects are evident on the blurb-writer—exploring something.
What's this remarkably motile tome spelunkin'? Why, "the possibil-
ities of bringing image to life"; presumably, this means that, unlike
Dr. Frankenstein, the book doesn't actually succeed in animating its
monsters. Pity, because that's a book someone might want to read.
Not only that, but, after negotiating a tortured stretch of syntax,
we learn that the book is "written in the language of the people."
Which language of which people? It's in English, right? Probably
not, because then we learn that the book—presumably, though
subject-object relationships in this sentence are hard to parse—is
"soaked in a heart of sapphire." Near as I can tell, this makes no
sense in my native tongue, so the book must be written in some
other lingo.

The explanation for this obscurity probably lies in the next
sentence, in which we learn that "the jury was intoxicated by this
book." Must be some kind of funky glue in the binding; I refer you
back to the earlier mention of the book's "stunning" properties.
The next sentence suggests perhaps that McCann has not won the
prize. The blurb writer insists that "this young writer should be
encouraged in every and all ways." Sic. And sic. Should be, but
hasn't been? I guess we'll have to wait and see. The concluding

clause of this sentence is priceless, "to the full extent" conjuring up the legal phrase "prosecuted to the full extent of the law." Perhaps encouraging young writers "in every and all ways" is tantamount to a prison sentence—I mean, that's a lot of ways, eh. What "the jury" means by "poetic promise" is bemusingly vague—is this some kind of grand Parnassian ideal, or is McCann's promise as a writer intended? The anti-genius of it is that it's impossible to say!

The brilliance continues in the blurb's last sentence, in which we are told that the language of this book—we're still not sure which language, but no matter—is not only "stark and meaningful" (which, as a phrase, is neither), but that its starkness and meaningfulness are equal to "the images [those poor stillborn things who weren't quite brought to life, recall] which express a lifestyle." Whether these images are to be found in McCann's book is by no means clear. Nor is it clear to whom the lifestyle belongs, but we do learn that it is simultaneously "hard-lived and yet as delicate as an origami bird." So, not a life hard-lived, but a lifestyle, which manages to make the book sound profound and shallow— AT THE SAME TIME! How a lifestyle can be "delicate as an origami bird" is equally baffling.

It's not nearly as egregious as the McCann citation, but the paragraph dealing with Marguerite Pigeon's *Inventory* is pretty awesome, too. Apparently, this intrepid little volume does a whole lot of exploring. I especially like the blurb's last two sentences:

> The jury loved this book and would like to gesture a large congratulations to Marguerite. All the best in the future.

Never mind the pure oddity of a direct address to the author in a text meant for an audience of everyone but the author. And never mind the "better luck next time" intimation. That's weird enough, but when I read "gesture a large congratulations," I had to wonder if the juror's mother tongue was something other than English, or if perhaps the blurb had been, in the name of poetic innovation, translated into Estonian using Babelfish and then returned to English. Because I don't know how a literate English speaker—much less a poet—could come up with that phrase unassisted.

And this, ladies and gentlemen, is why I have never joined the League of Canadian Poets. Though I've been taking the piss—because these citations are so dreadful as to be hilarious, when considered out of context—I think that allowing this crapola to be published is incredibly disrespectful to the shortlisted authors and makes the prize itself look like a joke. Which it probably is, but it shouldn't be. It should be a mark of distinction, the recognition that all of the author's years of apprenticeship have been well spent.

But when a juror uses words as if they can mean anything we want them to, it isn't much of a leap to think that the books she or he chose to honour were picked just as haphazardly. Can a juror who writes this ineptly possibly be qualified to choose the best books? Probably not, but their dubious skills are clearly enough to be a published, accredited poet in Canada, good enough to be appointed a "peer" to bona fide poets like Langer and Stewart and Hall. In a Q&A session following a recent reading, Langer told an eager young writer that publishing is not a brass ring. Shit like this proves it.

INTERVIEW

Naming, Maiming, Tourism, Travel
An Interview with Alessandro Porco

Alessandro Porco: Zach, your new collection of poetry is *Track & Trace*. First, could you talk a little about the book's title and central concerns, as well as how it relates—in the sense of continued or divergent areas of investigation—to your first book, *Unsettled*?

Zachariah Wells: The title is kind of a key to the book. As with the title of *Unsettled*, it doesn't refer to a specific phrase or poem title, but is something that links the poems, that accounts for these particular pieces being in this particular book. I think I first came up with the title after reading a passage in a story by Ivan Klíma (tr. Ewald Osers) in his book *My First Loves*. That passage, which resonates strongly with a lot of things in my poems, is now the epigraph of the book. But I might have had the title in mind already, then read the passage, not sure.

The poems, which I wrote over a period of ten or eleven years—during which time I was moving all over the place, between Halifax, PEI, Iqaluit, Montreal, Resolute Bay, Halifax again, Vancouver, and Halifax a third time—are mostly concerned with place and displacement, roots and rootlessness, flux and fixity. I don't tend to think of them in such terms—I'm generally more focused on how a given poem is working word to word, line to line than in how it relates to other poems or thematic concerns—but when it came time to put them together, those seemed to be the main things all of these poems had in common and they seemed to add up to a book. They're more or less the same preoccupations as most of the poems in *Unsettled*, I guess, but differently focused.

AP: Differently how?

ZW: Chronologically, there's significant overlap between *T&T* and *Unsettled*. The earliest poems in each book are pretty much contemporaries and the germ of *T&T* was a chapbook called *Fool's Errand*, which was actually published six months before *Unsettled* came out. So, not surprisingly, the poems have similar concerns. But I'd say that, generally, *Unsettled* is a more civic book and *T&T* a more lyric book. There are lyric poems in *Unsettled* and civic poems in *T&T*, so I wouldn't say that distinction is perfect. One of the poems in *T&T* is actually a revision of a poem that appears in two different versions in *Unsettled*, which is a way of pointing out that the sequence in which the two books have appeared is a bit deceptive.

I'd also say that *T&T* is a more refined book. *Unsettled* had over eighty poems in it, many of them quite rough and raw, some of which I'd disown now if I could, others of which still seem appropriate to the collection if not entirely successful as stand-alone works. I held on to the manuscript of *T&T*—or rather, the unassembled poems that might or might not go into that ms.—for quite a while because I wanted to have a book in which I was confident that each poem justified its own existence. It only has thirty-four poems in it and I don't think I'll feel as negative about any of them in five years as I do about some of the poems in *Unsettled*. *T&T* also reflects my growing interest in metrics and stanzaic structures. There are some rhymed and metred poems in *Unsettled*, but those things are foregrounded more in *T&T*.

A superficial but important difference is that *Unsettled*, being focused on the eastern Arctic, is more geographically unified than *T&T*, in which the poems take place on all three coasts, points in between and even in Orkney, Scotland. But that's kind of deceptive too, since the Arctic is such a massive place; I lived in two different towns there and it takes over two and a half hours to fly from one to the other by jet. *Unsettled* also has a tighter timeframe, since it's drawn primarily from the seven-odd years I spent in Nunavut, whereas *T&T* ranges from childhood to unspecified times in the future.

AP: Reading the collection, I had two questions that immediately came to mind: first, what does it mean—for you—to be, at times, a "nature" poet, keeping in mind (perhaps) your keen reading of, and affection for, poet John Clare. Second, and by extension, there is a gang of poems in the collection that really seem to be thinking through the act of intervention of man's hand into nature or into natural action: for example, "The Pond," which describes the transformation of the natural creek into the artificial pond; or, in "Fool's Errand," the job of interrupting or intervening in dogs in coitus; or "Leg-in-Boot Square," where the acts of intervention result in a "maiming." Could you discuss your interest into this difficult issue of intervention?

ZW: Now that I've been published in an anthology of nature poems, I guess I can't dodge this one, huh? "Nature," like just about any modifier for the term "poet,"—to say nothing of the term "poet" itself for that matter—is nettlesome. I grew up in the country, in a valley an eighth of a mile from a dirt road in the middle of Prince Edward Island. "Nature" there is not the wilderness of northern Ontario, Quebec, BC, Nunavut, etc. Milton Acorn said, very memorably, of the Island:

> Since I'm Island-born home's as precise
> as if a mumbly old carpenter,
> shoulder-straps crossed wrong,
> laid it out,
> refigured to the last three-eighths of shingle.

There's nothing in that landscape untouched by human hands. But this too is natural. I'm super leery of binary thinking about man-n-nature, I just don't buy it. Plastic is natural: it's made by organisms native to this planet from materials found on this planet. And dogs themselves are the product of human interventions—selective breeding—which are no less natural than willy-nilly fucking in a snowstorm. We tend to talk about human beings as though they're a special case apart from nature, and we tend to forget that we're not the only species capable of destruction and random acts of violence. The damming of a creek by a human with a machine is no more "artificial" than if it had been done by a beaver. Actually, I remember a big old beaver once wandering down our stream, only to encounter the dozer-built dam at the end. He turned around; guess he figured someone had beaten him to the punch, so he'd best look elsewhere.

Anyway, John Clare came from a similarly pastoral place, Northamptonshire, and he also wrote about certain intrusions and interventions into that place, most notably the Enclosure Movement. Those interventions, and Clare's reactions to them, have as much to do with social impact as they do with ecological impact: what they do to and say about a community. He hated Enclosure, but presumably had no qualms about the original clearing of woods to make room for fields. Then again, he never was very fond of working those fields, so maybe I'm wrong ... What I, and many other readers (including sensibilities as disparate as Seamus Heaney and John Ashbery), love about Clare's best poems, particularly his ornithological pieces, is their spontaneous, in-the-moment-as-if-you-were-there vividness. They positively reek of "naturalness." But they are, of course, artfully contrived constructions as well—that's how you get that *effect* of spontaneity. They're human interventions. Benign ones, surely, but interventions nonetheless.

A lot of what Clare does is straight description, but the description's so precise it seems to take on extra dimensions—*pace* Keats' objection that Clare's description prevailed too often over the sentiment—which is what makes him such a seemingly unlikely touchstone for John Ashbery: you don't just see what Clare sees, you see the process of his mind sifting what he sees. What I do in a lot of my poems, and it's something I've learned in part from Clare, as well as from Elizabeth Bishop, is just describe a scene, without offering any editorial insight; I try to let the language itself—the built-in metaphors of words rather than laboriously constructed figures that call attention to themselves—do the lifting. Something I see in a lot of contemporary poems, which I despise heartily, are these strained attempts to cram pseudo-profound and often abstract epiphanies, these nuggets of would-be wisdom, to say nothing of highly self-conscious figurative devices, into poems, to sum up and make sense of something seen, rather than just saying what's there. This isn't to say that I'm against the odd rhetorical flourish, but for me to buy it, it needs to feel organic, needs to feel earned by the poem itself and not just some grandiose Wordsworthian pronouncement handed down by the uber-wise poet to the no-doubt-less-wise reader. The kind of thing I'm talking about that I don't like often feels like the reason for writing a poem, rather than something that simply happened in the writing of the poem; the problem isn't that it's artificial, but that it's utterly without grace.

So yeah, you mention how I say that Leg-in-Boot Square is "maimed." Which is flirting with the kind of thing I hate, but I think it's justified because it's squarely in sync with the place's nomenclature, and it's that nomenclature, as much as the place itself, that I'm talking about. When I was living on Leg-in-Boot Square, which is in Vancouver's False Creek neighbourhood, I'd tell people my address and it would usually get a chuckle and the person would invariably say it was a cute name. But the name comes from an actual event that is far from fucking cute: the washing up on shore of a severed leg still in its boot (a kind of prefiguration of the recent rash of foot-in-sneaker discoveries). The maiming is therefore literal, but also has to do with people not knowing what's behind the name—such a perfect rhyme, ain't it—how this fashionable, upscale, beside-the-jogger-swarmed-seawall area, built on landfill bordering an inlet—again, the nomenclature of "False Creek" is almost too good to be true—that's been dammed/damned, how it used to be, not so long ago, one of the shadiest, shittiest places in a very rough-n-tumble logging town, which now constantly congratulates itself on being an affluent "world-class city" and is in the midst of trying to figure out how to hide its open sores (not so different as when Lowry wrote of "This place where chancres blossom like the rose") when the world comes to visit for the Olympics—in preparation for which another stretch of False Creek's industrial waterfront is undergoing a facelift. So me calling it "maimed" is really just compressed observation, peeling back the strata of construction and language and looking underneath. I do a similar sort of thing in my poem "White Trash" in *Unsettled*, which is all about the "rejectamenta disbursed in blizzard-spaced layers." (Carmine Starnino, who edited *T&T*, observed that I make a lot of poems, literally, out of garbage, which hadn't really occurred to me, but it's true.) It's as much or more a social thing as it is an ecological thing—not that they're ever separate. That civic impulse again, eh.

AP: I agree, very much, with your explicitly stated resistance above and implicitly stated resistance in the poems themselves to any clean natural-artificial binary, which is what makes the poems I alluded to, I think, worthy of re-reading and thinking through. But I'd like to jump off from comments at the end of your answer, specifically those about Leg-in-Boot Square. It seems you are critiquing here a sort of sentimentalism, i.e. "it was a cute name," which tends to forget—willfully or not—the historical fact, as you say, of the "severed leg." And in that poem you do connect this sort of thing to the impending tourist industry that is the "Olympics." In fact, there are a couple poems in the book that seem to be suspicious of tourism as an industry insofar as its success depends upon the repressed fact of labour and a sentimental relation to place. (You mentioned Bishop above; this suspicion of a certain kind of tourism, of course, seems to mark her influence on you.) Could you maybe talk a little more about these issues and how they play out in the book?

ZW: It's more a function of where I grew up and where I live and work now than Bishop's influence on me, I'd say. If anything, I have a kinship with Bishop because we shared this suspicion before I ever read her poems. John MacKenzie, in his poem "Lobster Boats, PEI," says "We have sold this Island so far into scenery / We have forgotten its landscape." PEI has ever had an ambivalent relationship with tourism. On the one hand, without it, the local economy'd be in even worse shape than it is. On the other hand, the tourist industry begets a lobster boatload of kitsch and tourists themselves can be super irritating.

I personally have put in a lot of time in the salt mines of tourism. As a teenager, I spent five summers working in Cavendish, the tourist mecca of PEI, slinging ice cream. That job features prominently in my poem "He Finds an Acceptable Way to Grieve." And for the past five years, the job I've worked most frequently on board passenger trains has been "Learning Coordinator"—basically, a host/guide providing bytes of info in charming packages to tourists travelling first class. That work has been seasonal—another mixture of blessing and curse—and one year I had to do some temp work to fill income gaps. One of the temp jobs I got was "collating documents" at a warehouse in Lower Sackville, a suburb of Halifax. Turns out the job involved folding and stuffing mail-out brochures, promoting Nova Scotia tourism. That brief assignment—it was supposed to be five days, but I quit after three—is the subject of one of *T&T*'s more satirical poems (I also wrote a brief memoir of the experience for *Maisonneuve*), "*Spend Time in Nova Scotia; Your Soul Will Thank You.*" The title's taken directly from the brochure; reading it over and over and over while folding them in a sodium-lit, windowless warehouse where one wasn't allowed to sit down because sitting was believed to decrease productivity—it was more than a little rich.

Like you say, sculpting things to suit the tourists leads to a sentimentalizing of place and people; at best to a highly selective edited version of a place. You hear all about the picturesque farmers and fishers, not so much about the unemployed and minimum wage drudges. Although I've done a lot of travelling myself, very little of it has been as a tourist and a lot of it has been on my own. It may well just be another brand of sentimentality, but I tend to favour the lone wanderer over the guided tour, as in "The Stranger," my version of a Rilke poem. When people travel in a group, they engage a lot less with their surroundings and a lot more with each other. Just yesterday, I got back from a train trip in which I was serving a group of fifty-four tourists travelling together on a guided tour. The sort of things I normally do went out the window, because they were clearly more into each other's conversation than anything I might have to tell them about the Maritimes. Another passenger was a guy from England who'd been travelling across Canada on his own and he had all kinds of stories about people he'd met and conversations he'd had. The contrast was striking.

A late addition to the ms. of *T&T* was "Orkney Report." While staying in Orkney (an archipelago north of mainland Scotland) with my wife and son, I struck off on my own one day to explore the Isle of Hoy. When the ferry docked, I got in my rental car and started it up in preparation to disembark. One of the ferry staff came over and told me that this was not Hoy, so I didn't want to get off here. When the gate came down on the ferry, I saw why: Flotta's basically one big tank farm for storage of North Sea oil and right in front of me was a huge gas flare. Not many tourists go to Flotta. Tourists go to pastoral Orkney for scenery and history, not industry. But oil is a huge part of present-day Orkney's reality. So I was playing with those tensions in the poem, linking the Flotta Flare with the eternal eye of a church and commenting wryly on the fatigue that sets in when you take in a lot of touristy activities in sequence.

Something I was struck by in Orkney was the ubiquity of quotations from the writings of George MacKay Brown, the Orcadian poet. They were etched in glass on the ferry, they were on the walls of museums and historical sites, to the same extent that you see Burns quotes on the Scottish mainland (on arrival at Edinburgh International, I remarked on the irony that Burns' "best laid schemes" line should be blazoned all around the baggage carousel; sure enough, KLM had mishandled one of our bags). I was reading a lot of Brown while I was in Orkney (we were staying across the square from his old flat in Stromness). Something that came up in *Letters from Hamnavoe*, a collection of his newspaper columns, was the disappointment of visitors who found out that he lived in a modern apartment in town and not in a stone croft. Understandable disappointment, because so much of Brown's writing is backward-looking, nostalgic.

I asked Tam MacPhail, the bookseller at Stromness Books and Prints—an excellent little shop, where I stumbled across signed copies of David O'Meara's *The Vicinity*, left over from David's visit there a few years earlier—I asked him how Brown was perceived locally and he told me that a lot of Orcadians didn't much appreciate Brown's portrayal of the place as a quaint relic of bygone days, that farmers were a forward-looking lot and had no interest in living in crofts and working their fields by hand if they didn't have to.

That disjunction between literary and/or official portrayals and actual social realities is fascinating and familiar to me, and I'm leery of writing anything that might be easily appropriated for promotional purposes. The Orkney poem complements a poem about PEI, "Water Works"; both contrast the transient goals of tourism bureaus—the "buttressed seawall" protecting the Neolithic village of Skara Brae on Orkney and the futile pouring of concrete to preserve an enormous elephant-shaped chunk of sandstone off the north shore of PEI—with the ineluctable geologic realities of erosion: "it'll all wind up in the sea."

AP: Your answer above has aesthetic implications, I think, especially in terms of the question of diction in your poems, which are clearly and purposely marked, at times, by taxonomic particularity (e.g., a great moment in the Al Purdy homage, "At the Rebecca Cohn Auditorium," in which the speaker makes a point of admitting the difference between his "poppies and saxifrage" and the received, consecrated flora, that is, Purdy's "Arctic rhododendrons") and local colloquialisms (e.g., in the poems "Cormorant" or "Old Gray Mare"). Why is this diction so significant, both to you and the poems?

ZW: It's the old question of the unity of structure and content. Too many poets, it seems to me, use the same register for every poem they write; having "found a voice" they become slaves to it and either write variants of the same poems over and over or try to shoehorn the same language into different subjects. I'm more of an equal-opportunity employer; I'm interested in finding the right words for the particular poems I'm writing. Sometimes, this involves, as you say, taxonomic particularity (another example is "The Exterminator's Song to the Silverfish" in my chapbook *Ludicrous Parole*); sometimes it involves mining veins of specialized jargon and sometimes it involves the incorporation of colloquialisms and/or profanity. (I wrote about this for *Quill & Quire* a few years ago and they edited out the phrase "old cunts and boxing gloves," with my approval, because they felt it would be just a bit too shocking for some of their readership; but I restored the phrase when I reprinted it as a statement of poetics for the University of Toronto's poetry site.) It often involves switching gears midstream, mixing more "poetic" diction with earthier words, exploiting the tensions that result from such juxtapositions.

Going back to "Orkney Report," I used a lot of local diction because it paired nicely with the local references. So there's "noust," "broch" and "peedie," for instance, which are words one's unlikely to encounter outside of Orkney. It would be strange and affected to use them in a poem about PEI, but they fit the bill just right in the proper context. They might send readers "scurrying" to a dictionary, but so be it. I've always loved the line from Peter Van Toorn's "Rune": "Like a bronze pope, it salutes no one." This use of local dialect is something I absolutely love in many of Jen Hadfield's poems about Shetland, where she lives, and of course something I'm drawn to in the work of Clare as well. Hopkins was also a dog for Lancashire dialect in his poems; "degged with dew" etc. I think I was first awakened to the possibilities of local, collo-quial speech by Seamus Heaney's essays in *The Redress of Poetry*, in which appears "John Clare's Prog," which was probably my intro-duction to Clare's work.

AP: In that short essay, "Workshop Lessons" (available through the University of Toronto's "Canadian Poetry" website), you worry that "It is altogether too easy, in the company of wordsmiths, to lose sight of things that matter to people other than writers and thereby produce texts that might appeal to writers but not much to other people." Could you, perhaps, talk about what might be dubbed your "populist" propensity? What are the benefits or dan-gers, as you see them, of this position, especially in a Canadian literary marketplace today that seems (for the most part) to auto-matically equate the "populist" with vacuity?

ZW: It's a source of no small amusement to me that I've been labelled both "populist" and "elitist." I have no interest in either ism, per se; I really only want to write the poems I'm capable of writing as well as I can.

People who want to read poems usually want to read well-writ-ten ones, regardless of what walk of life they come from. Despite having written a fair bit of verse on blue-collar subjects, I've gone on record more than once saying I have no truck with the poet-ics of Tom Wayman, who values accessibility and political propa-ganda over formal concerns and ambiguity, or "difficulties or mys-teries generated by tricks of language or poetic form," as he would have it. To me, those difficulties or mysteries are more intrinsic to poetry than Wayman's version of straight talk.

Making something easily accessible is rarely the same as mak-ing something people love, something that gets better the more you read it. Larkin's a pretty accessible poet, but that's not why he's so popular. If it was, then how on earth account for the continued popularity of Dylan Thomas, whose poems err on the side of den-sity? Or Dickinson, who could be incredibly gnomic and obscure.

Sure, you've got your Rod McKuens and your Mary Olivers, but their popularity tends to be short-term, transient.

What I was getting at in the essay is that, even if your only public seems to be fellow writers, it's artistic suicide to write as if this was the case and following a fast-track from undergrad to grad to teaching is a pretty likely way to wind up writing that way: people write from their social contexts.

Which isn't to say that poets necessarily pander intentionally, but that when you spend much or most of your time in the company of your pen-peers, and you value their opinion of your work, it will affect the kind of writing you produce. Edwin Muir touches on this:

> The smaller and more select the audience for poetry, the more the poet will be confined. The smallness of the audience cannot but discourage him, and in doing that diminish his imaginative scope: all this no doubt within limits. Those who now write poetry know that they are writing for a few, since few people will read them, and this must influence without their knowing it the poetry that they write. I do not mean that contemporary poets sacrifice their integrity for the shadow of a select reputation, or that when they are conceiving their poems they ever think of the audience. But they are aware of what is possible, given their small audience, and what is not.

If you're conscious of your readership being wise to the tricks of the trade, then any sense of the possibility of magic, it seems to me, has to evaporate and expectations for what is possible between a poem and its reader have to diminish considerably. You can see this, I think, in how many books poets publish and in how many poems they cram into their books; to me, this is the sort of self-indulgent behaviour one engages in—like masturbation—when one thinks no one is watching. My stance on this has a lot to do with my ethos as a critic/book reviewer, too. The way I see it, the people calling for a stay of execution on "negative reviews" are people who have given up on the idea of a public for poetry. I prefer to write reviews as if they might actually matter to people other than poets. Which is perverse, I know, but if I capitulate to the idea that no one outside our circles cares, I might as well quit altogether.

So much contemporary writing, from the mid 20th C. on, sounds more to me like essays in poetics than like actual poems. Writers are interested in poetics. General readers usually aren't. My first relationship with literature was as a reader and the defining feature of that relationship was pleasure (broadly, including instances in which reading caused me sorrow or pain). I hope that at least a few readers experience my writing in a similar fashion. So I cherish inordinately the points of contact I make with a non-specialist audience. In many ways, my favourite review of *Unsettled* is the one written by a journalist, John Thompson, in the *Nunatsiaq News*, the Nunavut weekly. He said my poems "describe a Nunavut that's familiar to those who live here, which is rarely captured on the written page." And that meant a great deal to me. While I knew that most of the people who'd be reading the book would be southern poets, I cared more about how it would be perceived by northern non-poets. That's the particular public I had to imagine for that book.

Similarly, one of my favourite publications was in *Eye Weekly*, because it got the poem out of the poetry ghetto. A friend of mine, a computer programmer in Toronto, said he was reading the poem while he was eating his cereal one morning and, before noting who wrote it, thought, hey, that's good, I wonder if Zach knows this guy. Unfortunately, I think *Eye* stopped publishing poems, which is really a pity, as there are so few print venues out there for getting a poem in front of non-specialist eyeballs. I wish newspapers made a bit of space for verse, but it's not surprising that they don't.

I also love talking and reading to high school students, because you can't take their interest in what you have to say for granted. If they're bored by you, you'll probably know it; there's no faked enthusiasm, no "good reading, man." I have no illusions of there being some kind of potential mass audience for my writing, if only I could get more media play or if only people weren't so opiated on

TV, movies and games. That's nonsense. The creation of a public happens in increments, and most poets, even if they're very good and worthy of an audience, are only going to have a small public, even if it is drawn from a broad spectrum of people. It can seem futile most of the time, but then I'll get an email or a non-generic comment after a reading that reminds me it's not a completely Sisyphean task.

AP: Returning to *Track & Trace*, in "He Finds an Acceptable Way to Grieve" and "There Is Something Intractable in Me," you dramatize the way verse-structure (e.g., an acrostic, rhymed couplets) has a way of keeping "emotion" in check in a poem. (This isn't a new idea, of course; Yvor Winters, for example, was a severe critic of such histrionics.) So, in a sense, you *are* theorizing a poetics in your work at times. Would you agree?

ZW: I see what you mean, but I wouldn't entirely agree, no. That dimension of those poems has more to do with my personality than it does with any thought-through theories of how poems should be written. When I've taken Meyer-Briggs personality tests, the result has been INTJ, and the profile fits me to a tee: phlegmatic, pragmatic, perfectionist, skeptical, judgmental. While at times I have a near-autistic inability to understand people's emotional reactions to certain things (e.g., writers who get upset by reviews of their books) and am generally deficient in the empathy department, I'm not a robot, nor do I have any "post-human" desire to banish the emotive dimension from writing. I also love to argue, not least of all with myself. So it's no surprise if such qualities manifest themselves in my poems.

Both of the poems you cite are indeed, as you say, dramatizations—specifically, they're dramatizations of a psychomachia, an inner conflict, between my alpha reason and my beta emotions. I don't believe in any perfect distinction between thought and feeling, but they are certainly mixed in different concentrations in different people. Nor do I believe that people's thoughts and deeds are slavishly determined by an immutable personality type, nor that people don't change. Since becoming a father last year, for example, I've experienced types and intensities of emotion completely new to me.

Any victory or even stalemate that emotion has in my poems is hard-won because any statement of feeling I make comes under the scrutiny of a rather hard-nosed internal auditor. There's no reason on earth anyone who doesn't know me should care about that, but it's my hope that the conflict and tension dramatized in those two poems you name, and in others, are interesting to a reader. Tension and conflict are intrinsically interesting and generally I find them wanting in the sort of essay-poem I was talking about before, where theory and praxis are too cleanly in sync, where poetics are both text and sub-text.

It comes back again to a struggle for authentic expression. For example, I wrote "There Is Something Intractable in Me," which is a poem to my son using his name as an acrostic, after reading what I thought was a very sappy father-son poem, a poem whose sentiment I couldn't swallow. Which got me thinking about how to write a poem about an infant that isn't pure treacle. Ultimately, I failed, because the poem isn't about the kid at all, but about the father's struggle with his thoughts and feelings, with what he'd like to say and what he's able to say, the tension between the constraints of art and the constraints of love. Which has a lot to do with Dickinson's "formal feeling."

Part of me would love to be able to write gushy slushy love poems; I envy someone like Neruda, for example. But it's too small a part of me for me to write gushy love poems that I could actually stomach or that would pass the sniff test for readers. I remember having an argument a while back with someone about the relative merits of Auden's "Funeral Blues" and Bishop's "One Art." Not surprisingly, my sympathies are with the latter; I find the restraint and irony Bishop brings to her expression of grief far more credible—and ultimately far more moving—than the hysterical hyperboles of Auden's poem. For someone on the other end of the emotional/intellectual spectrum, it would probably go the other way.

As for "He Finds an Acceptable Way to Grieve," while I agree that one could make certain inferences from it about its author's poetics, the poem is, first and foremost, a narrative, not an argument. There's a way in which just about any poem a person writes can be interpreted as a statement of poetics. Ideally, I think, that's actually the way it should be: i.e. poems should be the means by which a person—whether poet or reader—arrives at poetics, as opposed to poetics being the way one arrives at poems. If you know how, what and why you're going to write beforehand, I don't much see the point in following through. That's what I meant above when I said that some poems read like essays in poetics; the poem itself appears to be a programmatic extension of pre-formulated theoretical concepts. I write—and read—poems in large measure to work through things I haven't been able to figure out; insofar as the two poems named show a person in the process of working things out, sure, they're statements of poetics, but they're statements of poetics that I think apply to other realms. And they're statements of a poetics in progress, not of any fixed dogmatic position. Rarely does a poem actually provide me with solutions to problems, but poems often help me to ask better questions.

ESSAYS AND REVIEWS

FAULTY LINES
The Poetry and Poetics of Don McKay

I HAVE BEEN READING Don McKay's books for several years. My reading of them has not been dictated by any sense of cultural obligation. I have read McKay's books because I have enjoyed McKay's books. More specifically, I appreciate the improvisatory verve of his language, his humour and his refusal to draw a simple clean line between humankind and nature, technology and wilderness. His poems are fun, smart, easy to like. But, like a pleasant, engaging stranger you meet on a train, I don't think much about them afterwards. Why have I never had much of an urge to re-read McKay's books? Why do I have a hard time recalling specific McKay poems, or even lines? Why, when I think of excellent contemporary poets, does McKay's name not spring to mind? Why, when I do re-read his poems with a critical eye, do they mostly disappoint me?

A telling sign of the overall lack of distinction in McKay's work can be found in Méira Cook's selection of poems for *Field Marks: The Poetry of Don McKay*. With most poets who have been around for a while, a general consensus emerges as to what constitutes their best, most memorable poems. Cook's critical edition comes hot on the heels of a more comprehensive Selected Poems, *Camber*, but only twenty-one of *Field Marks'* thirty-five poems appear in the longer book, which contains a whopping 121 poems. This could mean that all of McKay's work is so uniformly good that it's impossible to whittle it down to an essential hits list, but this would make him one of the greatest poets ever to wield a pen, which I trust even his most ardent admirers would find too silly to say aloud. Reading and re-reading both of these books, as well as McKay's latest collection *Strike/Slip*, it seems to me a more plausible explanation is that McKay has written few, if any, truly exceptional poems and that any random selection from his oeuvre is as good as any other for illustrating his aims and accomplishments.

I don't mean to suggest that McKay is untalented or negligible—but it does seem to me that a significant rift exists between the claims made about his body of work and his actual achievements; that McKay is not, as Mark Frutkin has opined, "in the top rank of poets writing in English today," but rather, in Richard Greene's words, "a poet of considerable gifts, which are, in general, badly deployed."

*

In the introduction to *Field Marks*, Cook writes of McKay's "environmental poetics, his peculiarly gentle, un-grasping, dis-owning brand of nature poetry." She later enlists the aid of Robert Bringhurst to identify McKay's break from "the tradition of rapturous, nonspecific, pantheistic nature poetry inaugurated by ... Wordsworth." This sort of poetry is encapsulated by Wordsworth's famous lines from "The Recluse":

> ... my voice proclaims
> How exquisitely the individual Mind
> (And the progressive powers perhaps no less
> Of the whole species) to the external World
> Is fitted:—and how exquisitely, too,
> Theme this but little heard of among Men,
> The external World is fitted to the Mind[.][18]

18   Cook's Wordsworth, who "might recollect in tranquility images of 'tree' or 'bird,' [whereas] McKay painstakingly describes" specific species—a poet too enthralled by Big Themes to pay any attention to minute particulars—is a gross simplification. Ironically, she generalizes the poet in the same way she claims he generalizes nature. Were one to painstakingly describe Wordsworth's oeuvre, one would find ample

According to Cook, there is nothing of the Egotistical Sublime in McKay; in place of a proclaiming voice and Adamic naming, the poet " … 'discovers' but never appropriates the wilderness world. Gingerly, tactfully, reverently, McKay's watcher never 'becomes' bird." McKay himself advocates "listening through language" as an approach favourable to using language as a tool for dominance and ownership.

The problem is that the poems themselves betray these statements of authorial intention and critical explication in multiple ways. Let's start with this verb "discover." In Cook's essay, the word has a wholly positive connotation, which is echoed in McKay's afterword when he writes that the "form of a work is something it discovers." Just as the poet does not impose his ego on wilderness, neither does he impose domesticated form on the wilds of language. But if language is wild, then a significant portion of its wilderness must inhere in its evolutionary (viz. etymological) drift. McKay's gentle "discover" originally had a dark dimension, rooted as it is in malicious betrayal; a discoverer was, to use a more modern idiom, a stoolpigeon.

The word hauls with it to this day the heavy sea chest of its origins; when we speak of discovery in a North American context, we cannot tease from the word its association with destructive exploitation, with the subjugation of both the land and the aboriginal peoples who inhabit it, with the whole sordid business of the White Man's Burden. Cook extols McKay's "poems of ambling, wandering, and meandering, of taking the wrong road and getting 'there' anyway … of deviation, digression, excursion in landscape, and incursion in language, [which] represent various ways of knowing without

---

evidence to gainsay Cook's claim. Passages of "The Recluse" are studded with the names and habits of specific species. In particular, Wordsworth's treatment of the swan pair ("They strangers, and we strangers; they a pair, / And we a pair like them.") chimes with McKay's preoccupation with otherness and sameness between humans and animals. If anything, Wordsworth, in this passage, shows himself to be more "disowning" and "un-grasping" than McKay when he says the swans "require / No benediction from the Stranger's lips, / For they are blest already"—a sharp contrast to McKay's bestowals of blessings in his ongoing "Song for the Song of [X]" series.

claiming." At best, there is a sort of blithe naïveté about this, as if the Columbuses and Cartiers—not to mention the Franklins, Cooks and Pearys—weren't such mapless bumbling finders, as if discovery was an act inherently innocent of greed, ignorance and ambition.

Even if we ignore the philological inappropriateness of discovery as metaphor for non-possessive knowledge, the poems don't come near the ideal. McKay may not write with Wordsworthian confidence of the synthesizing genius of the human mind, but if you compare his nature poems with those of a true anti-Wordsworth such as John Clare, the gaps between stated poetics and poem become manifest. For Clare, poetry's preeminent ornithologist, the animal was never a mere trope, but a marvellous other to be admired, respected and accorded space. He was critical of Keats, of whom he said, "he often described Nature as she appeared to his fancies and not as he would have described her had he witnessed the things he described."[19] Clare's best bird poems are vivid, spontaneous play-by-play observations; the reader feels as though she's looking over the poet's shoulder as he describes the contents of one nest or another. The emphasis is squarely on the bird; the self-effacement of the poet is an organic (i.e. unintentional, un-self-conscious) by-product of his keen attention: he forgets himself or, more accurately, creates the impression of forgetting himself.

In an interview with Ken Babstock, McKay talks about "trying to make the appropriate gesture," but his poems often demonstrate that a failed attempt can result, against the poet's best wishes, in a gesture of appropriation. McKay's nature poems are distinctly literary, and more than a little Keatsian or Wordsworthian insofar as Idea or Sentiment come to dominate description—it came as no surprise to me to learn that McKay "could recite whole swatches of the Prelude"—by comparison with Clare's. In a poem like "How to Imagine an Albatross," McKay demonstrates that, like the Wordsworth of "The Recluse," "the Mind of Man" is his "haunt, and the main region of [his] song." The title is the first indication

---

19   The difference in sensibility was mutual, as Keats felt that in many of Clare's poems "the Description too much prevailed over the sentiment."

of the poem's concern with cerebration, which is heightened by the opening lines: "To imagine an albatross / a mind must widen to the breadth of the Pacific Ocean / dissolve its edges to admit a twelve foot wingspan." What is this if not fitting the mind to the external world and the external world to the mind? The bird arcs "thoughtlessly as an idea, as a phrase-mark holding notes," a simile McKay emphasizes by repeating it sixteen lines later. McKay rarely describes a scene in anything resembling its own terms, but fills land- and seascapes with the bric-a-brac "fancies" of his art- and culture-steeped mind:

> This might be
> dream without content or the opening of a film
> in which the credits never run no speck appears
> on the horizon fattening to Randolph Scott on horseback or the lost
> brown mole below your shoulderblade.

As Anne Szumigalski wrote in a review of *Apparatus*, "Out and about with McKay, I do not feel myself contemplating the landscape he is writing about—I feel myself contemplating his mind as he considers the natural order." Throughout McKay's oeuvre, from the earliest poems in *Field Marks* and *Camber* to the recent work in *Strike/Slip*, literary and cultural allusions proliferate and metaphor tends to make objects seem more arbitrarily weird than like themselves, as, say, Elizabeth Bishop does with such precision in a poem like "The Fish." Granted, this could be McKay's point: that animals and other non-human things are intrinsically strange to us because they are "other"; but when a deer's tail is likened to a fridge, we see neither a deer's tail nor a fridge, but a poet saying they are somehow related.[20] As with so many things in McKay's poetry, we must take the poet's word for it.

---

20   This sort of regimented "surprise" happens so often, so mechanically and habitually, in McKay's poems that we might accuse him, as Jarrell did Auden, of "The Bureaucratization of Perspective by Incongruity." Or we might instead call it Shake'n Bake Strangeness.

When McKay writes of releasing "the rage / which holds this pencil in itself, to prod things / until their atoms shift," I'm put in mind of Wallace Stevens'

> ... rage to order words of the sea,
> Words of the fragrant portals, dimly-starred,
> And of ourselves and of our origins,
> In ghostlier demarcations, keener sounds.

But perhaps even more, to plunder another Stevens poem, "The vital, arrogant, fatal, dominant X" seems *à propos*. Stan Dragland insists that "For ... Don McKay ... wilderness is anything but wasteland in need of stamping with the human imprint." This may well be McKay's political opinion or an echo of his own stated poetics, but in the poems, on the contrary, he insistently stamps his heated brand on the scenes and creatures he celebrates. How often in McKay's oeuvre are wild things described with metaphors drawn from art, text, technology and culture, as in the prose poem "Gneiss" from *Strike/Slip*. Here is the last paragraph:

> But close up it is more likely to be the commotion of stress lines swirling within each slab that clutches at the heart—each stone a pent rage, an agon. None of the uniform grey of limestone, that prehistoric version of ready-mix concrete, in which each laid-down layer adds to the accumulated weight that homogenizes its predecessors. Think instead of Münch's *The Scream* with its contour lines of terror; then subtract the face. Or you could turn on the weather channel to observe those irresponsible isobars scrawling across the planet. Imagine our ancestors tracing these surfaces, whorled fingertip to gnarled rock, reading the earth-energy they had levered into the air. They had locked the fury into the fugue and car crash into the high-school prom. They engineered this dangerous dance. Better stop here. Better spend some time.

Clutches at the heart, rage, agon, ready-mix concrete, The Scream, *weather channel, ancestors, fingertip, fury, fugue, car crash, high-school prom, engineered, dance.* The last two sentences are adapted from the poem's epigraph, drawn from a book called *Touring Scotland by Automobile.* Do the tropes make us see what he's talking about? Certainly. But they make us see it in our own terms; they domesticate rock into stone, make it ours, annex it to our experiences and emotions—they make it easy for us to "get," both in the sense of "understand" and "acquire." He also gets something badly wrong. Anyone who has stopped and spent some time with limestone knows well that it is anything but "uniform" in texture, colour and composition. It's a cutesy touch calling it a "prehistoric version of ready-mix concrete," since concrete is composed largely of, you guessed it, crushed limestone, but McKay seems to be cool with the fact that he has just verbally converted living stone into processed rock.

If, as McKay has claimed, "The first indicator of one's status as nature poet is that one does not invoke language right off when talking about poetry, but acknowledges some extra-linguistic condition as the poem's input, output, or both," one can only determine, from poking through this poetic creature's scat, that his "status" is something with which he is more preoccupied than he is with nature. The first lines of *Strike/Slip*'s opening poem, "Astonished"— also the terminal poem of the selection in *Field Marks*—is a sort of etymological meditation: "astounded, astonied, astunned, stopped short / and turned toward stone." Three lines down, stone "might be the symbol signifying eon." And in the final line, the ocean is "nameless." The problem is, when you call something "nameless," as McKay often does, you invoke the process of naming. It's a little like the scene in Polyphemus' cave, when Odysseus tells the Cyclops his name is "Nobody"—minus the dramatic irony.

The next poem, "Petrified," begins with "your heart's tongue seized / mid-syllable." In "Loss Creek" we find "The broken prose of the bush roads"; "raw drag without phrase / for the voice"; rapids speaking; "pauseless syntax." In "Alluvium" death is figured as having "letters [licked] from your name." In "Pond" water has "been possessed by every verb"; the pond "translates air as texture."

In "Devonian" "words / tap dance" into wilderness and "slur into is it sand or / is it snow that blows its messages across / the highway." In "Quartz Crystal" stones "call, in the various dialects of gravity" and the poet's poems are threatened with "depublication." I could go on, but all this, just in the book's first nine poems, should be sufficient to demonstrate that McKay is overtly obsessed with language. Yes, he most often refers to it as something to be shucked in order to better attend to the mute workings of nature, but he is so insistent about it that language becomes a sort of *occupatio* for him: "I won't 'invoke language right off,' but … "

I'm not saying that egocentrism or anthropocentrism—or heaven forfend, interest in language!—is wrongheaded. The business of art is, as both Northrop Frye and Wallace Stevens have suggested in works titled "The Motive for Metaphor," to make the world outside our minds make sense to us, a process which necessarily involves a kind of benign violence to the thing-itself through the medium of language. No, the problem is that McKay and Cook seem to be more deluded about the truth and beauty of this violent appropriation—and less clear or honest as to its nature, more precious and disingenuous—than Wordsworth or Stevens or Irving Layton, who queried: "How to dominate reality?" and answered himself, "Love is one way; / imagination another."

McKay and his apologists are in denial about some of the uglier aspects of human nature and consequently about the nature of art, which leads to untenable assertions in poetics and self-despising soft spots in poems, resulting in poems which are adequate to neither the "otherness" of the wild nor to the "selfness" of the mind. It's hard, in the light of McKay's poetics, not to see the attempted subversion of the guidebook clichés that end "Gneiss" as self-reproach, as the poet not having stopped long enough in his touring, not paying sufficient attention to see the rock in less human terms. To put it another way, the *raison d'être* of McKay's poems is to reiterate his poetics, rather than to *be poems*. Even if they occasionally piddle on the rug, they are domesticated animals, a kind of versified theory, and as such are more analogous with technology and the academic pursuit of knowledge than with the wisdom of wilderness. How much less persuasive—how much more "vestigial," to borrow McKay's own distinction—they are as homage than, say, the ingenious artifice of Les Murray's *Translations from the Natural World,* or the precisely described eroticism of Peter Van Toorn's "Dragonflies, Those Bluejays of the Water." McKay badly wants to be a "nature poet" of an un-Romantic bent but what he writes is not, even in his own terms, nature poetry so much as poetry in love with the idea of nature poetry.

Reading McKay brings to mind Christian Wiman's trenchant distinction between "poets" and "nature poets":

> Poets are interested in consciousness and how the natural world might reveal it; personality is not the point. Nature poets are interested in using the world to dramatize the self; each poem is a showcase for the poets' own dewy sensibilities. For poets, the emphasis is on the poem as event: it's important that they write well and originally. Nature poets emphasize whatever event occasioned the poem: it's important that they be very sincere. Because poets feel acutely the foreignness of nature, and because they recognize both the appeal and the danger of that unlikeness, there is usually some reluctance or ambivalence that makes itself felt in their work. Nature poets can't walk across the backyard without tripping over an epiphany. Poets make you see the world with new eyes, as the saying goes, and they make you want it more, too, though in a complicated way, fostering alike by beauty and by fear. Nature poets make you indifferent to both nature and poetry. Poets ... are rare ... Nature poets are everywhere.

McKay often seems uncomfortably caught between the ambition to be a poet and the ease of being a nature poet. The jocular self-mockery that is such a signature of his work is symptomatic of that inner schism, I think, but it is not altogether redemptive. McKay has succeeded in creating his own brand (and franchise) of nature poetry, but that brand does not transcend the clichés of the genre to which it belongs. That McKay on one level knows they are clichés makes his failure to reject them all the more disappointing.

McKay's wishful thinking might help to account for the real shortcomings of his poems, which are not thematic, but reside in the "habits and tricks," as McKay himself puts it, that are both what endear readers to his verse and what prevent his poems from fulfilling the potential augured by their more happily conceived moments. Prime among these distractions is the poet's persona, the self that speaks in the poems, which Cook describes approvingly as a "self-effacing ... off-handed, likeably self-mocking, endearingly modest poetic presence." The garrulous off-handedness of the McKay persona, like Al Purdy's but more exaggerated and ubiquitous, is so self-*conscious* that it can never really be "self-effacing" in any meaningful way; as Greene observes, this "is an obvious contradiction, and a pretentious one." We are constantly reminded of just how modest this character is and can therefore rarely forget that everything we're reading takes place on the proscenium stage of his braincase.

One of the manners in which we are thus cued is irony. Irony for McKay, to borrow Michael Schmidt's useful distinction, is more often stylistic than thematic; which is to say that irony is something perpetrated by the poet rather than by the anthro-in-different workings of the universe, as in the characteristic poems of Hardy or Larkin. Awe, astonishment and wonder are keynotes of McKay's poems and poetics. But they are moods he constantly subverts with jokiness, as he "rais[es] a fine / ironic eyebrow." It is as though the poet does not believe in what he's saying strongly enough to commit to the risk of saying it straight, or as though some culture-self is always waiting around the corner to knee-cap the wilderness-self. When Cook says that McKay employs "humour (joke, parody, irony, satire) to deflate pretension," she stumbles over, but passes by, a crucial question: whence this swelling pretension that needs such constant pricking?

Humour is a substance McKay adds liberally to his alembic to neutralize an equally substantial quantity of sentimental earnestness.

The clichéd phrase "clutches at your heart" from "Gneiss" is but one example of this predilection. In "Finger Pointing at the Moon," a poem from *Another Gravity* included in *Camber*, strains of trite pseudo-wisdom founded on a base of abstraction begin to seep in, and then take over, the poem. First, the "back-drag" of waves becomes a "drum kit from the far side of the blues / where loss begins to shuffle." The presence of the word "loss" is a predictable enough, if not necessarily fatal, flaw in a contemporary lyric poem, but then

> I think each memory is lit
> by its own small moon—a snowberry,
> a mothball, a dime—which regulates its tides
> and longings.

"Memory," "small moon" and "longings" are all stock tropes drawn from the common props closet. And then finally

> I think we come here so our words
> can fail us, get humbled by the stones, drown,
> be lost forever, then come back
> as beach glass, polished and anonymous,
> knowing everything.

This is nothing but egregious quasi-spiritualism, and rather sloppily executed at that. How can something be "lost forever"—bad cliché, that, reminding us of "My Darling Clementine"—but still "come back"? No wonder McKay feels the need to drag "your no-good Uncle Ray" and "lavish / sixties shag" into the poem, to puncture the sententiousness that would otherwise wash upon a reader's eyes and ears without distraction. Failing to evoke a sense of awe, McKay tends to spell it out for his readers; then, seemingly embarrassed by his strained efforts, he makes fun of himself for having done it.

Bearing in mind Yeats's distinction that "rhetoric is heard" whereas "poetry is overheard," there is far more rhetoric—even if it is a sort of anti-rhetoric—than poetry in the typical McKay poem, which seems to pitch its lines at the back row of an audience whose presence he can't ignore. As Greene puts it,

> At best, this is a failure of nerve: the poet feared his ironies would be concealed unless he advertised them. At worst, the whole poem ["Fates Worse than Death" from *Apparatus*, reprinted in *Vis à Vis, Camber* and *Field Marks*] ... is a piece of intellectual dishonesty on the part of a poet who loves the exaltations of language, but knows it is more fashionable to pose as a debunker of the big claims of art.[21]

*

Part of the wide appeal of McKay's poetry must be that, while having the surface sheen of erudition and deep thought, the poems rarely force a reader to think for herself. Reading a McKay poem, we feel smart because we recognize things from our own reading

---

21 I tend to think the truth lies somewhere in between. In *The Estate of Poetry*, Edwin Muir wrote:

> The smaller and more select the audience for poetry, the more the poet will be confined. The smallness of the audience cannot but discourage him, and in doing that diminish his imaginative scope: all this no doubt within limits. Those who now write poetry know that they are writing for a few, since few people will read them, and this must influence without their knowing it the poetry that they write. I do not mean that contemporary poets sacrifice their integrity for the shadow of a select reputation, or that when they are conceiving their poems they ever think of the audience. But they are aware of what is possible, given their small audience, and what is not.

That was in 1955, and if anything, the situation is even worse today because more thoroughly institutionalized. For McKay, who has spent his career immersed in the spheres of his limited audience of fellow-poets and -academics, it seems to me almost inevitable that an awareness of "what is possible ... and what is not" should have seeped into his practice. If one operates under the ingrained assumption that one's audience is wise to the tricks of the trade, one is far less apt to risk afflatus and more likely to seek refuge under the cover of ironic deflation.

and habits of thought, but our deeply imbedded assumptions are left untroubled. We read, we are charmed, we forget, we move on.

If McKay is a master of anything, it is of sublimating his faults as a poet and thinker into virtues: if he fails, it is because he is human and therefore finite and possesses only the limited resources of the English language in which to sing all the magnificent mysteries of the infinite universe. A noble sentiment, but unfortunately, it seems often to be an excuse for McKay to take shortcuts; if one's bound to fail, why bother with all the portage, eh? The most fundamental of his faults is his all-or-nothing adherence to randomness. Dragland insists that "McKay is no romantic," but recall his beliefs in the value of aimless wandering ("lonely as a cloud," perhaps?) and accidental discovery and in the highly romantic notion of form being something that a work "discovers" for itself (perhaps in the same way that Adam Smith's "invisible hand" supposedly regulates a capitalistic economy?).

If a poem must find its own form, then presumably the poet is, conveniently, off the hook for any faults in the final product. Shane Neilson has already taken McKay to task for line breaks which are "random and disconcertingly weak," but this is not the only stress fracture in McKay's prosody. He quotes Herakleitos to defend his chosen mode of *vers libre*: "The hidden attunement is better than the obvious one." In his book *Poetic Design*, Stephen Adams makes much of such "hidden attunements" in McKay's work, highlighting imbedded iambic pentameters in the poem "Softball." And it's true that at his best, McKay's rhythms are the strongest, most persuasive elements of his poems and his free verse lines don't often sound, as so many others' do, like chopped prose. But his eschewal of the discipline of metre, far from eliminating the padding evident in unskilled formal verse, seems to invite the superfluous in to stay. Consider "Song for the Song of the Coyote," from *Another Gravity* and reprinted in *Camber*:

Moondogs, moondogs,
tell me the difference between tricks
and wisdom, hunting
and grieving.
I listen in the tent, my ear
to the ground. There is a land even
more bare than this one, without sage,
or prickly pear, or greasewood. A land
that can only wear its scars, every crater
etched. Riverless. Treeless. You sing to its thin
used-up light, yips and floated tremolos and screams,
sculpted barks like fastballs of packed
air. Echoes that articulate the buttes and coulees and dissolve
into the darkness, which is always listening.

I know this piece has admirers, since I once received it in an email from another poet, but I have a hard time seeing how it transcends its flaws. The poem is fourteen lines, which calls to mind a sonnet. But as any student of prosody and poetic form will tell you, just because a poem has fourteen iambic pentameter lines and a set rhyme scheme doesn't mean it's a successful sonnet; by the same token, a poem that breaks or bends many of the strictures can still be, essentially, a sonnet—a version of a poem finding its own form, but not without guidance from the poet and tradition. This poem doesn't try to follow any of the sonnet rules, but it is marked nonetheless by the missteps of an eleven-line poem trying too hard to stretch itself into an orthodox sonnet. What is there in the first five and a half lines that can't be jettisoned for the betterment of the poem? What jumps out at me from the first incantatory repetition of "moondogs" is a white poet playing somewhat naively at native spirituality and the typical Romantic gambit of looking for symbolic meaning in the natural world. As McKay himself damningly puts it, "The romantic poet (or tourist, for that matter) desires to be spoken *to*, inspired by the other." In the fifth line, "ear to the ground," however literal it is in this context, is an egregious cliché.

I see no reason why the poem couldn't start with "There is a land" and be much the better for it. The lines that follow are far more interesting, even if unstructured by syllable, stress, syntax or sound and broken quite arbitrarily. The last half-line is also a poetical cliché screaming to be axed.

It seems odd that McKay, whose doctoral dissertation was on Dylan Thomas, one of the craftiest form-forgers in the history of English poetry, should cleave so willfully to a wishy-washy laissez-faire poetics of dubiously organic form. Another poet with whom Cook associates McKay is Hopkins. Like Thomas, who was influenced by him, Hopkins was a masterfully inventive manipulator of inherited forms. And those manipulations, far from being "unnatural," are actually reflective of nature's patterns and inscapes. As American critic Paul Lake has said, "Hopkins, like Coleridge, knew that it was rules or laws operating on chance—not chance alone—that gave nature its designs." A comparison of almost any McKay poem with almost any Hopkins poem is enough to burn any specious bridges built between the two poets by reputation-engineering critics. Just as Hopkins' deliberate pattern-making is a formal reflection of his reverence for the natural world, McKay's slipshod neglect of pattern discovers (in the old sense of "betrays") his touristic dilettantism.

His essential *in*attention is reinforced by the eccentricity of his approach to metaphor. McKay will often reel off a string of metaphorical possibilities, as in this passage from "Precambrian Shield":

> Would I go back to that time,
> that chaste and dangerous embrace?
> Not unless I was allowed,
> as carry-on, some sediment that has since
> accumulated, something to impede the
> passage of those days that ran through us
> like celluloid. Excerpts from the book of loss.
> Tendonitis. Second thoughts. Field guides.

This is more postmodern ADD than keen attentiveness. McKay rarely sustains focus throughout a poem; the attention he pays, both to the object of his attention and to the making of the poem, is desultory. As Richard Greene has observed of the poem "To Speak of Paths" (from *Apparatus,* reprinted in *Camber*), "The metaphors are not only mixed but, as occurs repeatedly in his poems, actually jumbled." Cook defends the weirdness of McKay's scattershot metaphors as evidence of "high tension" in his poetry: "Because of tension created between objects of comparison, between focus and frame, 'high tension' poetry promotes startling metaphoric effects, encouraging imagistic torque not readily legible in more habitual phrasing." But if "startling" is all that needs to be done to "reopen ... the question of reference," as McKay puts it, then strangeness is all that's required: "With a metaphor that works we're immediately convinced of the truth of the claim *because* it isn't rational." This isn't entirely incorrect, but it fails to account for a metaphor that doesn't "work," but is equally non-rational. Aptness, far more difficult to achieve and ultimately more durable in its ability to startle us awake, can be forgotten.

McKay's poems are full of contradictions, as I've said. A rebuttal to my criticisms above could be that, as per Emerson, consistency is the hobgoblin of my little mind. Perhaps McKay aligns himself with Whitman's "Do I contradict myself? Very well, then I contradict myself, I am large, I contain multitudes." But McKay's self-contradictions mostly lack the brazen self-awareness of Whitman's; he is constantly drawing our attention to them by apologizing for them, which makes them on the whole much less interesting than they might otherwise be. Far from containing multitudes, McKay contains his own inward-gazing particularity. As a general rule, McKay's contradictions aren't between one statement and another, but between statement of intention and formal execution, which strikes me more as an inadequacy—or "a failure of nerve," to recall Greene's phrase—than as a fruitful failure.

But roughly halfway through *Strike/Slip* I found a contradiction far more interesting in the form of a poem entitled "'Stress,

Shear, and Strain Theories of Failure.'" This is the poem from which the book takes its title, which refers to "a high-angle fault along which rocks on one side move horizontally in relation to rocks on the other side with a shearing motion." This is an unusual poem for McKay, not because of subject matter, but because of form: although irregularly-rhymed and -metred, the poem is, as it announces itself, a sonnet:

> They have never heard of lift
> and are—for no one, over and over—cleft. Riven,
> recrystallized. Ruined again. The earth-engine
> driving itself through death after death. Strike/slip,
> thrust, and the fault called normal, which occurs
> when two plates separate.
> Do they hearken unto Orpheus, whose song
> is said to make them move? Sure.
> This sonnet hereby sings that San Fran-
> cisco and L.A. shall, thanks to its chthonic shear,
> lie cheek by jowl in thirty million
> years. Count on it, mortals. Meanwhile,
> may stress shear strain attend us. Let us fail
> in all the styles established by our lithosphere.

In his afterword to *Field Marks*, McKay claims that he does not "identify [form] with those marvelous prosodic structures (sonnet, terza rima, glosas, pantoums, *cyghanned*) which have collected in the multicultural ragbag of the English tradition." Fair enough, but reading a sonnet like the one above, I wish he was not generally so thorough in divorcing those marvellous structures from his own methods. In this poem, the wit is integral rather than digressively apologetic, the internal rhymes complement the end-rhymes and the ragged pattern corresponds, in miniature, to the more-or-less predictable, but often dramatic, movement of tectonic plates. This is a poem in which McKay seems to have learned a lesson from Hopkins in design, in which he makes room for both the order of

Apollo and the "natural energies" of Dionysos, which divinities, as Nietzsche learned and taught, are more aspects of each other than mutually exclusive opposites. The poem finds its form within a frame that doesn't leave room for McKay's characteristic doodling outside of the lines. Unlike so many of McKay's poems, there is nothing in it I want changed, every word and formal choice feels necessary; even the abrupt truncation of "San Fran- / cisco" isn't done just to force a consonantal rhyme, but fits beautifully with the subject matter. The memorability of that final sentence is enhanced by the last line's being an alexandrine, an old trick of Spenser's, thumping its iambic pulse into blood and brain. Will this poem represent a strike/slip fault in McKay's poetics, or is it an anomaly, a rare eruption from an otherwise underachieving volcano?

ELLIPSES AND INTERSTICES
Richard Outram

IN HIS MONOGRAPH on the poetry of Richard Outram, Peter
Sanger says that Outram's book *Man in Love* "contains some
extremely, perhaps excessively compressed and abstract poems."
That qualified reservation is perhaps the only point at which
Sanger is at all skeptical of Outram's poetic practice. Later on
in the book he tells us that "in all of Outram's collections there
are some poems which require the most careful, patient reading,
word by word, tense by tense, antecedent by antecedent, within
the complete context of his work, before they start to yield some-
thing of their meaning." That the former qualm should come
from such a staunch admirer of Outram and from a poet who
is himself a writer of uncompromisingly compressed, sometimes
near-inscrutable poems, speaks volumes. The latter comment is
not intended as a criticism of Outram, but it might as well be as
far as the majority of not undedicated readers of poetry, this one
included, are concerned.

If readers balk at what Sanger calls their "cryptographic task"
it should not be blamed on indolence. While poetry is expected
to make greater demands on a reader's attention and intellectual
resources than other forms of writing, it isn't reasonable to expect
monastic dedication on the part of the average reader in order
for a poem to "*start* to yield *something* of [its] meaning." But if
this intellectual density of phrase and allusion is at the core of

Outram's not wholly undeserved reputation as an inaccessibly "difficult" poet—"where every rift," as Carmine Starnino puts it, "is ore'd with recondite details"—it is also at work in the generous handful—perhaps even an armload—of verses that should, in a just universe, secure Outram a permanent place in the hearts and minds of readers.

In a short essay[22] on Outram's "Story," the prefatory poem to his book *Turns and Other Poems*, Amanda Jernigan has done a wonderful job unpacking the significance with which the poem's twenty-six words are freighted:

> Let us begin with Death
> Overheard, in the cry
> Of the first breath,
>
> That for what it is worth,
> We may all thereby
> End with Birth.

I won't dwell on this poem at length, in part because Jernigan has left little for anyone else to say (although I am surprised she made no mention of the fact that the number twenty-six is of particular import for our alphabet, especially in a poem dealing explicitly with omegas et alphas). But primarily, I won't dwell on this poem, or others like it, because it's not the sort of thing in Outram's oeuvre that excites me. Here he has condensed things so radically that the poem, for all its formal brilliance and chronological prestidigitation, feels rather cool in its abstractions and generalities. I suppose I could be accused of being insensitive to the beauty of this sort of poem, but the shoulder-shrug it prompts in me is not the same reaction that I have to, say, Dickinson's "Because I would not stop for death," a poem far more intensely intimate in its speaker's relationship to Big Themes. And for me, it certainly does not come close to passing Miss Emily's acid test for poetry, that it make you

22　The essay can be found at http://arcpoetry.ca/?p=34/.

"feel physically as if the top of your head were taken off." Yes, it is accessible in a way that his more cryptic poems are not, poems like "Medium":

First O Sufficient
Image O Fire
Conveyed O Water
Burdened by Fire
We apprehend Other
Metaphor's Metaphor:
Man but abandoned
Momentum, language
Forsworn, that poem
As yet unbroken.

... and quite likely to remain unbroken. But accessibility is no more a poetic virtue in itself than difficulty and allusiveness are. Fortunately there are poems to be found throughout Outram's works that, while employing some of the compressive techniques of his more tortured work and the accessibility of poems like "Story," are deeply moving, heartfelt unities of thought and emotion.

Sanger tells us that the "accessible poems" in Outram's work are "grounded upon" the "difficult and densely written" ones, that to read Outram partially is to read him irresponsibly. It may well be that to gain a holistic scholarly apprehension of Outram's systems of thought and language, those knotted, gnomic, gnostic verses need plumbing. Edwin Muir insists that studying Yeats' barmy obsessions with fairies and gyres does nothing to improve upon our enjoyment of the man's best poems, even if the poems are by-products of the obsession. Similarly, I would advise non-scholarly readers of Outram not to bother fussing with his devil's knots, to skip the esoteric groundwork and go straight for the poems with broad appeal. Whither should we skip, then?

How about first to the unnamed Maritime isle on which the magical realist sequence *Hiram and Jenny* unrolls. This book, like many of Outram's, has delightful elements of farce, but at the heart of this comedy is a great "Grief":

> Jenny lost her baby.
> It was a small loss, and went almost unnoticed.
>
> Some people were kind and some were not.
>
> Now she can no longer walk past certain boulders
> or look at peonies.
>
> And sometimes, continuing along the shore, she seems
> to hesitate, as if about to turn back.
>
> Most evenings and first thing mornings.
>
> Her eyes, which were dark, have darkened.
>
> Hiram went out and split five cords
> of maple in three days.
>
> Sometimes exhaustion helps, a little.

Here, compression manifests itself, paradoxically, in gaps and absences. Not the sort of elisions and interstices that can be filled with erudition, but the kind of psychic hole that is palpably felt and can never be filled. Though the poem is simple and direct, there is great subtlety in the arrangement of phrases and images. How much is said, while nothing is explained away, by the trochaic directness of that first line, by the sad irony of "small loss," by "almost," by "certain boulders" and "peonies," by the fragmentary sentence of the fifth stanza, by the iteration in "dark, have darkened," by the comma before "a little," by the long pauses caused by end-stopped lines and stanzas. This poem, with its stoic refusal of easy sentiment, is heartbreaking. There isn't much to say about it if you're bent on scholarly exegesis, which is probably why Sanger says almost nothing about it in *Her Kindled Shadow*, but if anything it is such poems of lower ambiguity that provide a key to the locked chests of Outram's difficult work—and not the other way around. As with the more recondite of Outram's poems, the reader is left to fill the silent spaces between the lines of "Grief," but in this case does not require a pile of gear and tackle to do it.

Another poem in which Outram puts his aptitude for concision to brilliant use is "Barbed Wire," a piece more technically virtuosic than "Grief," but which is also one of the rare personal poems in Outram's oeuvre. This is not to say that the rest of his poetry is impersonal—much of it, in fact, is so personally encoded as to be downright private[23]—but that he does not often place himself explicitly inside his poem's narratives. Given the result in this instance, it is I hope not ungrateful to wish he had done so more often.

BARBED WIRE

Consists of two tight-twisted, separate strands
Conjoined as one: and not unlike, in fact,
Our own familiar silver wedding bands,
Though these are loosely woven, inexact,

With wide interstices, so that each makes
A circle of ellipses. Tightly caught
At random intervals, two little snakes
Of wire are crimped into a snaggled knot,

---

23 Sanger also acknowledges the privacy of Outram's ethics and aesthetics, related of course to Outram's involvement in Gauntlet, a "private press." For Sanger, privacy is not a problem in Outram's work, at least not one that bothers him. For scholars of Outram, I can see how this would be so, but speaking as I am here to more general amateurs of poetry, I can't agree.

That four short ends, sharp bevel-cut, present
Unsheathed, ingenious fangs. And when in place,
Stretched taut, or strewn in loose coils, may prevent
The passage through some designated space

Of beast, or man. You got used to the stench;
The mud was worse than being under fire,
My father said. A detail left the trench
At night, to get the dead back from the wire,

And no one volunteered. They stood, to view
Our brief exchange of rings and vows, for both
Our fathers had survived that war: and knew
Of death, and bright entanglement, and troth.

As with any Outram poem, intrication plays a key role in how "Barbed Wire" works. The poem is woven every bit as tightly as the titular wire; the ABAB quatrains are formally apt, being two lines twisted together with "four short ends, sharp bevel-cut." But there is also a looseness at play. "Interstices" are leitmotifs in Outram's work; as in "Grief, " he makes much of gaps, the spaces between people and things, the silences between words, sentences, lines and stanzas. The "ellipses" in the wedding rings do double-duty, as do many other words in the poem: they provide a sharp visual description of the bands, but they also alert the reader to the poem's procedures, as Outram shifts, with little to no warning, from one image to another, without the end-stopping and stanza breaks that help keep the reader oriented in "Grief."

The ambiguities created by Outram's choices and splices create the kind of bewildering verities identified by William Empson as integral to poetic linguistics. It's disconcerting to go from barbed wire, a tool used for involuntary containment and confinement, to wedding rings, symbols of voluntary loving union. And yet the poem convinces us, through the associative use of the word "conjoined," that the comparison is apposite as well as opposite, even if only at the points where the strands cross, suggesting that even the happiest and most imaginatively fertile of marriages involves some sacrifice of individuality. (It should be noted that Outram's marriage to visual artist Barbara Howard—hard to imagine that "barbed" is an accidental pun—was such a happy and fruitful union, as the two were not only devoted partners, but artistic collaborators as well.) This point is reinforced in the second and third stanzas, as it takes the reader a moment to realize that Outram has shifted back from rings to wire, creating a literal con-fusion of two images at the same time that it creates a confusion, however fleeting, in the mind of the reader.

Outram makes another unheralded associative leap from his treatise on barbed wire to his father's war experience, braiding violent death and degradation into the poem as counterpoint to love and loyalty. As with the comparison between wire and rings, this juxtaposition will not allow the reader to slip into complacent thought habits; the poem suggests that war is bound as closely to loyalty and love as it is to death and destruction—a fact that should come as no surprise to readers of war poets like Wilfred Owen—and that both are hard-wired into our minds. They are non-adaptive by-products of our evolution we stick with fiercely, even when they seem to compromise our own chances for survival and reproduction. Even if "no one volunteered," the killed were still brought back from the wire for burial; even if marriage is a voluntary union, it can still be, as the old chestnut has it, war. Art here is the formal rite sanctifying the formal rites of both funeral and wedding, often the only events that bring an extended family together in one place at the same time. As Eric Ormsby has observed in his reading of this poem, these "[o]pposites coincide ... without sacrifice of integrity." Outram affirms what we all know on one level, but tend to elide with dichotomous thought schemes: that the circular wholeness of existence not only accommodates opposites, but actually twists, blends and welds them into an indissoluble unity.

The final surprise shift occurs in the first line of the last stanza. We think at first that "they" refers to the soldiers on the battlefield, but learn in short order that they are two specific soldiers, Outram's and Howard's fathers, standing not in mourning for their fallen comrades, but, having survived, in celebration of their children's union. In the poem's gorgeous final line, Outram twists the poem's strands, themes and tropes back together, "death" and "troth" both separated and united by a "bright entanglement," a phrase that summarizes the poem as a whole with its beautifully original combination of disparate terms. As in "Story," Outram deals here with the union of apparent opposites. He wastes no space and no words in doing so, but unlike "Story," "Barbed Wire," by combining technical excellence and verbal compression with particular experience, narrative and emotional resonance—by telling a story—leaves the door open to a reader's own emotions and experience. Here compression is not hermetic, but enables a fruitful expansion.

There is something quintessentially poetic about Richard Outram's approach to Coleridge's ideal of "the best possible words in the best possible order." This is consistently admirable, but as with ideals of all sorts not always easy to love. A great poem can't be paraphrased without something—usually much—being lost in the process. But it isn't necessarily unparaphraseable, and unparaphraseability does not in and of itself a great poem make; most of the disposable dreck of contemporary academic poetry and avant-garde experimentation is unparsable and inexplicable, but it is also unenjoyable, formally skint and imaginatively sterile. Many of Outram's poems are so compressed, so allusive, so resistant to paraphrase, that the reader who comes to them unequipped goes away unrewarded, either confused or indifferent; less secure readers might even be made to feel stupid by their inability to get what's going on.

Such poems actually disable the connection that a poem should make with a reader—the space in which Poetry happens—unless that reader has taken significant pains to attune her antenna to the HF channels on which Outram broadcasts. Ardent fans and specialists will always have time for such poems, which may well be the *sine qua non* of his more accessibly moving and beautiful efforts. But it is those latter poems, poems such as "Grief" and "Barbed Wire"—and many others scattered throughout his oeuvre, but concentrated, as Starnino maintains, in his later books—which should help Outram overcome his reputation as an intellectual oddity. As with all great poems, they are perfect unities of structure and content, emotion and technical excellence. They should endure.

PORNO FOR PORCO

Alessandro Porco
The Jill Kelly Poems

UBIQUITOUS AS MASS MEDIA pop culture is, it's no surprise that more and more poets are writing about professional sports, music, fast food, movies and TV. When everyone's selling something and every second phrase in the public sphere is trademarked, the artistic dilemma for a poet who wants to exploit pop cultural allusions for poetic ends is—or should be—how to do it without annexing yourself to the commercial machine, just another slickly packaged faddish ephemeron. Where do you position yourself between the poles of shrill condemnation and half-awake celebration and still maintain integrity?

In his debut collection, Alessandro Porco goes whole hawg on popular culture. His poems overflow with references to music, sports, television, film and, especially, pornography (the Jill Kelly of the title is a porn starlet). Porco strikes an iconoclastic pose with poems that celebrate such rebels as the rapper Eazy E and literary cum film character Rambo, with diction that is unapologetically salty and with poems that poke fun at the staid conventions of Canadian "poesie." Porco displays a wealth of technical skill, a good ear for the erotic rub of word on word and cheeky wit. But are bad boy bravado and bravura versification sufficient conditions for poetry?

The problems start before we even read the title of the first poem. The first section of *The Jill Kelly Poems* is entitled "Bad Boys." This gives us a preview of the iconoclasm to come, but it also, ironically, establishes a paradigm of rebellion rendered tame by packaging—"Bad Boys" being evocative of the recently sequelled Hollywood comedy of the same title (starring Will Smith, whom Porco derides as "Big Willy" in the book's first poem) and the theme song for the reality TV show "Cops."

We encounter our first bad boy in an elegy for the former NWA rapper Eazy E. In Porco's portrait, E is uncompromisingly authentic, no "mass sucker," never going "in for / PG rated big-pimpin' or gettin' jiggy" and "if he were alive today, / he'd hard-knock life Jay-Z back to reality / & send Big Willy's willy styles back to west Philly." Even though he's on the brink of death, E is "defiant to the end, he refused to wear / the regulation hospital-blue gown. Rigged-up / in Raider gear instead." "Rigged" here conveys another unintentional irony, since E's defiance allows him what? Inimitable personal expression? No, it allows him to advertise merchandise until the day he dies.

E's rebel image in life was merchandise itself. The feuds between members of the disbanded NWA generated untold millions of dollars in revenue for the rappers and their labels, selling Compton ghetto "hard knock life" to white kids in the suburbs, for whom the gangsta life of "real G's" provided an exotic fantasy to alleviate the tedium of ticky-tacky McMansions and manicured lawns. In his earnest tribute to Eazy E, contrasting him with the supposedly phony sellouts of today, Porco indulges in *nostalgie de la boue*, and mistakes the bluster and bombast of a nonconformist image for the real G thing.

But maybe it's misguided to be looking for any "real thing" in this book. The publicity bumph accompanying it proclaims that it contains "a poetry of surfaces" written "in gonzo fashion"; clearly, what we are to expect is an unholy hybrid of John Ashbery (who wrote in "Self-Portrait in a Convex Mirror" that "the surface is everything") and Hunter S. Thompson. It seems especially likely that Porco would align himself with Ashbery, since he quotes the American poet twice in the book, going so far as to say that "*A randomness, a darkness of one's own* sent me on my way."

In a programmatic triolet, Porco insists "This poem includes the word somnambulist / Because I like the way it sounds. / There's no meaning to be derived by formalists." And in "Ode to Balzac," the speaker reveals that the poem is not about the French novelist at all: "I just get a kick out of saying Balzac, // emphasis on the homophonic *entendre*. Ball. Sack." The eschewal of substance and depth, of "moral imperative[s]," in favour of slick surface and parody is Porco's aim, so we should evaluate his book, if we are to evaluate it at all, on those terms. And there is a strong case to be made that all poetry should be, first and foremost, read according to the Ashberian/Porconian prescription, because poetry will always succeed or fail on the strength or weakness of its surface qualities.

But it is precisely Porco's felt need to tell his readers how to read his poems that signals his failure to live up to his own superficial ambitions. Ashbery presents his *ars poetica* obliquely, through an ekphrastic interpretation of a painting by Francesco Parmigianino. His crucial statement is a paradox the complexity of which enacts the hall of mirrors he sets up by writing a warped poem about a painting done in a warped mirror:

> And just as there are no words for the surface, that is,
> No words to say what it really is, that it is not
> Superficial but a visible core, then there is
> No way out of the problem of pathos vs. experience.
> You will stay on, restive, serene in
> Your gesture which is neither embrace nor warning
> But which holds something of both in pure
> Affirmation that doesn't affirm anything.

Ashbery eschews attempts to access depth, but affirms the creation of the illusion of depth, using the "laws of perspective," highlighting Parmigianino's "extreme care in rendering / The velleities of the rounded reflecting surface ... / So that you could be fooled for a moment / Before you realize the reflection / Isn't yours." Porco, by contrast, is far more blunt:

… my title's
a smokescreen, a MacGuffin, man without country, poem without
    subject—

"There are no lions in the highlands of Scotland!"
The aphorism delimits a theory of suspense put forth by
    Hitchcock—
it would be a shame not to … Hitch. *Cock.*
—where style is visible substance, some invisible hand

pens *The End* in elegant cursive, but
by then no lesson's learned—crisis averted—no moral imperative
    imparted

Whereas Ashbery's paradox complicates the relationship between
reader and poem, Porco's simplifies and trivializes it. The result
is precisely what he says poetry should not be: didactic; not true
to surfaces, but to the author's intentions. Porco would do well
to heed Ashbery's observation that "works of art [are] so unlike /
What the artist intended." Instead, the overwhelming impression
this book gives is of a poet less concerned with what and how he is
writing than with what and how he is *not* writing. Theory's in the
driver's seat, praxis rides shotgun.

Both poet and publisher insist that we read *The Jill Kelly Poems*
as a provocative backhand to the face of the poetry establishment.
Besides the author's resolutely foul language and frank depic-
tions of sex acts, we have a trio of jacket endorsements. David
McGimpsey opines that "Alessandro Porco vitalizes contemporary
poetry with timely smack." Sex columnist Josey Vogels—whose
blurb was no doubt solicited to show how this book can be a
"crossover" hit with appeal to non-traditional poetry audiences—
calls the book "A daring, bright and downright smutty collection."
And Mary di Michele gushes: "Not since Irving Layton has poetry
of such erotic gusto and music both dazzled and disturbed me.
The Jill Kelly Poems is not for 'vegans nor Marxists nor Puritans.'

Alessandro Porco will surprise and shock and seduce readers with his 'darlings of xxx lingo.'"

The story these blurbs really tell us, however, is not a tale of brash nonconformity, but of chummy coteries and academic fads. McGimpsey and di Michele, both of whom are thanked by Porco in his acknowledgments, are faculty members of the English/Creative Writing Department at Concordia University, where Porco obtained his MA. His acknowledgments are chock-a-block with the names of professors and fellow students. Porco has also extended this collegial camaraderie beyond the bounds of his first book by publishing praiseful essays of his friends Carolyn Smart (the director of CW at Queen's University, where Porco studied as an undergrad) and McGimpsey. The question begs to be asked: What would Eazy E make of all this mutual congratulation and institutionalized favour-trading? It's cool. No it ain't.

Porco's preoccupation with porn and other staples of popular culture, far from being risqué, is standard currency in the trade economy of academic discourse. On the preoccupation of many scholars with "shocking" sexual topics at the most recent Modern Languages Association conference, John Strausbaugh writes in *The New York Times*, "There is, in fact, something achingly '90s about the whole affair. The association has come to resemble a hyperactive child who, having interrupted the grownups' conversation by dancing on the coffee table, can't be made to stop."

The Jill Kelly Poems is just such a coffee table lap dance. What is unfortunate, however, is not what Porco is writing about, but how little he does with what could be powerful and provocative subject matter—had he only locked horns with it. The kind of engagement I'm thinking of is shown nowhere better than in David Foster Wallace's essay about the American porn industry, "Big Red Son," a piece of writing that is both hilarious and humane, while Porco rarely does better than scurrilous and jejune. I get the sense reading his poems that he doesn't much care about the things—or the people—he writes of.

The title sequence, for example, is not really, as it suggests, an engagement with Jill Kelly as a character, but uses her as a glossy pin-up to ornament poems that are for the most part only nominally concerned with her. I suspect his motivation to write "The Jill Kelly Poems" was to send up books like Stephanie Bolster's *White Stone: The Alice Poems*. But there has to be something more to a project than its being *un*-genteel for it to gain real traction. Porco might have given his satire more bite if, for instance, he'd been able to bring on board an observation of Foster Wallace's:

> [O]ccasionally, in a hard-core scene, the hidden self appears. It's sort of the opposite of acting. You can see the porn performer's whole face change as self-consciousness (in most females) or crazed blankness (in most males) yields to some genuinely felt erotic joy in what's going on; the sighs and moans change from automatic to expressive. It happens only once in a while, but ... the effect on the viewer is electric. And the adult performers who can do this a lot—allow themselves to feel and enjoy what's taking place, cameras or not—become huge, legendary stars. The 1980s' Ginger Lynn and Keisha could do this, and now sometimes Jill Kelly and Rocco Siffredi can. Jenna Jameson and T.T. Boy cannot. They remain just bodies.

Instead, we have "Jill Kelly's Titty-Bop Sonnet":

> What's to stop me, say, from writing
>   A beauty's-best blazon, never looking
> Above, below, or beyond gianormous
>   Jugs jugging-in at a C-cup 36?
>
> Well, sure, some critic might claim,
>   *Porco è porcu*, his pen unable to sustain
> A poetic argument of "real" value;
>   But that's no reason not to do as I do,

Which is express a love of bib-bubs
    In a fourteen-line song to the God of
Titty-bops—*hast thou forsaken me?*
    Why not hand over a naked Jill Kelly

So as I can finally stop writing this
    Thing & slide my this between her thats?

Porco's pre-emptive strike against a critic like me makes it clear that at least he knows his poems are throwaway squibs, but that doesn't make a throwaway squib equal to something more nuanced and challenging. Shallow by design still be shallow. And it doesn't make his two-dimensional Jill Kelly anything more than "just a body." If Porco is playing at Catullus, then Jill Kelly makes for a pretty dull Lesbia. To borrow from Ashbery again, Porco's "way of telling … intrude[s], twisting the end result / Into a caricature of itself."

A comparison of Porco's book of blue verse with the multi-faceted oeuvres of some of the poets he alludes to and quotes—including Catullus, Herrick, Campion, Ashbery, Sappho—only reinforces how one-note the tune Porco plays on his pan pipes is. Notable exceptions include "MacGuffin" and "Solarium," a version of a poem by Quasimodo, which give a glimmer of what Porco might be capable of should he relinquish his apparent need to strike a pose:

A tectonic shift
Broke the heart of the Earth
Like a back—disks
Slip, ring weighs on ring, the
Cartilaginous sting
As blinding as the Sun,
And, suddenly it is evening.

It's hard to figure where such a sublimely beautiful poem came from, in the midst of all the bad-boy fronting that fills the rest of the book. Mary di Michele compares Porco with Layton, but it is with Layton the shock-jockey alone that this comparison is valid; most of Porco's work doesn't hold a candle to the magisterial poems of Layton the maestro at his sublime best—and without the maestro, the shock-jockey gets no air time whatever. Porco follows Ashbery's lead as far as not "affirming anything," but missing almost entirely is the "pure affirmation." The "exposed core" of his surfaces rings regrettably hollow.

No Mere Whistlepunk

Peter Trower
Haunted Hills & Hanging Valleys: Selected Poems 1969–2004

PETER TROWER IS OFTEN COMPARED to that British Columbia legend of logging doggerel, Robert Swanson, and to Swanson's antecedent Robert Service. Trower is definitely tuned in to the singsong ballad metres of the two Roberts, but, as Don McKay states in his forward to Trower's *Selected Poems*, "all labels mislead, especially those that are partly true," and Trower's classification as a "logger poet" in the land of TISH has unjustly limited his audience to date.

If we must engage in odious games of poetic phylogeny, it seems to me that Trower's poetry has stronger affinities to the verse of Thomas Hardy than to the more tonally and formally limited ballads of Service and Swanson. This comparison is made all the more appealing by a coincidence of geography. Trower, who at age ten immigrated to Canada with his widowed mother in 1940, was born at St. Leonard's-on-Sea, England, on the eastern edge of Hardy's Wessex, two years after the great writer died.

Like Hardy, the elegiac is a key mode for Trower. As the title of this book suggests, ghosts (of people, machines, buildings and whole towns) wander in and out of Trower's poems and the book as a whole is suffused with an affecting nostalgia that usually steers clear of the pitfalls of sentimentality—a vice to which Hardy was also prone. Trower shares Hardy's preoccupations with time and mortality, which is reflected very nicely by the organization of *Haunted Hills and Hanging Valleys*. Rather than being organized chronologically, as many retrospective selections are, the poems are presented in a loosely thematic weave between old poems and new. Appropriately, it begins with "As Long as the Wheel Turns Us":

> We're all another year
> closer to our comeuppances—
> the carpenters the cat the gulls
> the bees the ghosts and me—
> riding with time through the carousel seasons
> as long as the wheel turns us.

and ends with "Ghostcamp":

> I have come full circle—
> across the inlet lies Misery Creek
> where my brother and I watched camp
> one fireseason summer two decades back.
> The dead camp sprawls around us.
> I can't speak. It's too strange.
> Log long enough, you're bound to stumble
> across your own bootprints in the end.

The first poem is from the 1986 collection *The Slidingback Hills*, the last from *Between the Sky and the Splinters* (1974). Trower's work has at times been uneven, especially in more recent books, but the great strength of this gathering is its demonstration that the vernacular vigour and sweat- and sawdust-impregnated empathy that generated his most powerful work in the 1970s are far from tapped out, as thirteen of the ninety-six poems have been drawn from Trower's most recent book, *There Are Many Ways*. The newer poems are quieter, more contemplative, and as such they complement nicely the raw-edged work of Trower's early books.

Trower the erstwhile whistlepunk and feller shares also with Hardy, the one-time stonemason, a thoroughgoing sympathy with the working classes and an emphasis on the regional. Trower sets his poems in either logging camps and factories or in the skid road beer halls and low-rent hotels of downtown East Vancouver. He can be almost anti-poetic at times in his depiction of brutal scenes:

> She said:
> "I got wrists
> like anyone else, see?"
> and she showed them to me.
>
> There were five white worms
> across one
> and three
> across the other.
>
> She said:
> "You're supposed to be a poet,
> baby.
> What do you think of those poems?"
>
> I said:
> "Those are the saddest poems
> I've ever read,"
> and watched my buddy, bleak boy,
> screwing her with his eyes.

If you're not paying close attention, it's easy to miss the self-inculpating irony of the poem's closing lines. Trower's apparent artlessness here is the means of conveying, with utmost subtlety, a very tense little drama.

Trower is not always so plain. Hardy, following the example of William Barnes, was almost fanatical about purging Latinate words from his poetic vocabulary and would invent compound Anglo-Saxon kennings where a simple noun didn't exist. Trower shows similar favour to local diction, his poems chock-full of specialized logging jargon like crummy, donkey, spar-tree, guthammer, choker, whistlepunk, handfeller; and he has a propensity for invented compounds that rivals Hardy or Hopkins: a forest fire's breath is a "cinderwind"; burning trees are "sap-factories exploding"; clearcut hills are "stump-chimneyed slopes"—and these are just from one poem. He does overplay it by times—Carmine Starnino has zeroed in on Trower's use of alliteration, in particular, as an "all-purpose anti-boredom device"—but Trower is hardly unique in having strengths that manifest occasionally as mistakes.

Another formal kinship between Hardy and Trower is their rhythms, which, in spite of homebuilt folksiness, are far more complex than the regular foot-stomping beat of a ballad. Hardy caught flak for what critics took to be a bad ear, but the roughness of his metre was perfectly deliberate, as reflected by a passage in *Life*:

Years earlier he had decided that too regular a beat was bad art. He had fortified himself in his opinion by thinking of the analogy of architecture, between which art and that of poetry he had discovered, to use his own words, that there existed a close and curious parallel, each art unlike some others, having to carry a rational content inside its artistic form. He knew that in architecture cunning irregularity is of enormous worth, and it is obvious that he carried on into his verse, perhaps unconsciously, the Gothic art-principle in which he had been trained—the principle of spontaneity, found in mouldings, tracery and suchlike—resulting in the "unforeseen" (as it has been called) character of his metres and stanzas, that of stress rather than of syllable, poetic texture rather than poetic veneer; the latter kind of thing, under the name of "constructed ornament," being what he, in common with every Gothic student, had been taught to avoid as the plague. He shaped his poetry accordingly, introducing metrical pauses, and reversed beats; and found for his trouble that some particular line of a poem exemplifying this principle was greeted with a would-be jocular remark that such a line "did not make for immortality." The same critic might have gone to one of our cathedrals (to follow the analogy of architecture), and on discovering that the carved leafage of some capital or spandrel in the best period of

Gothic art strayed freakishly out of its bounds over the moulding, where by rule it had no business to be, or that the enrichments of a string-course were not accurately spaced; or that there was a sudden blank in a wall where a window was expected from formal measurement, have declared with equally merry conviction, "This does not make for immortality."

We see this sort of "cunning irregularity" everywhere in Trower's work, too. Consider "Industrial Poem":

That night, Slim Abernathy
pushed the wrong button and wrapped his best friend
three times round a driveshaft
in directions bones won't bend.

They shut her down and eased him out
broken most ways a man can break
yet he clung to his ruin for twenty-four hours
like a man to a liferaft for his death's sake.

They'd hardly hurried him away from there
as we stood around shockdrunk, incapable of help
when they cranked those expensive wheels up again,
started rolling more goddamn pulp.

"Hamburger for lunch tonight, boys!"
joked a foreman to the crew.
I wish he'd smelled our hate but he never even flinched
as the red-flecked sheets came through.

The poem is an anachronism: a ballad, first published in 1978. Originating in medieval traditions of oral folk song, the first printed ballads date back to the early 16th Century and the form was often adopted by poets well into the 19th Century. In the 20th Century, however, the ballad, rooted in straightforward narrative, lockstep rhythms and regular rhymes, fell into disrepute as a vessel for serious poetry, and was relegated to the ghetto of popular doggerel. Trower, fashions of the day be damned, wields the ballad stanza like a fine old rust-flecked sword. Often used to convey outrage against social and economic injustice, particularly during the Industrial Revolution, the ballad is a fitting structure for the content of this poem.

But Trower is no rustic naïf, and "Industrial Poem" no old-fashioned exercise in metrical finger-stretching or unsophisticated protest. In some respects, this poem does adhere to the prescriptions of balladry (it tells an action-focused story, briskly and plainly, employing simple stanzaic and syntactic structures), but close reading shows that Trower has also made it new. The metre Trower employs consists basically of the three and four-beat iambic lines typical of balladry, but, in Hardyesque fashion, he diverges from it so often and goes so far afield that the traditional metre and rhyme-scheme is like a frame showing through free verse cladding (recalling Eliot's admonition that "the ghost of some simple metre should lurk behind the arras of even the 'freest' verse").

These deviations might seem like evidence of a tin ear, but besides the fact that irregularity of metre is a hallmark of pre-Victorian balladry, I would argue that Trower, steeped in the ballads of Service, Kipling and Swanson, jars their rhythms strategically. The five beats of line eight for instance—four of them awkwardly clumped in the spondees "liferaft" and "death's sake"—mime the injured man's deathbed struggles, like the irregular blips of a heart monitor, as he "[clings] to his ruin." The rhythmically and syntactically clumsy phrase in line ten, "incapable of help," is a perfect reflection of the workers' "shockdrunk" state. He could easily have changed the line to conform to the metre, such as "we stood around shocked, unable to help," but such an option would have sterilized the poem and dulled its emotional force. Similarly, the six beats of line fifteen, three of them in the terminal trochaic phrase "never even flinched," limn the workers' brimming hatred for the cold-blooded foreman, whose gallingly prosaic speech in line thirteen serves to underline his crassness.

With all of these subtle touches, Trower updates and personalizes the ballad for his purposes. The speaker's position in relation to the subject is the other major departure of this poem from ballad conventions. Normally, a ballad, often composed by an anonymous author—or authors—is narrated either in the third person by a party not directly involved in the action, or indirectly through dialogue. In this poem, however, the speaker, as we realize in line ten, is very much implicated in the scene he describes, and therefore incapable of retelling it in a cool, smooth, metrical fashion.

Trower no more loosens the ballad stanza for the mere sake of appearing modern than he chooses the structure in order to be traditional. Rather, he crafts his lines in response to the particular formal demands of the subject matter he has tackled. The result, all questions of prosody aside, is a chilling indictment of industry's capacity for dehumanization and an affirmation of art's capacity for redress. One can readily imagine a draught of this poem penned on a red-flecked sheet from that very mill.

The point of all this comparison is not to say that Trower is "Canada's Hardy," for it's sufficient that he's Canada's Trower. He may not be a "major poet," but I know of no other poet like him. Hardy's writing was sneered at by many contemporaneous critics as the product of a regional rustic. Peter Trower's work has suffered a more polite, if no less dismissive, neglect. It's high time he was recognized more widely as the gifted and versatile force in Canadian poetry that he is.

Step Right Up!
Michael Harris
Circus

Peter Norman
At the Gates of the Theme Park

LADIES AND GENTLEMEN, boys and girls, children of all ages! Titles aside, it would seem at first glance that we have before us two very different volumes of verse: one a first trade book by a writer under 40, the other a seventh collection by a belaurelled senior poet; one edited by the guy who put out an anthology called *Surreal Estate,* the other by the fella who assembled *The New Canon.* But don't be fooled, folks, these two wily versifiers and their books share more common ground than you'd think. Both Peter Norman and Michael Harris are masters of impersonation, wearing many masks and speaking in a range of distinct voices; as their respective titles promise, they make of poetry a spectacular multifarious performance. (I have seen both of these fellows read and I recommend going to hear them if they come to a venue near you.) Both poets are great formal experimenters, as adept at following the rules as they are at reinventing them. Both poets are wits with a sneaky knack for making you laugh just before delivering a sucker punch straight to the blood pump. Both men have worked as editors and their scrupulous attention to detail is evident at all levels of their collections. And both of these books are wonderful, entertaining additions to 21st Century poetry in Canada, so let's take a look, shall we?

Although *At the Gates of the Theme Park* is Peter Norman's first perfect-bound book, he is no literary neophyte. I first encountered his poems in the delightful limited edition chapbook *Wild Clover*

Honey and the Beehive: 28 Sonnets on the Sonnet (2003). In that publication, Norman and Stephen Brockwell engaged in a game of duelling sonnets, with Brockwell arguing, somewhat perversely, against the form and Norman crafting pro-sonnet quatorzains. It was clear from Norman's inventive facility with the form and from the witty metaphysical gambits he deployed within it, that this was a poet with serious chops. Those chops were also in evidence in Norman's e-chapbook *The Shape Inside: 12 Sonnets* (2003), which includes his ingeniously funny "Bolshevik Tennis!" a poem I included in *Jailbreaks: 99 Canadian Sonnets*. Work that appeared later in magazines demonstrated that Norman was just as good in looser forms as he was within the so-called fixed constraints of traditional structures. (Most poets who write free verse well know their way around a metrical line.) His poem "Up Near Wawa" won *Arc* magazine's Confederation Poets Prize in 2008 and "Playground Incident" and "The Super" appeared in the first two editions of *The Best Canadian Poetry in English* anthology.

It is striking that none of the poems I've just named—all of which are very good—grace the pages of this book. As I've suggested, Norman has been writing poetry at a high level for some years, during which time he has also been earning a living as a freelance editor. Perhaps this is why he gave Mansfield Press poetry editor Stuart Ross a free hand in curating the selection of poems for *Theme Park*: to give himself a break! (And perhaps to experience vicariously what is every editor's dream: working with an author who does everything you tell him to ...) This is also likely why we've had to wait so long for a book from Norman; there is nothing like editing to make a poet cautious about publishing their own work too early or too often.

Something of the editorial sensibility is on display in a street-cleaning truck that "bears down on the one outstanding flaw," as well as in "Little Rejection Slips," a disarmingly moving poem, balanced on the knife edge of satire and pathos. It's a piece that should resonate with most people involved in small magazines, and particularly with anyone who has received one of the handwritten no-thank-yous for which this journal[24] is famous.

---

24   This review was first published in *The Fiddlehead*.

The poem begins with an editor addressing another editor who is thanked by submitting writers "for gentle rejection" and continues:

> A man sent a play.
> He's grateful for your note last time.
> Hopes for another.
> Says he has to live on those.

> I have read and read again
> your letter. Held it to the light
> in case you'd watermarked a change of mind.

> The note was written in pen.
> Felt. Blue.
> I dare not write him back:
> "She's gone.

> You'll have to learn to live on something else."

Whatever Norman's reasons for trusting Ross to shape the book, the result is a gathering of forty-one poems that is not just tight and accomplished, but which also reflects the tastes of its editor. Had someone like Carmine Starnino (who edited Harris's book) been given carte blanche to cobble together sixty pages from the same pile of typescripts, I have the feeling we'd be looking at a collection with only partial overlap that was just as strong, but with a subtly different flavour.

Theme Park contains four sonnets, including one, "Nesting Doll," from Norman's 2003 chapbook; a couple of pieces in rhymed quatrains; and a few other rhyming stanzas, but most of its poems are more loosely built and many tend towards the kind of oneiric soft surrealism favoured by Ross. One piece, "The Sun," is actually a riff off a poem by Ross that riffs off a poem by Georg Trakl:

Something like soup is drooled from high clouds.
Ears flick to attention: a ray sneaks past.
Here is an overturned bug. Here is a syringe filled with sugar.

Even the sonnets are apt to have irregular rhyme schemes and shaggy line lengths. Anyone who has followed Norman's career to-date might be surprised to discover this "other Norman." But, unless they're dogmatic formalists, they shouldn't be disappointed. It would take a pretty narrow mind, for instance, to miss the formal brilliance in a poem such as "Recursion," which proceeds like a rewound film:

I fall awake alone. Outside,
nocturnal rain ascends.

Alarms rage, summoning a thief
who hurries to the store,
unpacks his duffel sack,
replaces items on the shelf.

Morning. The plane dispenses you.
We enfold each other,
celebrating your undeparture.
Tears scroll up our cheeks,
nestle into ducts.

And ends with this memorable image:

Outside, a robin
cocks her head,
feeds worms
to the hungry soil.

A lot of the poems in this book are clever ideas put into motion, ingenious little purpose-built verbal machines. Norman seems to like setting himself a challenge and taking a run at it. Sometimes more than once. Not only do we find here "Recursion: The Outtake Reel," but we also have "Winter Morning: The Next Morning" as a sequel to an earlier "Winter Morning." The mechanics of thinking are as much or more Norman's concern as finished thoughts. As he puts it in the paradoxically titled "Still Life with Action": "I've got life lined up in my scopes, / but the damn thing won't keep still." One thinks here of Gotthold Lessing's observation that poetry, because it is a time-based artform, is better suited to the depiction of action than to the representation of static objects.

If cleverness occasionally seems to be too much the point, however, it must be acknowledged that more often—as in "Little Rejection Slips" above, as well as in the beautifully sad list poems "What He Found in the Vacuum Bag" and "My Collection"—wit is apposed with feeling and the two often fuse into a single poetic substance. The conflicting imperatives of technical proficiency and human feeling form the vexed subtext of Norman's devastating sonnet "The Pilot," which is a kind of negative image to Randall Jarrell's "Death of the Ball Turret Gunner." Note the writing metaphors:

I carve
my autograph in earth. It's too bad
for those down there. Almost sad.
Who aren't blown up will starve
or go mad with grief. You serve
the enemy, you gag on the enemy's feast.
Some guys loop back, drop extra. It's a waste.
I stick to the flight plan, play it safe.

Once, on a low pass, I could see detail.
That's a day I'd rather blot out.
A building spilled children like shelled peas;
my payload threw them to their knees—
the siren had come too late.
I turned back to base to refuel.

That kind of Yeatsian click-shut ending is something Norman is very good at, but he doesn't lean too heavily on it. He is just as likely to end a poem in uncertainty:

> I think I can see
> a shift
> in the map,
> a trickle
> or twitch
> in its compass of fronds.

Or bewilderment:

> I hear the slinking of small things.
> They are going about their business.
> The cliff's shoulder is cold with moss.
> I don't remember where I was before this.

Norman is also a fiction writer; no surprise, then, that many of these poems are written from the perspective of characters who clearly are not to be confused with the poet. The speaker of "Nesting Doll" is the father of a young girl, for instance, whereas "Boy Germs" is spoken *by* a young girl. It's impossible to tell with any certainty if Norman is ever, like his pilot, carving his own autograph. In an interview with Jacob Mooney, Norman has maintained that "very few of my poems are pure autobiography," but there is an unfakeable degree of personal investment in very many of them. Whatever the case, his mistrust of lyric self-absorption does nothing to diminish the emotional pull of *Theme Park*.

Masks, ventriloquism and poetic artifice are things Michael Harris's *Circus* has in common with Norman's book. Harris assembles a motley cast of improbable freaks and virtuoso performers, whose exceptional oddities are often juxtaposed with the banalities of quotidian existence, in such a way that one can't help thinking that performative brio is so much stage paint barely concealing intense private pain. The speaker of one poem, "Mephisto, the Human Pincushion," makes this plain:

Poetry. Never managed to figure out poetry. Managed
to separate the literal from the metaphoric, the visceral
from the imaginative, ended up going into business anyhow
as "Mephisto, the Human Pincushion!" Go figure. The blood, by
    the way,
is insensate. Hard to see it in this light, but I can report
that it's an itchy little trickle, quite as irritating
as the wound itself. As if the shimmering liquid
on my arm were not the result of very clever lighting,
but real blood, wet and shining. Chameleonic,
wouldn't you say—how one can abandon oneself
so easily and become someone else, if only
for the length of this performance, right here on this stage.

Harris (the founding editor of the Signal Editions imprint under which his book is published) is, like Mephisto, a battle-scarred veteran. One might be forgiven for thinking, prior to the appearance of *Circus*, that its author had retired from the ring. His last book was published in 1992, and that was his *New and Selected Poems*. His last collection of entirely new work came out in 1985. I first encountered some of these "new" poems more than ten years ago, when I heard Harris read them on a couple of occasions in Montreal, where I was a grad student at Concordia. He also came to talk to our poetry class and told us not to be in any hurry to publish our work. Clearly, advice he stands behind!

It's been worth the wait. *Circus*, a distilled gathering of just 35 loosely linked poems, has already won considerable acclaim, making the shortlists for both the Quebec Writers' Federation A.M. Klein Award (full disclosure: I was one of the jurors) and the Governor General's Award for Poetry. Prize listings are notoriously arbitrary, but the proof of the poetry is in the reading. I'd like to take a close look at one of the book's best poems, "Concentrate," which follows immediately on the heels of Mephisto's soliloquy. The poem begins with an aural feast:

> With dusk come creeping as it does across the provinces,
> raccoons descend from their roosts in the trees;
> moose big as Ozymandias settle up to their bellies in water
>
> and begin, one huge scoop of tongue at a time,
> to drink the lake.

Free verse doesn't get much more gorgeous than this, with all the subtle sonic densities of consonant and vowel Harris deploys in the service of sharp, evocative imagery and a well-integrated allusion to Bishop and Shelley in a single simile. But just as you're settling in to enjoy the music, Harris falters:

> But once the wire is set and the rigging steady,
> there should be little to make you hesitate but a want of confidence—

Ugh. What happened? This is so wordy and clunky, so clogged with articles and prepositions, so utilitarian and provisional. And it gets worse:

> unless you were to slip into musing about the various malaises
> of domesticity, say, the kids and their adventures in the quotidian
> messinesses, the ex-wife, money and whatnot. Sex
>
> is a distraction, you might as well admit that once and for all,
> what with its swoons and perfumes, its loosenings and
>   tightenings—
> admit that one, then, and then move on.

If "various malaises / of domesticity" is a pretty awful mouthful, then "quotidian / messinesses" is an almost unsayable train wreck of a phrase. "[M]oney and whatnot" is so disposable it's been thrown out before it's even spoken; "admit that once and for all" is an off-the-rack cliché; and what's with those clumsy plural gerunds, anyway? Those "swoons" and "perfumes" seem almost a parody of the assonant "oo" sounds of the poem's beginning. How could the same poet have written this crap and those gracile opening lines—in the same poem? It's almost as if Harris is *trying* to write badly.

Which is precisely what makes this poem brilliant. He *is* trying to write badly. And then he "move[s] on." The writing smoothes out, but then seizes again, and the poem concludes much as it began:

> Just
> concentrate and all will be well, the hawks will settle in their nests
>
> in the stilled rivers of bark, the car spark into life with one turn of
> the key,
> the goal, as ever, that little plot of platform at the end of your
> leisurely walk,
> never the fame bestowed by those upturned faces, nor their dark
> hope
>
> that they will be the lucky ones to see you fall.

The injunction to "concentrate" is directed as much at the reader as it is at the speaker. You have to be paying proper attention to appreciate how cagey Harris's technique is here. Just when he talks about losing concentration on the tightrope—and what is a long free-verse line but a tightrope?—his own line goes slack. And when he returns to concentration, the line tautens again. This is formal brilliance, risky and brave, that has nothing to do with "formalism" or any other aesthetic dogma.

Part of why I wanted to home in on this aspect of Harris's technique is that it's a microcosm of the book as a whole. Immediately following "Concentrate" is "Hang in There," which begins

> Who among us has managed the high-wire
> with its gyroscopic soul?
> Not I, says Ms Wobbily-Bobbily:
> I should have used the pole.

Silly doggerel! But if we've payed proper attention to "Concentrate," we might suspect that Harris is up to something. That suspicion is confirmed by the last stanza:

> Who lived through the crash
> of the Krazy Kops car? I did,
> and I'm fine, says Benji the Clown:
> there's an art to falling down.

It's an art that Harris nails time and again in this book, vacillating between poles we might label Yeats and Nash, often within the confines of a single poem. There is, indeed, something of Elizabeth Bishop's blend of the "awful, but cheerful" "art of losing" in the last line of "Hang in There." Harris keeps his chin up, only to be slapped in the face with a trout. Nowhere does this happen more poignantly— and hilariously—than in "The Beller of Cats," in which the toothless, cuckolded speaker, suffers the "final indignity" of catching his leg

> on the neighbour's picket fence,
> while attempting to catch the cat
> whose single reaction at hearing one's heartfelt
> *Here, kittykittykitty—*
> is to bolt.

> One must not call the cat-catchers
> with their ladders and hooks and smug-mugged looks;
> one did not resort to the lawyers, their fingers
> tapping like scorpions on the boardroom table;
> one eschewed the therapists with their asps
> of assessment, their anacondas of advice.

> One must maintain
> whatever dignity is left.

> One must temper torment with sanguinity
> and sing out: *Here Kitty Kitty Kitty.*

The triple feminine rhyme of dignity/sangunity/*Kitty Kitty Kitty* is just the right self-ironical manoeuvre with which to end the poem—a light touch with a sting in its tail.

There are several masterpieces of light verse in this book, including the virtuosic ninety-two line, "Hoodiddit," reminiscent of T.S. Eliot in Ol' Possum mode:

> That noise in the night's not a bedspring—
> for alive in the shadows and dust,
> a monster stirs down in the basement
> and his yawns are loudsqueakers of rust.

> The sleepers upstairs in their bedrooms
> think it's the furnace that roared;
> they don't understand it's Hoodiddit,
> who's hungry and cranky and bored.

But there are also poems that are just plain dark, none more so than "The House of Horrors," which is "fuller than the bag full of ears, / the ditch full of Jews," demonstrating that Harris's circus ring is broad enough to accommodate the personal and domestic as well as the world-historical; farce as well as tragedy. There is also the short verse essay "On Beheading," which has all of the sangfroid of Keith Douglas's "How to Kill." Harris's poem ends with a "scimitar-wielder" "swishing his razor-thin blade through the throat of a standing man, / such that the head would remain aligned, at rest on the dead man's neck." A morbid reprise of the art of tightrope walking.

There are several outstanding individual poems in the book, but I'd like to end by paying some attention to what is probably the best of them. "Molivos," a bravura performance in forty loose tercets with just a hint of terza rima, is suggestive of Dante. But instead of Virgil, Harris is accompanied by Ray Liotta (an actor who, like Harris, has proven adept at self-parody), who comes across as part Zen-master, part Jungian analyst. The poem is presented as a dream, which licenses its more idiosyncratic elements and allows Harris to proceed according to a logic that is more associative than linear; it permits him, like Weary Willy in another poem to "see ... the world sideways."

"Molivos" is also highly allusive, with references of varying degrees of subtlety to Homer, Sappho, Matthew Arnold, Coleridge and many more besides. Although written from a mountain-top perspective above Molivos, the poem is concerned with the implausibility of Parnassian verse in modern Greece where, as Liotta in his capacity as guide says, "'folks drive scooters as well as donkeys, import bananas, / and seldom squat to shit even though the European / flush toilet uses gallons of precious water.'"

Liotta goes on to say that "the whole town is the self / one needs to rise above to see properly—though, really, / what you see from the Castle is Turkey." This play of transcendence punctured humorously by the matter-of-fact is what both Harris and Norman do very well, each in his own way. Which would be impressive enough on its own, but it is to both poets' credit that the sublime is occasionally allowed to blow the ludicrous away.

DISASTER TOURISM
Anne Simpson
Loop

ANNE SIMPSON HAS QUICKLY become one of the usual suspects in the poetry prize sweepstakes. Her first collection of poems, *Light Falls Through You*, was shortlisted for three prizes, winning two, and her most recent effort, *Loop*, is the only collection to have made the shortlist for both the 2003 Governor General's Award and the Griffin Prize for Excellence in Poetry.

It's easy to see why the compass needles of jurists are drawn to Simpson's work like it was Lodestone Mountain. Her verse is rife with elements that insist: This Is Excellent Poetry to Be Taken Very Seriously. She tackles subjects of great moment and casually show-cases her erudition with references to literary classics and oriental culture. She employs clever, complex structures as well as honed *vers libre*: in her first book, the Trojan War is retold in a sequence of poems about punctuation marks; in *Loop*, the World Trade Center disaster is depicted in a crown of sonnets inspired by the paintings of Brueghel. She makes statements that seem to bear the weight of hard-won wisdom and pain: "Now you wind yourself in the cloth of suffering, cloth of twilight, but it does no good."

But there are many things I find phony and off-putting about this poet's work. Let's start with the line I just quoted, which contains not one, but two instances of a formula Pound very rightly proscribed—viz. "the [concrete noun] of [abstract noun]"— because it "dulls the image"; the only thing that partially redeems

Simpson in this instance is adjectival restraint. Lines like this, pregnant with gravitas, make for poeticism, not for poetry.

For all its apparent profundity, Simpson's verse is remarkably shallow. Looking over both of her books, a disturbing pattern emerges. She seems to have scoured literature and history for scenes of wreckage and death which she can then turn into cool, arm's-length poems. In her first book, she writes not only about the Trojan War, but also the Montreal Massacre, a 19th Century train wreck and the genocide in Rwanda. In Loop, besides a slew of references to literary tragedies, we find September 11, a meditation on the Swiss Air Crash at Peggy's Cove, as well as glibly dropped references to the war in Kosovo and the Chernobyl nuclear disaster, with a graphic second-person rape sonnet thrown in for good measure.

Now, as I said, these are weighty topics, and certainly merit poetic treatment, but in poetry, it's not the subject that matters, but, as Irving Layton put it, "it's all in the manner of the done." And Simpson does not do these subjects justice. She flits from one tragedy (to employ the ubiquitous bastardized sense of the term) to another, exploiting them as opportunities for lyric insight, becoming in the process what Seamus Heaney termed, in a self-incriminating aperçu the likes of which you won't find in Simpson's work, an "artistic voyeur." Ironically, in the Twin Towers sequence, we find these lines: "Half- / heard, the phantoms speak: *No, you weren't there*— / We turn; we sleep. But once there was a prayer" (emphasis added). In a villanelle on "The Grand Canyon," she uses the following refrain lines: "I haven't gone there: tell me what you've seen" and "We think we know it, but we've never been."

Not having been there never slows Simpson down. She betrays faint awareness of her own inability to do justice to objects and events she hasn't witnessed—and yet she proceeds anyway, digging up the dead and making them sing and dance for her. As a poet she, like Anne Michaels before her, is a tourist in the realms of human misery and suffering. She makes sure to show us how choked up she is about it all with a distracting tendency towards syntactic disruption, miming her disingenuous incapacity for articulation through the excessive deployment of portentous full-stopped sentence fragments:

> These watches. Ticking, still. Each hour is cold:
> the rims surround quick voices. Shut in rooms.
> Gone. *Tick.* The towers. *Tock.* Of fire. A fold
> in air. We're smoke, drifting. A painted doom
> where cities burn and ships go down. Death's
> dark sky—a grainy docudrama.

Her catchpenny treatment of these events, her reduction of them to tropes and occasions for—as she herself says in a press release from her publisher—indulging in "the play of poetic forms," constitutes gross artistic and moral irresponsibility. With no irony whatsoever, she complains that "ordinary lives are always embellished by the papers"; she seems to possess no awareness that she does the same thing herself, again and again. Perhaps she thinks that because she has hung out her shingle as a poet, she is therefore immunized from committing the sins of mass media. I'm sure she doesn't mean to be so gruesome, that her intentions are noble. Unfortunately, she haphazardly sabotages those honourable intentions at every turn. She deserves some credit for taking risks that other poets wouldn't dare to, but those risks lead most often to spectacular failure. Her work is proof that mere craft and liberal ideals are insufficient to the writing of Excellent Poetry.

Unfortunately, this year's Griffin jury, which has awarded the grand prize to *Loop*, seems equally blind to the demerits of Simpson's disaster tourism. It's hard to blame them, I suppose. I consider myself an avid reader of poetry, but I doubt that I read much more than one or two hundred individual collections a year. The jury, on the other hand, had precisely one year—probably much less, in practice—to read and evaluate 423 collections (over a hundred of which were Canadian), many of which were no doubt retrospective gatherings thicker than the standard slim tome of verse. Poetry is simply not a commodity meant to be consumed in such quantities. It would be uncharitable to expect our overworked jurors, all three of whom must have other things with which to occupy their time, to make subtle distinctions between competent craft paired with ambition and actual artistic achievement.

CLEAR VISION
Goran Simić (translator Amela Simić)
From Sarajevo, with Sorrow

DECEPTIVELY SIMPLE: the shopworn phrase of the blurbing alche-
mist who would gild a leaden text with an effortless attribution of
hidden complexity. Deceptive simplicity is often attempted and
often diagnosed but rarely achieved. The world has many more
Rod McKuens than Robert Frosts. Deceptively simple is decep-
tively hard. So when Goran Simić announces that he "would like
to write poems which resemble newspaper reports," the connois-
seur of poetry is apt to balk. Why ever would anyone want that?
Should not the rich, deliberate language of poetry oppose the
rushed, plain, fact-obsessed prose of journalism? Isn't this asking
of poetry something that it cannot and should not be made to do?

Nine times out of ten, the connoisseur is probably right. But
the majority of British or North American poetry readers bring to a
book a privileged set of assumptions forged in relative peace, secu-
rity and prosperity. For most Western poets, writing about war and
genocide is a voluntary act and can only be done abstractly. But
for a poet who has witnessed a period of horrible violence—and
the florid rhetoric that invariably accompanies such tumult—the
exigencies of her craft are radically different. As Theodor Adorno
famously said, "writing poetry after Auschwitz is barbaric."

Paul Celan, a Holocaust survivor writing in the language of
that atrocity's perpetrators, responded by writing poems of hyper-
compressed indirection. As a Bosnian Serb who lived through the

siege of Sarajevo and whose brother was killed by a sniper, Simić, now resident in Toronto as a PEN writer in exile,[25] takes a radically different tack: "I simply wrote what I saw." Indeed, "What I Saw" is the title of one poem and vision is one of several leitmotifs that give *From Sarajevo, with Sorrow* its form.

Twenty-nine of the forty-four poems in this new collection appeared in 1997 in very different English translations. These versions were written by David Harsent, who worked from "cribs" prepared by Amela Simić. Reading Harsent's adaptations, published by Oxford University Press as *Sprinting from the Graveyard*, beside these new/old versions (as translated by Amela Simić alone), one quickly gets the sense that Harsent was uncomfortable staying true to what Goran Simić saw and to the poet's own stated aims. Harsent writes in his foreword that he used Amela Simić's "literal texts ... to get what I wanted. My purpose was to make new poems in English from this raw material. ... I made changes, some extravagant; excisions, some radical; and additions, some substantial. ... There's nothing particularly new about this technique, though I think I may have taken it further than most."

There's nothing inherently wrong with such a technique. The loose adaptation of extant texts is a literary staple and poets such as Robert Lowell, Robert Bly and Peter Van Toorn have created wonderful poems in English by taking liberties with a text in another language. But context matters. The spirit of the original poem matters. When the subject of a work to be translated is the very "raw material" of an actual war zone, as witnessed firsthand by the poet himself who is still living—*pace* a newspaper report to the contrary published during the siege—then greater sensitivity to formal intention is required of a translator, lest he be guilty of the sort of lyrical barbarism of which Adorno is rightfully leery. "Taking it further" in such a context is nothing to brag about; "extravagant" changes are unforgivable. What the translator wants *must* be secondary to what the source poem demands.

25 Review originally published in 2005.

Looking at the differences between two translations of one poem is a good way to get a sense of how Harsent went wrong and why the "new" version, if less polished, is superior. The first poem in *From Sarajevo* is "The Beginning, After Everything." In *Sprinting*, this is the thirteenth poem and Harsent has shorn the definite article from the title to accommodate the move. Opening with this poem is crucial because it contains the programmatic statement of artistic intention I quoted above; this is *the* beginning, not merely *a* beginning, setting the stage for what follows.

Most of the poems that were published in *Sprinting* are typeset in *From Sarajevo* as columnar prose paragraphs "which resemble newspaper reports." They *look* more like cribs than poems. Harsent breaks prose into verse lines and paragraphs into stanzas, so that the poems are now only "*like* newspaper reports" (emphasis added). In *From Sarajevo*, Simić wants his poems to be "so bare and cold that I could forget them the very moment a stranger asks: Why do you write poems which resemble newspaper reports?" Harsent, bareness be damned, has jazzed this up with emphatic repetitions to read "so heartless, so cold, / that I could forget them, forget them / in the same moment that someone might ask me, / 'Why do you write poems like newspaper reports?'" Elsewhere, a "hungry dog licking the blood of a man lying at a crossing" becomes a "ravenous dog / feasting on blood / (just another corpse in snipers' alley)." The melodramatic phrasing—ravenous, feasting, corpse—and loaded place name are so patently opposed to the chilled restraint Simić espouses that one feels embarrassed for Harsent's enthusiastic adornments. It's regrettably ironic that Harsent changed Amela Simić's "stranger" to "someone" because it reinforces the message of the poem that strangers can't possibly understand the situation and the poet's response to it.

Comparative reading suggests that some of the "radical excisions" Harsent has permitted himself function to cleanse the poems of references that might be particularly offensive to outside observers. This is most evident in "Love Story," a poem about two lovers from opposite sides of a bridge who are killed trying to cross it. The new English version contains the following paragraph:

> Newspapers from around the world wrote about them. Italian dailies published stories about the Bosnian Romeo and Juliet. French journalists wrote about a romantic love which surpassed political boundaries. Americans saw in them the symbol of two nations on a divided bridge. And the British illustrated the absurdity of war with their bodies. Only the Russians were silent. Then the photographs of the dead lovers moved into peaceful Springs.

The poem ends with "Spring winds" carrying the "stench" of the lovers' bodies; "No newspapers wrote about that." In his adaptation, Harsent deliberately excludes Simić's damning critique of Western nations' (which countries Simić says in his preface "compensated for their dirty consciences by feeding our walking dead, while they did nothing to stop the siege") aestheticization of a war story; no countries are named and the final sentence is dropped. This is censorious editorializing, not translation, and Harsent is guilty of it on several occasions. In the unexpurgated translation, we see one very clear reason why Simić wants to write poems "which resemble newspaper reports": because newspaper reports too often indulge in the barbaric lyrical fancies of poetry.

But we should be careful of taking Simić's stated intention too literally. A poet's manner of seeing is not the same as someone else's vision. The poet has "X-ray eyes"; he sees in metaphors, in images, in allegories. And he sees not so much in pictures as in words. There are references in these poems to a gremlinesque angel who "rewrote the prescription for my glasses" and "officers with gold buttons for eyes [who] enter my back door and look for my glasses." For Simić, keeping his vision clear is crucial and constantly threatened by partisan propaganda and the psychological trauma of life in a combat zone. Besides the cold bare facts of war, Simić's poems, as the above-quoted lines illustrate, are full of hallucinatory, paranoid nightmares. Which are also facts of war.

Simić is never aloof or self-righteous in his role as witness. In his preface, he sounds like Joseph Conrad's Marlowe when he writes that, for all the "horror that I went through … as a poet, I would be deeply sorry if I hadn't stayed, in the middle of horror, a witness to how cheap life can be." There is inevitably something parasitically self-serving and self-consuming in the poet's transformation of life into art, regardless of how noble that art ends up being, an irony to which Simić, ever clear-sighted, is not blind. He captures it with sangfroid in the very unjournalistic sonnet, "I Was a Fool":

I was a fool to guard my family house in vain
watching over the hill somebody else's house shine,
and, screaming, die in flames. I felt no sorrow and no pain
until I saw the torches coming. The next house will be mine.

If I wasn't somebody else, as all my life I've been,
I wouldn't say to my neighbour that I feel perfectly fine
upon seeing his beaten body. I should offer my own skin
as a tarp. Will the next beaten body be mine?

I was a fool. I love this sentence. Long live Goran and his sin.
There is no house or beaten man. There is no poetry, no line,
there is no war, there are no neighbours. There's no tarp made of skin.
But there's a pain in my stomach as I write this. It's only mine,

this sentence, the one I swallowed, whose every word
is each of the flames I saw, every scream a sword.

Here, the poet looks back on the conflict—both external and internal—and manages simultaneously to damn and praise his role in it. It is significant that he does this in a form more conspicuously poetic than the prose columns that predominate in *From Sarajevo*. This marks the poet's transition from a poetry of immediate witness to a poetry of reflection and recollection, inhabiting traumatic spots of time. It also marks the migration from one home and language to another, the Shakespearean sonnet being a quintes-sentially English form. Simić tells us in his acknowledgments that sixteen of the poems in this book he "either wrote in English or translated into English himself." Coyly, he doesn't specify which ones and I would have a hard time trying to guess them all. If, as I suspect, "I Was a Fool" is an original English poem, then I would have to say that Canada and the English language are the recipients of a great blessing improbably born of a brutal war.

Jabbed with Plenty
Peter Van Toorn and the Canadian Condition

OUR NATIONAL FOUNDATION myths tell us that when European settlers first arrived in Canada, they found a vast empty land. If it was full of anything in the eyes of pioneers, it was the raw potential of resources—and the anxiety-causing potential of failure and death. As schematic syntheses like Margaret Atwood's *Survival* demonstrate, much of our literature has been obsessed with making sense of the putative vacuum, with recording the ways in which we have attempted to fill the void and with negotiating our psychological sense of inferiority or victimhood, wedged as we are between the mute rock of northern nature on the one hand and the intimidating cultural hard places of Great Britain and the USA on the other. Atwood's wary approach to a theory of Canadian Literature is in fact uncannily similar to early settlers' notions of their new found land. She tells us that her assumption prior to beginning *Survival* was that there was no such thing as Canadian Literature, that it was a dearth, a shapeless scatter of texts bound together by no single theme or myth. Even if there was a pattern to be discerned—and not merely one to be superimposed, as David Solway maintains— perhaps we'd be better off now if Atwood had pretended otherwise, for despite her repeated disclaimers that she does not consider *Survival* to be the final word in delineating a Canadian literature, any such attempt at a critical meta-narrative inevitably involves the fixing of perimeters and parameters, establishing not-so-ghostly demarcations between what is "literature written by Canada" and what is not.

This is the theoretical equivalent to clearing brush and wood-land to build a homestead. Atwood says that the Canadian pioneer

> is a square man in a round whole; he faces the problem of trying to fit a straight line into a curved space. Of course, the *necessity* for the straight lines is not in Nature but in his own head; he might have had a happier time if he'd tried to fit himself into Nature, not the other way round.

That Atwood's pioneering study is such a neat analogue for the literal breaking of ground by main force is the cen-tral unintended irony of *Survival*. It is hard not to see her as Paul Bunyan and her book as Babe the Blue Ox, bound and determined to pull the bows out of the laughing Mississippi of literature. Her book gives handy thematic shortcuts to aca-demic specialists and to writers seeking to curry the favour of a university audience,[26] but the straight line it takes elides the essential curviness of the literary enterprise and thereby excludes much undomesticated writing that doesn't fit into the established paradigm—whilst promoting less accomplished, but thematically correct, texts to canonical status. *Edible plants inside, weeds outside*: a tautology that renders anything that grows on one side of the fence foison and anything on the other side poison, so that if one comes across an unidentifiable plant in one's wanderings beyond the well-hoed rows of the garden, one will be automatically suspicious of it, though it be the most delectable fruit in the forest.

---

26   As Solway says, "What begins to unite us is not so much the search [for roots] but the recognition that the search is good business. It helps politicians get elected, enables merchants to peddle their wares, provides media and university jobs, and hands over to the poets a ready-made subject ... " This is of course not a new argument, as it was voiced by AJM Smith, in very similar terms, as long ago as 1928.

The problem with a literature based on themes of survival and victimhood is a Maslovian one.[27] When the basic requirements of staying alive occupy the mind, the higher functions of self-actualization—including aesthetic pleasure and grace, including the manic elation of inspiration—go unfulfilled. Can there be a greater failing for an artist than this? The dogged cultivation of stunted crops in soil and weather ill-suited to their growth is stupid—tragically so—when richer nourishment hangs ripe and ignored on the bough.

Several critics have objected to the bare-bones, unadorned survivalist ethic in recent decades. In 1985, thirteen years after the publication of *Survival*, M. Travis Lane wrote in a review of George Elliott Clarke's *Saltwater Spirituals and Deeper Blues*, that

> Many of our contemporary Canadian poets have adopted for their verse a deliberately plain style, whose lack of ornamentation, allusion, and musical grace is intended, in most cases, to portray a sense of newness, of emptiness—what they perceive as the linguistic and cultural barrenness of the Canadian "landscape," the Canadian experience. This style conveys a sense of cultural de-racination, but, sometimes, also a kind of cultural inhibition—as if a turn of speech natural to an educated mind might be somehow un-Canadian. At its best (Atwood, Kroetsch) this style of heightened simplicity can be powerful, but, as in the comparable paintings of Colville, it is not so much a representation of reality as it is *an artificial conventionalization of reality*. The adoption of this plain style may have helped our poetry sever its colonial roots, and, as practiced by its masters, it need never be rejected. But a mature literature needs to use the whole of its inheritance. (Emphasis added.)

---

27 It's worth noting in this context that Maslow developed his theory of human motivation as a reaction to orthodox behaviourism and psychoanalysis, dominant procedural modes which he deemed to have an unhealthy preoccupation with pathology, in much the same way that orthodox approaches to Canadian literature—if not the bulk of the literature itself, as Atwood diagnoses it—have a morbid obsession with survival and victimhood, precluding the achievement of full human potential.

Lane points out the central fallacy of the Canadian plain style: that it is somehow more natural and native than showy imports using meter, metaphorical flourishes and patterns of rhyme. Metrical verse, it must be understood, is actually less artificial and synthetic than prose, which evolved as a literary form along with other sophisticated technological developments, such as the printing press. Thus, the deliberate prosiness of Canadian poetry, far from being aligned with the "barren emptiness" of Canadian nature, is the kissing cousin of Western industrialization, of humankind's alienation from the earth's natural rhythms and patterns.

Another writer taking issue with orthodox Canadian poetics in the '80s was Peter Van Toorn, whose seminal work *Mountain Tea* was published in 1984. The critical neglect of Van Toorn's poetry is perhaps the grossest instance of the literary establishment's blind husbandry and bad diet. On the surface, at least according to Survivalist logic, Van Toorn is the most un-Canadian of poets. Whereas the pioneer poet has a puritanical suspicion of "superfluous" ornamentation, Van Toorn deploys a "baroque artillery" of catholic technique. Whereas Canadian settlers seem to lack the vocabulary to identify the elements of their environment, Van Toorn's improvisatory and often inventorial poems are overbrimming fonts of aboriginal nomenclature.[28] Whereas *Survival* poets focus on the here and now, Van Toorn ranges widely and travels in time by translating poems from other eras and by adapting classical forms into his own idiom.

---

28   As Atwood says, "In a lot of early Canadian poetry you find this desire to name struggling against a terminology which is foreign and completely inadequate to describe what is actually being seen. Part of the delight of reading Canadian poetry chronologically is watching the gradual emergence of a language appropriate to its objects." This is to me a rather dubious assertion of literary evolution that begs the question of teleological progress and makes excuses for studying what would otherwise be dismissed as bad poetry. A more parsimonious, and therefore probable, account is that a hardscrabble colony exerted no great pull on poets of real ability, but was more attractive to the unlettered, pragmatic poor on the one hand and to gentleman adventurers who happened to dabble in verse on the other. It's only as middle class comfort is established in the colony that education and culture take root and a local literature sends out its first tender shoots.

In short, it's no small temptation to see Van Toorn as an alien in a strange land. Certainly, he seems to have been perceived as such, if the grudging praise and dismissive skepticism of *Mountain Tea*'s early reviews and the subsequent critical silence[29] are anything to go by. But it is my contention that the superabundance of his verse, his proclivities for catalogue and neologism, are the formal answer to a land that is not in fact harsh and empty, but bountiful and populous. His globetrotting and time-travelling quests for antecedents do not so much constitute a negation of Canadian identity as a mature awareness that our collective character is not singular but prismatically various; that we are not at the awkward early stages of history rising out of primeval mud, but the heirs of a wide range of traditions—traditions which ought not to be rejected as foreign baggage, but sifted through and borrowed from as a great treasure trove. The brash swagger of Van Toorn's virtuosity does not reflect a hubristic failure to recognize the meanness of our colonial condition, but is proof that this status is more psychological affliction—an internalized, atavistic victim complex—than objective reality.

Early reviews of *Mountain Tea* give the distinct impression that the reviewers didn't quite know what to make of Van Toorn's writing. Tom Marshall, who finds Van Toorn "impressive even when he is most irritating," advises that "one has to get used to his style, his unusual and rich diction" and that "diction and rhythmic shape are foregrounded, 'content' somewhat submerged." Similarly, John Tucker observes that "images ... do not resolve themselves. The landscapes that are his frequent subject remain elusive. Sonic gain ... seems to entail semantic loss." Tucker finds in *Mountain Tea* a "singleness of style" and Marshall feels the book does not contain "a particularly compelling vision of life." What is most interesting about these baffled and bemused readings is the extent to which they echo the settler's responses to the foreign landscapes and cultures he encounters upon arrival in the Canadian wilderness: the need to adapt, to "get used to" strange new surroundings; the absence or non-disclosure of significance; the overwhelming

---

29   With the exception of one essay, by Douglas Burnet Smith.

sameness; the dearth of coherent culture, of "vision." In their efforts to make sense of *Mountain Tea*, Marshall and Tucker attempt to plough straight furrows through knotty, "bouldershot" "taiga / full of elbow holes / and timber." The strain shows.

The beautiful irony here is the extent to which Van Toorn anticipates such square peg criticism. "In Guildenstern County" and "Epic Talk," the two sequences framing the first section of *Mountain Tea*, are, besides being catalogues of, and meditations on, Canadian landscapes, reproaches to the "bad brush" of Canadian poets and the "orthodox trajectories / of historians // whose assymptotes [sic] / never meet"—to artists and thinkers who have failed to do justice to their surroundings. Wind, linked through breath to inspiration, is a unifying motif of the book as a whole and blows especially fiercely through "In Guildenstern County":

> In guildenstern county
> where there's hardly any wind
> to go by
> you can smell the poem in a thing for miles
> when wind wins.
> Wins,
> handsdown, right out of nowhere: given
> good grass out front,
> bad brush behind.
> Even so,
> not counting wind in the pines,
> wind in the brakeslams,
> there's hardly any
> to go by. Go
> by, put arms around, smoke on, ride off, bounce
> on a blanket about. Just
> miles and miles
> to crash
> and keep crashing through.

A passage like this could be interpreted as an orthodox settler perspective, with nothing but "miles and miles" of empty space to crash through and the poet clearing "bad brush" to plant "good grass." But if you look more closely, you see that Van Toorn has turned these tropes on their heads. There is "no wind" (inspiration) *except* "in the pines" and "brakeslams"; it's official Canadian culture (as represented by "guildenstern cojunct county") that's lacking in wind; when it does blow, it "carries ... bluster," not beauty. There's "So much to trip out on" in nature, full of the "honkiest names." What "suck[s] your eyes out" is not the landscape's curviness, but the straight lines of "trackpoles and lineside" and "Dewline"[30] cutting through it.

In case he hasn't made his point sufficiently clear through the oblique jazz riffs of "In Guildenstern County," Van Toorn is more explicit in "Epic Talk." In "Bee's Eye," the fourth poem of the sequence, George, a "guide" (someone therefore with intimate knowledge of the wilderness), leads a "vip's wife" into the bush,

> with her old man
> complaining
>
> of the humid subzero sting
> and snowy
>
> blindmaking
> of this damned climate
>
> it was as if you were
> walking

---

30   This is an especially Canadian reference. The DEW (Distant Early Warning) Line is a string of radar sites in remote northern regions, established by NORAD to detect a possible Soviet attack of North America from the Arctic. When Van Toorn writes of "radar caught up in the Queen's fuddy lace," he encapsulates the Survival theme of Canada caught between the USA and the UK. Unlike Atwood and others, however, he dismisses this situation as "Nothing to get stung up about"—an allusion to the Beatles' song "Strawberry Fields" in which "nothing is real, and nothing to get hungabout."

in a ping pong ball
she said

and George he nodded
and smiled

as the wind removed
a right pawfull

of snow
off the trees and slammed

it like snowthoughts
on the ground

on she complained
about

the winter air's
prickle

and never noticed how
something

sound of drumskin
on fire

the lemon sparkle in
the eyes

the old pride
at seeing

not a missing of
moisture

but a firing
of that same moisture

into diamondiest flakes
a trout sparkle

it took an eye
his eye

compound
as a bee's eye

to grasp a wealth
instead

of a relative
vacuum

I'm reminded here of Marshall's inability to see any "compelling vision" in Van Toorn's poems. A poem like this one—and many others in which eyes and tropes of vision appear—reveals that it is critics like Marshall, dazzled by the "blindmaking" surface of *Mountain Tea* and hobbled by received conventional wisdom, who, too caught up in their talk, lack the vision required to see clearly. It takes a true local like George (a stand-in here for the seeing and naming poet) to perceive the "wealth" of his supposedly blank surroundings. If Marshall and others fail to detect *a* vision, it's because Van Toorn does not restrict himself to any single focal point. Note the third- and fourth-last couplets quoted above, in which three of four lines end with "eye" and the odd line out with "compound." Always true to the details, Van Toorn has created a small picture in words of a bee's eye to reinforce the visionary theme of the poem. This trio of eyes should also be read as a trinity of "I's": ever the protean conjurer, Van Toorn, who "can tell nothing about me" does not confine himself to a singular identity.

At the risk of setting off alarm bells in the headquarters of the politically correct, I would call Van Toorn's techniques of seeing and naming aboriginal. By this I don't mean that he uses native themes or figures symbolically,[31] a trait of Canadian Literature identified and explicated by Atwood in Chapter Four of *Survival* and lambasted by Solway in "The Flight from Canada." Nor do I mean that he attempts to speak in an Authentic Native Voice in the manner that has been with no small justice called the "appropriation of voice." Unlike many an achingly righteous liberal, Van Toorn does not claim special access to the spiritual life or cultural plight of dispossessed Native Canadians. Rather, his relationships to landscape and language exist in a fluent comfort zone that runs *parallel* to aboriginal peoples' symbiotic rapport with the extra-human natural world—prior to European colonization and interference.

The aboriginality of *Mountain Tea* is most obviously embodied in its author's use of language. In part, this involves his adoption of words from various native idioms, especially "wawa," the windy theme of "In Guildenstern County's" jazz variations. More to the point, however, aboriginality inheres in Van Toorn's insistence on "iconic" instead of "referential" language.[32] He sees much contemporary poetry as having

31 I concede that the "crone Huron on Bear / Island" in part 3 of "Epic Talk" could be construed as a symbol. It seems to me, however, that Van Toorn's portrait is imbued with a degree of disillusioned realism that renders it credible. At any rate, this instance, whether symbolic or not, is not strictly related to Van Toorn's native fluency as I intend to define and describe it.

32 For my ideas about Van Toorn's aboriginality of idiom, I am in part indebted to Milton Acorn's notion of "Ojibway" as a universal language of poetry, as articulated in "On Speaking Ojibway":

In speaking Ojibway you've got to watch the clouds
turning, twisting, raising their heads
to look at each other and you.
You've got to have their thoughts for them
and thoughts there'll be which would never
exist had there been no clouds.

been impoverished by reliance on the sort of stripped down "blandly referential" "utility prose" appropriate to survival and rational analysis, but not to fulfillment and spiritual ecstasy:

> In utility prose words 'go public' and have the inertia and complacency of conventionalized life. Their function is so referential that their value is mainly utilitarian: the reader notes the point they make and dispenses with them. The iconic qualities of language are absent from utility prose—rhythm, sound word play, metaphor, idiom, etc.—so that the reader or listener feels no ripple in his consciousness at these

Best speak in the woods beside a lake
getting in time with the watersounds.
Let vibrations of waves sing right through you
and always be alert for the next word
which will be yours but also the water's.

No beast or bird gives a call
which can't be translated into Ojibway.
Therefore be sure Ojibway lives.
There's no bending or breaking in the wind
no egg hatching, no seed spring
that isn't part of Ojibway.
Therefore be sure Ojibway lives.

The stars at night, their winking signals;
the dawn long coming; the first
thin cut of the sun at the horizon.
Words always steeped in memory
and hope that makes sure
by action that it's more than hope,
That's Ojibway, which you can speak in any language.

As with many ars poetica statements in verse, Acorn's is, paradoxically, more about how to "speak Ojibway" than it is an example of same (much as Archibald MacLeish's famous poem, when it says that "A poem should not mean / But be," contradicts itself). Many instances in Van Toorn's poetry, by contrast, could be construed as statements of purpose, but he makes most of his statements analogically rather than didactically, as in, for instance, "Mountain Leaf," discussed below. Generally, Van Toorn is more inclined to make overt statements of poetics in prose essays.

very things being described. Utility prose describes the mechanism of a goose pimple, even how it feels, but it cannot make you feel it.

Rather, "Poetry, whose units of sound, image, significance and spiritual flow are aboriginally tiny, condenses as it slows down or accelerates into a time whose locus it shares with song and dance." Occasionally, this means that Van Toorn appears to put down words for the pure play of sound, as in "Mountain Boogie," an anaphoric—and euphoric—litany of sensory delight:

> O peppermint moon behind the loud running clouds!
> O aspirin violets!
> O the cue to look up splickering out there in the U-sphere!
> O aspirin ivories!
> O nick nock of madder smoosh!
> O the sparks when she peels her sweater in the dark!
> O sepia blush!
> O pink pink: the fingers' rinks winking with quick!

And so on, over forty-six more lines. This poem, for all its non-linear elements, does have formal antecedents in public prayer and ritual chant. Its title announces that it will be more dance than essay, eschewing analysis in favour of apostrophe, enumeration and celebration. Presumably it's this sort of writing that leads critics like Tucker and Marshall to complain of sense subordinated to sound, of "semantic loss" and the absence of "a compelling vision."[33]

---

33 There is a historical parallel to this kind of critical failure of eye and ear to perceive the value and validity of "unorthodox" means of communication. In the 1980s, in Gitxsan land claims hearings in Smithers, BC, Chief Justice Allen McEachern deemed inadmissible hundreds of hours of testimony in the form of Gitxsan oral history and song. In *The Other Side of Eden: Hunters, Farmers, and the Shaping of the World*, anthropologist Hugh Brody reproduces part of the courtroom transcript from the case, in which an elder, Mary Johnson, wishes to include a traditional song as part of her testimony. McEachern's response is: "I have a tin ear ... It's not going to do any good to sing to me. ... I don't think that this is the way this part of the trial should be conducted. I just don't think it's necessary. I think it is not the right way to present

Leaving aside the fact that such thoroughgoing absorption in 'pure sound' is far from Van Toorn's only, or even usual method, the inability to perceive the transcendent sense of a poem like "Mountain Boogie" signals a singular failure of the imagination on the part of *Mountain Tea*'s reviewers. As Douglas Burnet Smith writes of another of Van Toorn's catalogue poems, "The Cattle," "the rhetorical and the figurative represent one another coming to life as each description is added to the next to make an accumulated epiphany." The epiphany that gradually reveals itself is a strong contrast to the explicit, anecdotal epiphany that has become such a cliché of contemporary lyric verse. Again, Smith has it right when he says of "Mountain Boogie" that for Van Toorn, "the bombastic is the vessel of the subtle." By downplaying the referential function of language and stepping up its iconic quotient, by refusing to pander to the Canadian reader's expectations, Van Toorn sidesteps the decidedly unsubtle options of exposition, analysis and declaration. He thereby comes closer than almost any modern era poet (with the possible exceptions of Clare and Hopkins) to defying Wittgenstein by bridging the gap between language and the world it is supposed to represent, and to fulfilling Archibald MacLeish's axiom that

> A poem should be equal to:
> Not true.
>
> For all the history of grief
> An empty doorway and a maple leaf.
>
> For love
> The leaning grasses and two lights above the sea—
>
> A poem should not mean
> But be.

---

the case." Brody writes much as Atwood does about the straight-line, square-peg mentality of European agriculturalists in Canada and about the incompatibility of such approaches with aboriginal hunter-gatherer mores and with nature itself.

Through the rhythmic accumulation of minute particulars (lists of all sorts abound in *Mountain Tea*), Peter Van Toorn broaches the cosmic. He makes the reader, supposing she is already sufficiently attuned, *see* differently.

He accomplishes this transport not only through linguistic play, but also through precise observation, in which mode his language downshifts from the outright "bombastic" to the minutely rigorous. Consider this description of dragonfly courtship rituals:

> ... Those wings
> and spiny forelegs must have been battered stiff
> by every kind of twist in wind on deck,
> while she slipped her steering end into U-curves
> under the floating fabric; and battered stiff
> from trying out so long, racing for solid
> hours between beds, often landing just to check
> and take off again. Nine times out of ten
> something in the bed blocked the way solid.
> She'd arch and strain her whole fuselage
> dipping it under again and again
> (sometimes rocking the fabric apart, stage
> by stage: water splashing up all around her
> and priming the air with a rainbow)
> trying to up and around where his began.
> And he'd be doing a standstill solo
> in the air, wings pitched at fortyfive degrees
> from her lock-in sockets, and doing ninety
> to keep the whole thing balanced. Then off again
> when it wouldn't work. She with her sounder
> ochre butt, he with a longer, more pliable
> end of sorts.

As with the best nature poems of John Clare ("The Nightingale's Nest" comes to mind), the sharp focus zoom of the vision and inobtrusive colloquial fitness of the diction create the illusion that there is no text mediating between the reader and the event described. The writing, in fact, does not so much *de*scribe as *in*scribe and enact the aerial flirtation and fornication of the two insects, as though the poet had hitched a ride on one of their backs, hanging on for dear life and taking notes with his free hand.

Van Toorn extends such tactics radically in his remarkable sonnet, "Mountain Leaf":

> A bird pushes a leaf on a red roof,
> aiming for ground, so it falls—not the roof,
> but the leaf a bird pushes; and the more
> it pushes (crisp beak and twig toes), the more
> it pushes a still bronze leaf, all curled up
> in a cone (showing a beak all curled up
> in a cone too, aiming a bronze baked leaf)
> for grounds that roll the curls out of a leaf,
> grounds which, though rolling round a huger sound,
> nevertheless snap twigs in leaf's own sound,
> so that, round on round, the red roof, while not
> waiting for a leaf to fall, is still not
> tongue-tied either, but stands by, push for push,
> ready for leafy bird's stiff, crisp, bronze push.

On one level, this poem is a piece of virtuoso stuntwork. The diction is Frostian in the extreme: the sonnet's 140 syllables are deployed in 123 words, only fifteen of which have more than one syllable (counting "tongue-tied" as a single word). It is the intricate patterns of repetition Van Toorn builds out of this sparse language that make this poem such a dizzying bit of craftsmanship. Most obviously, this repetition takes the form of the identically rhymed couplets, an unusual strategy to see employed once in a poem, never mind seven consecutive times. This alone goes against all conventional workshop wisdom. But that's not all. Of the poem's 123 words, only twenty-three occur uniquely; the other one hundred are repetitions of thirty-two other words. Whole phrases ("a bird pushes"; "red roof") get recycled; and just look at the enjamb-ments in lines three through six: "the more / it pushes"; "all curled up / in a cone."

The way the poem unfurls is quietly spectacular. In the first six lines, we find only two of the uniquely occurring words, whereas twenty-one appear in the following eight lines, giving the sense of a movement out of sheer neurotic repetition into more confidently purposeful—if still without obvious reason—activity, beyond the mere pushing of boundaries into the realm of art. Chief among the repetitions of single words is "push," which makes seven appear-ances; also notable is eight instances of words ending in "ound" (sound, round, ground). In a poem so intentionally and tightly wound, it can hardly be accidental that these specific reiterations stand out: Van Toorn is pushing the limits of sense and sound, just as the bird is pushing the leaf across the roof, and likewise just for the sheer perverse pleasure of the labour, the end result of which, for both bird and poet, is a "stiff, crisp, bronze push."

Van Toorn's capacity for identification with his subjects in a manner that is at once spontaneous and highly wrought[34] is one of the most sophisticated examples I've seen of Keatsian negative capability. Van Toorn is keenly aware of what he's doing, as he quotes Keats's famous remark ("If a sparrow comes before my win-dow, I … pick about the gravel.") as an epigraph to "Mountain Rain," a poem in which the poet follows the path of rain "washing cracks / in worms' backs." In "Mountain Maple" there is a perfect reversal of subject and object as the poet literally enters the epony-mous tree, which speaks the poem to the poet:

> On me you scratch and blot your bitter ink.
> I make the matches, handles, and boxes
> you burn me, cut me, and bury me with.
> I am a cross between man and grass, and

---

34 Solway has said of Van Toorn that he is "what we might call a natural poet, at one with the concrete world around him, and yet at the same time the most rigorous of verbal disciplinarians, one who still remembers how to gaffle a line."

grow in the thought of him from the ground up.
Is it for cutting me down for no use,
for letting too many of us go, till
everything's up to the nostrils in snow,
that you sing and cry and write down this thing?

I would call this fluid plasticity of identity shamanic. As
Hugh Brody explains, "shaman" is a word used by the Tungus
of Siberia "to denote a person who has the power to cross from
the human to the spirit world, and to make journeys in a disem-
bodied form." And elsewhere, "[s]hamans are the people whose
special skills and techniques allow them to move from the prac-
tical realm to the spiritual, from the everyday to the metaphys-
ical." Note the emphasis here on "special skills and techniques"
and recall Marshall's opinion that Van Toorn's technique is "often
gratuitous and a little empty." Many Canadian poets espouse a
shamanistic ethos and strike a shamanistic pose,[35] but with very
few exceptions, the reader is not allowed to forget that they are
reading a poet shamming at shamanism because their visions lack
the immediacy and verbal authenticity required to make their
cartoonish caricatures of medicine men and women credible. As
we have already seen above, Van Toorn, through improvisatory
language, imaginative leaps and precise observation—in short,
through *technique*—is a poet able to cross, in Brody's phrasing,
the porous "boundaries around the human world" effortlessly
and at will, becoming possessed by the life energy of insects,
birds, foxes, trees and other humans.

Brody also tells us that "all those who rely on shamans believe
it is possible for especially gifted men and women to visit places
beyond the reach of ordinary travel; they also believe that shamans
can make journeys to other times." Van Toorn performs such tran-
sit in two different, but related, ways. The first method is highly
metaphysical and can be seen in a handful of oneiric, hallucinatory

---

35   E.g., Susan Musgrave, of whom Carmine Starnino has said that "few Canadian
poets have written poetry that boasts such a full quotient of shamanistic glamour."

poems, such as "Russia Home," "The Snow Remover Is Coming," "Kora's High," "Baudelaire," and "Mountain Tea." These are poems in which the poet taps into the subconscious, often with the help of mind-altering drugs, as is made explicit in "Baudelaire" (who was himself, of course, a notorious experimenter with narcotics), with its "black and gold logic." Significant also that pride of place is given to "Mountain Tea"—*tea* of course being a slang term for cannabis—a sonnet in which the subject of the poem, addressed in the second person but probably the shaman-self of the poet, literally loses his head and goes

> ... falling a few planets deep,
> and deeper, where nothing warns you straight out,
> a pair of hands, pulled by the pull of sleep,
> won't meet, to pour mountain tea out, without
> fire that air, earth that water, dreams that sleep
> pour out deeper than a few planets deep.

John Tucker, with the defensive unease of the unsettled settler, finds it "puzzling" that this poem, which "successfully defends its obscurities from the probings of the 'utility prose' intellect," should share its title with the book. But the strange imagery of poems like this one are only "obscure" to Joe Friday minds resolutely dedicated to the dichotomies of fact and fantasy, reality and dream. In contrast, as Brody tells us, there are for people with faith in shamanic wisdom "facts about things and facts about spirits. And the wall between these two kinds of entity is not solid." He elaborates:

> [D]reaming ... allows a form of knowledge that in effect processes all other knowledge. ... Dreams take the dreamer not to some surreal universe in which the natural order is transcended or reversed, not to a land of fantasy, but to the place and creatures he or she knows best. ... By escaping mere facts, [hunter-gatherers] discover the most important facts of all.

This statement could easily be a prose paraphrase for "dreams that sleep / pour out deeper than a few planets deep." It's not much of a stretch to say that Van Toorn is primarily concerned, as artist and thinker, with opposing the "merely factual"—which, as Solway says, is "[i]n poetry … merely factitious"—with dream journeying. Consider a few choice quotations from *Mountain Tea*. In "Pigeon Feeder," the eponymous character (like the guide, George, a poet figure) is surrounded by "dumb and cruel" birds (surrogates for poetasters or blind critics) who "Peck peck, crabbing for *facts* / those spic and span beaks knurly with cancers." (Emphasis added.) Their empty talk, their "peckerblab hangs [in the air] like a neurosis." The association of "spic and span" beaks[36] with "cancers" and "neurosis" is no accident: the neat and tidy straight line of utility prose leads us mentally and physically astray from profounder insights into our psyches and environment and is apt to occasion pathological disorders and physical illness. In "Metaphor," the sixth poem in the "Epic Talk" sequence, Van Toorn praises the poet who provides "an // endless / chain of mysteries," as opposed to those who have on offer "mere barbarities."

In case you think I'm stretching Van Toorn's poems to accommodate pet theories, consider the poet's plain prose assertion that "[a]n age prone to stichic assimilation in verse betrays a predilection for reason over rhyme, statement over suggestion, definition over rune, and confession over apostrophe." The title of *Mountain Tea*'s prefatory poem is "Rune," in which Van Toorn lays out his poetic principles in opposition to contemporary convention. He describes the "rumour that starts like a rune / in the earth" as a "heresy." The rumour is further associated with nature and music ("like a frog, a bird, a song / or a stone"), dreams and ego displacement ("it's a walk / in somebody's bones"). It is both precise and spontaneous ("runs like a clock / but keeps changing time"), prismatic ("In a poem it boasts all colours of the sun."), and finally independent and defiant ("Like a bronze pope, it salutes

---

36   It is noteworthy that Marshall praises George Bowering's language, in contrast to Van Toorn's, for its cleanness.

no one."). Clearly, Van Toorn is on the warpath against the predominant trends in contemporary—and particularly contemporary Canadian—poetry and poetics. In this programmatic poem, as in his prose writings, he insists on the primacy of icon over reference, of outward attention and address—as in "The Cattle" and "Mountain Boogie"—over inward self-examination, the extraordinary and miraculous over the banal and quotidian.[37]

Waldo Frank, in an essay on Hart Crane (one of Van Toorn's exemplars) writes that "Whitman's challenge was not widely accepted; the plain-minded folk, the fact-minded poets of his time and ours resisted him. Hart Crane shares Whitman's fate." So, too, does Peter Van Toorn. Consider Atwood's assertion that

> a reader must *face the fact* that Canadian literature is undeniably sombre and negative, and that this to a large extent is both a reflection and a chosen definition of the national sensibility. ... [I]n Canadian literature, a character who does much more than survive stands out almost as an anomaly, whereas in other literatures ... his presence would be unremarkable. (Emphasis added.)

Atwood earlier mixes praise and complaint when she observes that

> The really positive virtue is the insistence ... on *facing the facts*, grim though they may be. Romanticism and idealism are usually slapped down fairly hard ... What one misses, though, is joy. After a few of these books you start wanting someone, sometime, to find something worth celebrating. Or at least to have fun. (Emphasis added.)

---

37 For contemporary poems that exemplify what Van Toorn opposes, see Sharon Thesen's "Mean Drunk Poem" and "Hello Goodbye." In the former, Thesen writes "I get drunk // to lubricate my brain & all that comes out / of my Gap / is more bloody writing"; in the latter, "Helpless, / I yearn for this one or that one / happy in their houses or unhappy / as the case may be." Thesen is, admittedly, an arbitrary choice; one could pick any number of poems from the 1980s preserved in any number of anthologies to illustrate the case that what poets like Van Toorn and M. Travis Lane were objecting to was ubiquitous and is still prevalent and valued by many critics.

Note the reiterated emphasis on the settler virtue of facing the perceived facts. The problem is of course that Atwood begs the question of factuality. She and so many others are caught in an unimaginative dichotomous thought-system which sees only the polar opposites of "facts" and "romantic ideals." Small wonder that a character such as Van Toorn, who "does so much more than survive," gets, if not "slapped down pretty hard," widely ignored by his contemporaries. If there is insufficient joy to be found in Atwood's reading, as she complains, her thesis does nothing to remedy the *fact*.

Van Toorn's war is also against the parochial inwardness and self-referentiality of most Canadian verse, which brings us to the other principal means employed by him to travel through space and time: translation. The poet returns from his shamanic wanderings with news that stays news from Ancient Rome, Medieval France, Renaissance Germany and 19th Century Japan, to name but a few of his plunders. Thirty-eight of *Mountain Tea's* eighty-six poems are versions of pieces written originally in a language other than English. Other poems, such as "Baudelaire," "Icarus Like Crane" and "Swinburne's Garden," are significant tributes to, and engagements with, the work of past masters. Whereas pioneer poets are obsessed with forging an original Canadian style and identity, Van Toorn writes of becoming through translation "unencumbered by the burden of originality." Although he loves his "Snoweyes country, / surly over flag debates," he knows that a poet's true north strong and free has no fixed boundaries because it is poetry itself. And he knows that to have a proper perspective on his here and now, the poet must be steeped in past and elsewhere. As he puts it "a translation can provide the poet with a perspective lacking in his culturally inherited situation... it can allow him elbow room for interpretation of values which his native culture will only allow if sanctioned by exotic sources." He likens translation's capacity for imaginative expansion to travelling in time and draws distinctions between "literal translation," which involves "travelling backward in time" and "original and innovative translation" which moves old poems "forward in time."

Van Toorn's translations are of the "original and innovative" variety. In resolutely un-Canadian fashion, he "approaches the celebrated poet of the past as an equal," as John Tucker puts it. Tucker's evaluation, tainted by settler prejudice, is not praiseful. He calls Van Toorn's adaptations "as much acts of defiance as acts of homage" and wonders what the authors of the originals would make of his "melodies from different periods played on the saxophone." The default Canadian position being deference, assertions of creative will, speeches made from a position of strength, are seen as artistically and ethically suspect. Tucker seems to be echoing the title of Alice Munro's famous story collection in asking, "Who does Van Toorn think he is?"

In Atwood's terminology, most if not all of the poetry in *Mountain Tea* should be categorized under "Position Four" in the hierarchy of "Basic Victim Positions": "a position not for victims but for those who have never been victims at all, or for ex-victims." For the non-victim, "creative activity of all kinds becomes possible" and nature "exists as a living process which includes opposites: life and death, 'gentleness' and 'hostility.'" Van Toorn is not, as discussed above, alienated by or from his surroundings or his sexuality, but sees himself, in Atwood's terms "as part of the process." The catch of course is that, although such moments are "imaginable and therefore possible," they "are few in Canadian poetry," obsessed as it is—or at least as its critics are—with victimization and oppression. The emergence of a Position Four poet—of an artist perfectly at ease in his skin[38] and environment: Bloom's "strong

---

38   Sex and the erotic in *Mountain Tea* would make a rich topic for future discussion. Among Canadian poets, Irving Layton and Milton Acorn are perhaps Van Toorn's only rivals for sheer gusto of writing on the subject. When he digresses to comment on his own performance of dragonfly sex—

> ... As a whole
> much more truly quotable,
> more strictly independent and severe
> (though less essential, and with more art)
> than an elephant with one-storey shoulders
> and bouldering mind, swinging
> a rubber boom.

—it's hard not to read it as a playful jab at Acorn's "The Natural History of Elephants."

poet"; Nietzsche's *ubermensch*—in a too-human culture syllogistically preoccupied with its imagined victim status on the one hand and its oppression of other cultures on the other, is bound to be mistaken for something less than it is, or even resented, much as a country boy who makes good in the big city comes to be seen as "too big for his britches" back home.

The clarity of Van Toorn's perspective on Canada no doubt has much to do with the fact that, as an emigrant from the Netherlands, he is not burdened by prior generations of inward-focused Canuck roots-seeking, nation-building and meaning-making. He glosses this in the penultimate poem of "Epic Talk":

> a people's genius
> emerges
>
> from a black felt hat
> upside down
>
> not when a rack is placed
> for its hanging
>
> but when a violence
> of metaphor
>
> a soil's flower
> dragged up by the roots
>
> hangs fire
> on the lapel of an outsider
>
> whose unique ability
> to yank
>
> more than mere barbarities
> from the hat

gives him an insider's right
to wear that hat

a people's genius
emerges

when an outsider can wear
a felt hat

inside out
ably yanking from it an

endless
chain of mysteries

that grow on them
as

flowers grow
on a woman's breast

or pollen rubs off on
the bee's leg

The self-confidence implicit in writing like this is alone suf-
ficient to brand Van Toorn un-Canadian. It is precisely his "out-
sider" status, however, his turning inside-out of what is commonly
held to be Canadian—as embodied by the straight-line "rack"—
that makes him the ideal Canadian citizen and artist. "Genius"
here has a triple connotation: as defined in the *Canadian Oxford
Dictionary*, it encompasses "exceptional creative power" as well as
"the tutelary spirit of a place" and "the prevalent feeling or asso-
ciations etc. of a nation, age, etc." Poetic genius and the spirit[39]

---

39   The word "spirit" is often poo-pooed in this ironic and pragmatic age as mystically
vague, but it bears remembering that the word's origins are by no means metaphysical.

of the land are one. And it is important to note that Van Toorn does not restrict the spirit of the land to "the deep country," but locates it also in "urban / spaces." Like his Montreal pigeon feeder, Van Toorn wears both the "overalls" of the hick rural bard and the "black beret" of the hip urban poet. I doubt that anyone has limned the simultaneous beauty and *laideur* of a Montreal winter—"Snowbound / in a stolen newness, swaggering in goo"— as memorably as Van Toorn does in the first section of "Icarus Like Crane." As with the virtuoso description of dragonfly sex this kind of scene painting is highly innovative, but is not, *pace* Marshall, "gratuitous." Rather, Van Toorn's virtuosity serves to bridge the gap between reader and scene, to collapse the boundary between language and objective reality; one hardly needs to have experienced a Montreal winter to get a vivid picture and feel for it when reading this poem—which is crucial for communicating Canadian reality and not merely warped tomographs of the "Canadian psyche" to the world outside our borders.

Canada is a staggeringly diverse mix of geographies and peoples. Most of the literature that has been identified as characteristically Canadian has not been equal to the formidable challenge of representing that diversity. Small wonder if we have, as is often complained, produced no Yeats. Too often what we get—what we settle for—is a grainy Polaroid of our own intimidation in the face of that challenge. This isn't to say that the settler perspective is invalid, but that as a paradigm Survivalism is inadequate and constricting. Now, though Alden Nowlan's observation that "this is a country / where a man can die / simply from being / caught outside" is still technically accurate, it is hardly reflective of daily life for the vast majority of our citizens. Rather, statements like Nowlan's, in all their no-nonsense, stripped down prosiness, do little more than convey a stray thought that happened to pass through the poet's mind as he was walking home to his heated flat after work. To restrict oneself to a narrow range of subjects

---

Rather, spirit is etymologically related to inspiration, and hence to breath, or "wind" in Van Toorn's symbological universe.

and styles is to remain in the garrison. It takes a more innovative vocabulary, a greater attention to form, a broader frame of geographic, historical and literary reference, a comfort within—but also an ability to step out of—one's own skin and skull, to *embody* the "genius" of the Canadian people.

This heady mix is just what we have had under our noses since 1984, when *Mountain Tea* was first published. David Solway puts it perfectly in describing Peter Van Toorn as "an architectonic magpie gathering his materials from everywhere and arranging them in the best, most startling and yet wholly appropriate order." He demonstrates in poem after poem that he is at once profoundly spiritual and wittily urbane; that he is rigorously disciplined and wildly freewheeling; that he is attuned to the value of both innovation and tradition; that he is both indigene and immigrant; that he is a poet of Nature as well as a poet of Society; that his verse embodies, in short, the kernel of what Canada has been, can be and should be, with all the chaff left on the threshing floor. My hope (on better days, my belief) is that we are at last—or at least—approaching the level of cultural maturity and self-confidence required to move beyond mere survival and our preoccupation with identity, to recognize that Van Toorn and other singular talents have already done much to define our culture without delimiting it, and not to dismiss their superior skill and vision as alien because they refuse to conform to easily commodified package concepts of Canada.

SMALL IS POWERFUL
Souvankham Thammavongsa
Found

> They got little cars
> That go beep beep beep.
> They got little voices
> Goin' peep peep peep.
> –Randy Newman

IF SHORT PEOPLE GOT NOBODY to love, the plight of short poems is, all too often, that they got nobody to love 'em. In a crowded literary marketplace, the large and the loud tend to drown out the wee. Our arbiters of literary excellence, not to mention general readers, so often equate big and sprawling with ambition that they dismiss the small as slight. Very rarely will you see a handful of lines conveying a single image walk off with a prize in one of our ubiquitous poetry contests. Just to be eligible for the CBC Literary Award, a poem or sequence must be at least 1000 words (making the prize worth, at best, six bucks a word—I suppose any more would look like a bad bargain). Small wonder, then, that very few poets dedicate themselves to the very short poem. Sure, lots pepper their well-padded books with epigrams or sprinkle in the occasional haiku for contrast, but how many go small or go home?

One poet who has pitched her single laurel leaf against the tsunami of published poetry is Souvankham Thammavongsa. Not only has she avoided being crushed in the process, but she has ridden the crest of the wave to considerable acclaim. Her first trade collection, *Small Arguments*, won the ReLit Award (appropriately, a prize reserved for *small* presses), has gone into a second printing, and the book's elegantly simple construction—the work of Elizabeth Hobart of Zab Typography and Design—was honoured with an Alcuin citation.

Thammavongsa is a hyper-minimalist. *Small Arguments* is a sequence of thirty-one very spare poems, most of which focus on little things and creatures that typically escape our notice. They "show the strangeness and wonder lying just below the surface even in the commonest things in daily life," to use the words of Bertrand Russell, quoted in the book's epigraph. The collection's title comes from "A Firefly," which

> casts its body
> into the night
>
>
> arguing
> against darkness and its taking
>
> It is a small argument
> lending itself to silence,
>
> a small argument
> the sun will never come to hear.

In his review of *Small Arguments*, John Baglow said: "It is as though permission were being asked to speak, similar to the rising inflection. The arguments are indeed small, indirect, not really arguments at all, more tremulous suggestions."

I don't think he could have misread Thammavongsa more thoroughly. "A Firefly" concludes:

Darkness,
    unable to hold against

        such tiny elegant speeches,

     opens its palm
       to set free a fire

        its body could not put down.

Far from a "tremulous suggestion" or a shy request for permission to speak, this is a statement of willful defiance, the firefly emblematically standing in for Thammavongsa's work as a whole—if not for her life.

If you can't hear that in the poems, you're probably, like the sun in "A Firefly," not coming to listen. There's plenty of corroboration to be found in Thammavongsa's biography and interviews. After a perilous journey from Laos on a homemade bamboo raft, her parents arrived at a refugee camp in Nong Khai, Thailand, in 1978. In August of that year, Thammavongsa was born prematurely, weighing less than two pounds, her body, in her own words, "the size of a pop can." Her parents were unable to afford an incubator, without which the doctor said she would not survive. He was probably the first person to misread her.

Thammavongsa describes herself as "a fighter"; she is unapologetically proud of what she has accomplished and makes a point of saying that she has done it "alone." Her minimalist approach is an extension of that mentality. "One word," she says, "has to do what five more words could do, but must do it alone." Far from being soft and pretty, "[m]inimalism is a work of violence. It targets the fluffy or meaty stuff of language and rips it out." "A Coconut," she writes, "does not know / tenderness." Again, she tips us off that this is oblique autobiography in an interview: "I'm not about handling things with tenderness." She describes her poems as the product of focused thinking, which "means ordering, reordering, arranging, rearranging, orchestrating, getting dirty. It means choosing for yourself." This is what Stevens called "the rage for order"—writ small, perhaps, but all the more fierce for it—and Thammavongsa is deeply invested in "ghostlier demarcations, keener sounds."

It may come as a surprise to the casual reader of Thammavongsa's work that she admires Irving Layton, but the more time I spend with her poems, the more her affinity for an embattled little immigrant kid striking Napoleonic poses makes perfect sense. Some of the statements she's made in interviews sound as though she's channelling Layton's ghost: "I know that there are expectations for me to write a poor immigrant story or about my pussy or about making jam sandwiches by the window while staring out at the snow." Or: "I don't really like poets. They are awfully boring and not honest about anything at all." Or:

> Poets or poems that flatter, flatter themselves and each other. These are the ones I don't like so much. The kind that makes people go "oooh" or "ahhhh" as if it were aromatherapy or cute and sweet. ... The poems I do like don't care about being liked, because to be good, to be different, you can't care about that. They care about telling you who you are and who you might be.

Tremulous suggestions, indeed.

If her *Small Arguments* "tend towards silence," Thammavongsa's second book, *Found*, plunges straight into the heart of it. The entire text of the book, including a prefatory note and the titles of poems (which often, true to economical form, double as first lines), is about 830 words. If that factoid doesn't strike you immediately, consider this: I published a sequence of seven sonnets—a form prized for its compactness—as a chapbook last year. Word-count: 733. And don't forget the rules for the CBC Literary Award; this entire book would be a bad bargain by their reckoning. In *Small Arguments*, Thammavongsa's previous benchmark for sparseness, we hit the 830th word halfway through the book. *Found* is minimalism as extreme sport.

So much for statistics, what's the story? Best to quote Thammavongsa's preface in full:

> In 1978, my parents lived in building #48. Nong Khai, Thailand, a Lao refugee camp. My father kept a scrapbook filled with doodles, addresses, postage stamps, maps, measurements. He threw it out and when he did, I took it and found this.

Here we find ourselves in familiar Canadian territory: the diasporic (auto)biographical long poem. Right? Knowing what we know about Thammavongsa, probably not. For one thing—apologies for the spoiler—we already know it's not long, in the usual sense of the word. For another, this is not "found poetry" of the sort we've come to expect. In an interview on the CBC, Thammavongsa repudiates the poetic legitimacy of such methods, insisting that her book consists, by contrast, of "real writing." It is her response to her father's scrapbook, not the "poor immigrant story" of her father in the refugee camp. A critical factor is that what writing there is in the scrapbook is Laotian, a language the poet speaks, but cannot read or write; nor did she seek to have the text translated. Instead, she approaches the scrapbook—which she describes in the CBC interview as "tiny"—like one of the minuscule objects of *Small Arguments*.

And indeed, this second book starts off sounding much like the first, with a two-sentence untitled poem built in a slender column aligned on the left-hand margin:

I took only
bone

built half
your face

left
skull and rib

as they came

If you knew
love

these
do not say

but of life
your life

it was small and brief

Again, a veiled statement of poetics, the deliberate choice to take "only / bone," cutting away and discarding the fat and meat of the long poem. Again, the assertion of importance on behalf of the "small and brief." But we have to look more closely. What's different here is that this is not just a poem about "life," but a very specific "your life." The "you" addressed is not only the generic second person of some *Small Arguments* poems, but also the poet's father.

The anthropocentric focus is something very different for Thammavongsa. The next poem, "Thermometer, a Diagram of," affirms that this will be the subject of an extended small argument to come:

The human body
is set

between
two points

[...]

This
is where

it lives
and how

Somewhere between
two points

Those points are, explicitly, the boiling and freezing points of water but they are also birth and death. We are reminded how close together those points almost were for Thammavongsa and how crucial temperature—in the incubator, or out—was for her survival.

We make this connection, of course, only if we know her story, which she has no intention of telling in straightforward terms, at least not in her poems. What about the poem itself? First of all, for all its parsimony, it contains a wild overstatement. The human body actually lives in a subset of the range between boiling and freezing—a narrow subset. The poem reminds us, obliquely, how fine a line we walk and how great the perils on either side. This is also analogous to a minimalist poem's survival. She describes writing a poem as being "like a tightrope. My job is to walk across that air and not fall off." Too close to silence (freezing) or rhetorical sentimentality (boiling) and the rope snaps or goes slack; the poet falls.

Having built a frame in the first poem and established the terms for life in the second, Thammavongsa next goes inside the body:

The Heart,

    the real

        heart,

           is ugly

      Nothing

          here

   can break,

      or be broken

And nothing

can come

from here

but blood.

This is, on the surface, a rejection of sentimentality and its worn-out tropes (i.e. fake hearts) in favour of objectivity. Forget the metaphor, we are talking about meat. But it is also another statement of defiance; she might have left it at "can break," but by carrying on to "or be broken," she makes one think also of what is done to a horse to render it tame. While banishing sentimentality, the poem still honours true sentiment. That idea of loyalty and the double iteration of "nothing" swing us sideways into *King Lear*:

KING LEAR
… Now, our joy,
Although the last, not least; to whose young love
The vines of France and milk of Burgundy
Strive to be interess'd; what can you say to draw
A third more opulent than your sisters? Speak.

CORDELIA
Nothing, my lord.

KING LEAR
Nothing!

CORDELIA
Nothing.

KING LEAR
Nothing will come of nothing: speak again.

CORDELIA
Unhappy that I am, I cannot heave
My heart into my mouth: I love your majesty
According to my bond; nor more nor less.

Found, like *Lear*, is a story about a father and a daughter. Thammavongsa can no more heave her heart into her mouth than can Cordelia. "Love, and be silent" might well be the motto of this book. She is too keenly aware of a double duty: to poetry on the one hand, and to her father on the other (don't forget the synecdochic sense—family—of the poem's last word). Two more points between which to balance.

In the next poem

The Lung

takes

what it has

always taken

What

work it does

it has done

and has been doing

all these years

alone

and in the dark

you carried here.

Blood comes from the heart, breath comes from the lung. Since Thammavongsa is set on being literal, we should keep in mind that the lung is the source of inspiration. Note also the presence of "alone" all by itself—a one-word stanza, an almost empty room—and remember Thammavongsa's insistence that her work has been done by her alone. Something that is striking about this image in this poem is its paradox, since lungs typically work in pairs; as always, the absent details are as telling as those that are present.

Poetry and biography intertwine in these organic poems. The cardiovascular pairing of heart and lung correspond to something Thammavongsa has said in an interview:

> I went to a lecture on the sonata by Professor Woodland, and he said that the thing that makes a sonata remarkable is the composer's ability to draw out material from the most simple and basic notes. When he said this, I thought about my own life, and about writing. I thought about what my parents told me: that when I was born, they could see my lungs, my heart, all through a very thin layer of skin.

Found, like *Small Arguments* before it, is an echo chamber, in which art amplifies life amplifying art.

But for the constraints of space, we could continue to wander down that hall, teasing out the layers of Thammavongsa's miniatures. Her poems demand this kind of intense looking as much as they enact it. But let's skip ahead. After thirty pages of pared-to-the-bone but straightforwardly textual poems, we arrive, on page forty-three, at the beginning of a sequence of calendar leaves: "January, 1978," which reads:

> This month
> has
>
> [large hand-drawn X]
>
> This
> the mark
>
> of
> a hurried hand.

As we proceed chronologically, sometimes skipping several months at a time, we get more and more hand-drawn symbols (lines and slashes). At "January, 1979":

The first day
here

is
circled

then

[large hand-drawn slash]

takes out
the month.

The next seven months, over seven pages, have no text besides the title—no text, that is, beyond a hand-drawn slash. Then we have "September, 1979":

This
is the first

month
left unmarked

The ones
after

are
the same.

And indeed, October-December, covering three full pages of *Found*, are blank, but for the title.

This seventeen-page stretch of tightrope is the part of Thammavongsa's book that courts dismissal most stubbornly. Here she no longer "tend[s] toward silence," but, like John Cage in his famous anti-composition of *4'33"*, plunges right into its depths.

It's worth noting that Cage also favoured the sonata. What distinguishes Thammavongsa's silence from Cage's silence, however—what saves it from being a repeat of an unrepeatable stunt—is that one has no sense whatsoever of this being what Cage called "purposeless play." Rather, it is more like Frost's "serious play," another example of what Thammavongsa calls "real writing."

Certainly, part of the point has to be to reproduce in the reader of *Found* the same feelings of curiosity and unease, perhaps frustration, that the reader of the inscrutable scrapbook must have felt. But there's more to it than that. These are visual poems, but visual poems quite unlike the *horror vacui* of many examples of the form. Nor do they exist, as much visual poetry is supposed to, in order to frustrate a reader's analytical desire for meaning, but they are included to assist the attentive reader in finding it, however tattered it might be.

Thammavongsa uses an aphorism of Wittgenstein's as the book's epigraph: "The work of a philosopher consists of assembling reminders for a particular purpose." And that is precisely what she has done. If one looks closely at the facsimiles of hand-drawn signs, one realizes that they aren't identical to each other, but have subtle differences of length and angle, and very slight bends in different spots. One might also notice that they bear a resemblance to the step-staggered lines in the book's earliest poems. As part of "My Father's Scrapbook," an essay published in *The New Quarterly* (105), Thammavongsa provides marked-up copies of three of her poems, illustrating each piece's orchestrations. Two of those poems are the slash-marks of July and August, 1979, with three circular orchestrating marks on each line, in markedly different places. *4'33"* also had three movements. Just as Cage's silence and Thammavongsa's silence are not the same, just as the five trochaic "nevers" of Lear's famous line make for one of the greatest interpretive challenges a Shakespearean actor can face, no two silences in *Found* are alike—Cage said "no two Coca-Cola bottles are the same"—and we can detect this by paying close attention to something our instincts and habits tell us to dismiss.

Cage might as well have been talking about the anechoic chamber of *Found* when he said: "There is no such thing as silence. Something is always happening that makes a sound." We don't know why the keeper of the scrapbook started slashing whole months after previously crossing out each day meticulously. We don't know why he stopped marking the months altogether. Was he bored? Desperate? Hopeless? Or did life get too busy to keep recording the passage of time? Rather than presume to tell us, rather than filling in the gaps and interpreting the slashes, Thammavongsa does something far bolder, far more arrogant even, by leaving us to interpret the silence for ourselves—by making us think about it as she has thought about it.

"Small talk" is the phrase we use for inconsequential babble used to fill what would otherwise be an awkward silence. Thammavongsa's often unspeakable, but deeply articulated poems are the opposite of this sort of small.

Peeing Unrepentantly into Infinity
John Smith
Fireflies in the Magnolia Grove

JOHN SMITH, PRINCE EDWARD ISLAND'S inaugural poet laureate, has been publishing books of poetry since 1972. In spite of his on-Island acclaim, and despite the fact that a Google search of his name—in quotation marks!—turns up nearly sixteen million hits, he remains very little known outside the cozy confines of the Maritime peninsula still known as PEI. Moses Berger's harsh words to his father in Mordecai Richler's *Solomon Gursky Was Here* spring to mind, by way of objection: "Not all neglected writers are unjustifiably neglected." While I wouldn't argue that John Smith is one of Canada's *greatest* poets, nor that he deserves the same attention as, for example, his neighbour and contemporary Milton Acorn, I do think his work is excellent and, more importantly in some ways, perfectly unique in the largely homogeneous world of contemporary verse.

His obscurity can be chalked up to several factors, besides a name that sounds like it was invented by an unimaginative adulterer for the guest registry at a no-tell motel. For one, until recently Smith has published his books with very small regional presses. His 1982 collection *Sucking-Stones* (which incorporates two chapbooks published in the '70s by Réshard Gool's Charlottetown press, Square Deal), was published by Gary Geddes' subscription press Quadrant Editions; PEI's Ragweed Press published both *Midnight Found You Dancing* (1986) and *Strands the Length of the Wind*

(1993); Ragweed's successor Acorn Press published *Fireflies in the Magnolia Grove* (2004), which was shortlisted for the Atlantic Poetry Prize. 2005 marked Smith's first publication by a bigger publisher, with Fitzhenry & Whiteside's publication of *Maps of Invariance*, a sequence of essayistic prose poems.

A more cynical explanation for his lack of renown is that unlike other Maritime poets who have transcended geographical obscurity to achieve notoriety—Acorn, Nowlan and Thompson—Smith has neither the eccentric public persona nor the turbulent biography of the iconoclastic bad boy, which, for better or for worse, can help put a poet's work under the public eye. But I think the *causa prima* of his unpopularity is that Smith has over the course of his career followed a path (references abound in Smith's oeuvre to "The Road Not Taken," which is clearly a touchstone for him) down which few readers are intellectually prepared to follow.

Which is to say that Smith's poetry is unabashedly brainy; as Ross Leckie has said, it "does not apologize for its massive intelligence." This goes against the grain of the Purdyesque self-effacement and plain speech that has had so much currency in Canada. To give you an idea of Smith's register, the section headings of *Fireflies in the Magnolia Grove* are "Specifications," "Contributions to a Theory of Identity," "Histories," "Reports of Sexual Dimorphism," "Epistemologies" and "Disquisitions on the Question of Being." He deploys a complex polysyllabic vocabulary and his poems range over vast swaths of human endeavour, including, to name a few, philosophy, theology, geology, mathematics, physics, music and dance.

Smith's is a style that few poets can manage convincingly because it is a style that is founded on enormous knowledge. Certainly, few have tried. But Smith's uncommon breadth of learning (although he is Professor Emeritus of English, he also has a degree in Mathematics and Physics and has studied, in his own words, "numerous things both systematically and otherwise") and nimble, capacious mind, in concert with an elegant formal touch and keen ear for the music of a line, make his best work appeal to both aesthetic and intellectual brain regions. Smith *occupies* realms of investigation; he doesn't merely visit them for brief walking tours to retrieve metaphors, as do so many contemporary writers incorporating science and philosophy into their poems. (The fact that science is hot for younger poets now bodes well for a renaissance of interest in Smith's work.) Take, for example, "Mind Insists":

Mind insists on rambling. The mountain, after all, is so
vast, so intimately fissured, so accommodating.
There are so many ways of getting to the top, it's hard
to stay fixed on the flower of one asketic microcleft.

Trickles can start at any point where conditions are right
for condensation. They come to meet you with disarming
merriment, most of them dedicated to the deepening of
features already on record, but a few to true innovation.

When a rockface does break free, you go catatonic and cling
together. Once admit there's no escape, you're gratified
to have so much time to watch the avalanche approach. A wall

of air hits you first. Death is in effect spontaneous.
Or, both saved, you're bridged over by a boulder. Climbing out
reincarnate, the mountainside is a frozen surge of raw

seafloor. You don't get down to make a new start from the valley
till you've been parched and mummified by the naked dust of
the catastrophe. The other option would have you go extinct in the
    rubble

and so, as it were, achieve the summit by euphemism only.
But on a still summer's day, you're oblivious to such extremities.
Slopes compacted of ancient tragedies are simmering with bees.

Rocks here have been locked in place for more lives than you
    remember.

I've quoted the poem in its entirety because Smith's syntactically sinuous work is particularly difficult to excerpt, in spite of such brilliant phrases as "frozen surge of raw / seafloor" and "mummified by the naked dust of / the catastrophe" and the deft assonance and consonance of a line like "When a rockface does break free, you go catatonic and cling," with its cracking and clutching structures of sound. What I find most impressive about a poem like this is the poet's sustained control of the extended metaphor, the smaller metaphorical nuggets embedded within it, the contrapuntal interplay of abstract general statement and concrete particular detail. "[H]ard / to stay fixed on the flower of one asketic microcleft," indeed. In the introduction to *Maps of Invariance*, Smith writes of "a metaphor that is not actually stated, but rather is acted out, phrase by phrase, as the very body of the poem." It's precisely such an enactment embodied in a poem like "Mind Insists," which puts the lie to any false binaries of "process" and "product."

The nature of that metaphor and its enactment has long been a preoccupation of Smith's. It appears, for instance, in one of his finest sonnets, "There is one," from *Midnight Found You Dancing*:

There is one metaphor for everything. If it is money,
then poetry is redundant. If not—ah, if not, then
is it that single nonsense syllable sung by the indefatigable
oarsman setting his back against the tide of things,

groaning out the strokes of his trade, but hearing
in each groan a new thwack of the sea ring
like an unstoppable tonic chord reached at the last
expiring bar in the last sonata of a long career

as the boat turns to flotsam? Yes, it is that.
There is one metaphor that serves for everything in turn,
and it is like enough to all metaphors at once that it hardly differs
from

the things themselves that hardly differ from the effort to achieve
   them.
Bend, address the moment—this is an old see-saw—drop
—get it right—heave, breathe, groan, hear, swing up, again, again.

It could be validly argued that Smith's poetry suffers from a
restricted range of tone, subject and form, that one John Smith
poem too closely resembles any other, particularly since *Midnight
Found You Dancing*. It's true that Smith has explored similar the-
matic territory over the course of his career and has done so using
primarily a sort of meditative free verse sonnet, whether in four-
teen lines or in caudated variations thereof. Smith himself says of
Strands the Length of the Wind, "I tend to think of these poems
as individual pieces in an open mosaic. Each piece of the mosaic
is an abbreviated meditation that takes a run, often from what
I think may be an unexpected angle, at one or more traditional
themes." In a more recent statement of poetics he referred to his
sonnets as "randomly ordered facets of a polyhedron, a polyhedron
constantly in process of extending the number of its facets. That
polyhedron represents the wholeness, uncompleted and perhaps
defiant of completion, that these privileged moments and their
sonnet-embodiments compose."

A poet's appraisal of his own work is always to be taken with
a grain of salt, and I would hesitate to say that such an explana-
tion necessarily justifies repetition. I think in this case, however,
that Smith's statement provides the key to an appreciation of his
tessellated oeuvre, or "the art of perfect repetition," as he puts it
in the opening poem of *Fireflies*. Each piece is on the surface sim-
ilar in colour and texture, but contains important subtle variances
that make it integral to the picture as a whole. Seen from above,
the assembled fragments coalesce into a hologram-like image that
changes depending on the angle of the observer; from up-close, the
overall picture is lost, but one becomes aware that each individual
tile is a similarly variegated whole, that "the part / also contains
the whole." Certainly, the sonnet is nothing resembling a "closed

form" in Smith's hands, not simply because he does not feel bound to restrict himself to fourteen decasyllabic lines in fixed rhyme schemes, but because his three volumes of sonnets are the very essence of expansiveness.

Another aspect of expansiveness in Smith's work is performance. "Inevitably," he says, "a poem is performed, whether by a reader on a public platform, by a member of a coterie, or, most likely, by a solitary encounterer in the silent cave of the private mind." While there's nothing stopping those silent solitary encounters from taking place, anyone who has never heard Smith read his own poems—or others', as he often does—is missing out. Smith, whose style is antithetical to the drone of the dreaded "poet voice," is one of the best performers of poems in the country. His readings add dimensions and colours to his poems, making explicit their multiple voices, their coy ironies and farcically authoritative pronouncements. His dramatic readings often clarify the reasons for quicksilver shifts and disjunctions; they concretize beautifully the manifold abstractions that jostle about in his sonnets and offer invaluable clues as to how one might go about performing one's own readings of his work.

Fortunately, for readers who haven't yet had the pleasure of encountering Smith's poems live and out loud, the University of Prince Edward Island—where Smith is Professor Emeritus of English—has published a multimedia package, including two DVDs of Smith reading his own poems and a CD containing an hour-long lecture-with-readings: "This Hour Has 1338 Years: A Quick Journey Through Thirteen Centuries of English Poetry." During Smith's term as Poet Laureate, there were some poets on PEI who grumbled that he should have used the position to promote local writers. But Smith's mountain-top perspective reveals the here and now to be but a speck; his lectures on canonical poets are the very model of what a laureate might do to serve his community—a community that comprises more than just his peers.

Through electron microscope and Hubble telescope—a device to which Richard Lemm has compared Smith's work—John Smith probes the opposite realms of infinity and nothingness, the self becoming, as in Pascal's *Pensées*, "*un milieu entre rien et tout.*" Reading Smith's oeuvre, which belongs as much to the Renaissance (or for that matter, to the thought of the pre-Socratics, especially Heraclitus) as to our own age, I am put in mind also of Newton's supremely humble statement that he seemed to himself "to have been only like a boy playing on the seashore, and diverting myself in now and then finding a smoother pebble or a prettier shell than ordinary, whilst the great ocean of truth lay all undiscovered before me." This is another way of accounting for Smith's lack of stature in the Canadian canon. So much of what has been anthologized is poetry of the individuated ego or "voice," strong-stanced poetry of passionate conviction, evocations of specific places and times. Smith's work in no way lacks passion or intensity, but for him it is not glorification of the self and its credos, not specific landscapes, but "the need ... // for the hook of questioning / and quest" that animates his writing. His poetry thus bears marked affinities to Hopkins, Dickinson, Borges and Stevens, and is bound to be appreciated by admirers of such masters, as well as by readers of contemporary Canadian poets like A.F. Moritz and Robert Bringhurst, who value inquiry over easy answers and who find wonder and joy and terror at every touch and turn.

Song of the Salmon

Tim Bowling

The Lost Coast: Salmon, Memory and the Death of Wild Culture

EVER SINCE THE PUBLICATION of *Low Water Slack* in 1995, Tim Bowling has been singing the song of the salmon. Born and raised in the Fraser Delta fishing town of Ladner (now absorbed by Vancouver's sprawl), long resident in Edmonton, Bowling is one of our most gifted poets and possibly the country's finest elegist. The song he's been singing is a dirge, both for the salmon itself and for the salmon-fishing industry and the "wild culture" in which he grew up. After seven poetry collections and three novels, he turns to non-fiction for *The Lost Coast*, giving us his most in-depth and extended work on the history and fate of the Fraser River.

A legatee of Henry David Thoreau, with this book Bowling joins the ranks of prose masters of the ethics of place, such as Barry Lopez, Bruce Chatwin, Robert Bringhurst, Hugh Brody, Harry Thurston, Peter Sanger and Annie Dillard. Yes, this is a strong claim—one best defended by the author's own words:

> In 1969, a hundred feet from the surface of the earth, the river to the north still rippling with giant spring salmon and sturgeon, the ocean to the west still humming with the secret lives of rock and ling cod and crab and abalone, the town directly below in gentle decline, one muddy boot still in the nineteenth century, the other a shoe being shined for the glossy, modern, fast-food corporate future, I knew, in my body, exactly everything I needed to know to live in an intimate

way with the place of my being, and did not know anything about the massing forces of the world that would kill that intimate knowledge in me.

Anyone who can handle the long sentence that beautifully is worth listening to for style alone.

But there is much more than mere style to this book. Bowling blends personal memoir with local and provincial history, social commentary and salmon science into a narrative that is both forceful and informative. He paints a damning picture of government and industry's mismanagement of salmon stocks, disregard for the riparian ecology of BC's river systems, and mistreatment of First Nations and immigrant Asian peoples. Into this big picture, he weaves episodes from his childhood in the late '60s (the 1969 lunar landing is a leitmotif, providing a poignant contrast between humanity's simultaneous accomplishments and failures, and artfully calling to mind the clichéd moan that we can put a man on the moon, but …), his own experiences of fishing on the Fraser with his father and brothers, and his present-day life as a writer and family man.

Throughout, he laments the diminishment and destruction of wildness—both in its literal manifestations (salmon stocks) and in terms of the independence of his father and various Ladner characters Bowling vividly recalls from his youth—and hints at how we might go about recovering the wild in our lives today. Bowling's is a high Romantic soul and "wild" is for him, unsurprisingly, a term wholly positive in its connotations. It stands in opposition to such slurs as "civilized" and, especially, "farmed." Just as the wild sockeye are disappearing, replaced by farmed alien varieties, so too are the free-spirited dockside characters replaced with corporate fishing enterprises and salmon farmers: "A bureaucrat can manage a farmed fish and a farmed man a lot more easily than he can a wild salmon or a Rod Beveridge [a Ladner fisherman]. The wild is an embarrassment to the un-wild; the truly free offends the caged."

The wild is a sword by which Bowling lives—he describes this book as "a school of wild words"—but it is also one on which he falls at times. On the level of style, wild can mean erratic, a net flung too far, snagging on deadheads. Bowling is on his game when he hews to concrete specifics—to "[r]iver, salmon, brine, blood, blossoms, earth"—which he experiences through "the great gift of hands-on sensory involvement with the world." Late in the book, he says, "What poets say is too easily dismissed by the world. I'd rather speak as a man who has come from one place and loves it, year by year, more than any other, even as he watches it disappear."

Had he stayed true to this aim, *The Lost Coast* would have been stronger for it, but he strays repeatedly, inserting precious assertions of the poet's vital role: "Poets ... dangle on fragile ropes over dark, rushing water and build our flumes of words to carry something beyond ourselves." He also delivers a number of bilious eco-political harangues in a mode that Steve Noyes, writing in *The Vancouver Sun*, aptly dubbed "salmon evangelism." And Terry Glavin, while acknowledging Bowling as "one of Canada's greatest living poets," is critical of him for fudging facts and for naively exculpating "the small-boat gill-net fishermen who went about their quiet work in the spring and the fall."

It's not because I disagree with Bowling that his indulgences are irritating, but because the arguments are made so much more eloquently and assuredly in other parts of the book, and because digressions into self-important rhapsodies and condescending lectures only drive wedges between writer and reader. Disrupting narrative flow to sledgehammer points home is overkill analogous to that which left dead salmon rotting on the docks outside glutted canneries at the nadir of the Fraser fishery.

But Bowling's weaknesses as a romantic writer have always been tied to his strengths.[40] "[T]hose who rail against 'romanticism,'" he says, "are really railing against the joy that is as real in memory as sorrow and pain are"— almost all of his writing,

---

40   Carmine Starnino, in a review of Bowling's *Selected Poems*, has said that Bowling's "failings ... are also responsible for glorious effects he would never achieve otherwise."

successful and otherwise, has an unusually high heat signature. He might not know when he's at his best, but he understands the risks he takes, stating that "the unwillingness to sacrifice myth to mundanity … inform[s] everything I write." For him, the salmon are totemic gods and the Fraser takes on dimensions that make it confluent with the Styx, Thames, Congo and Lethe. There is always something vital at stake in Bowling's work, and rarely do the trivia of modern writers' preoccupations seep in. He could fairly be accused of being humourless and it occasionally seems as if he lives somewhere other than the real world, but since dissatisfaction with the real world is at the root of his concerns, he can hardly be dismissed as delusional. As per Longinus, a flawed sublimity is infinitely superior to an impeccable mediocrity, and this book, whatever its faults, is a work of transcendent beauty and anger.

Somewhat surprisingly, it is also a work of hope. Bowling, a father of three, has not given up. *The Lost Coast*, as its title insists, is predominantly elegiac, or what its author would call melancholic ("Melancholy, in my definition, simply means a constant attentiveness to what has been"). But Bowling clings stubbornly to joy and celebration, and offers glimpses into his own present-day existence—car-free (in Alberta!), TV-free, independent—as a simple example of how one might go about re-staking a claim to wildness and severing ties to the massing unsustainable forces of infinite economic expansion. The more of us who follow his counsel and ways, the better off we'll be. The days of wild salmon in turbid Fraser waters may be numbered, but some of us might yet find our way home.

RESPONSIBILITIES AND OBLIGATIONS, MASKS AND ALTERITIES

Peter Sanger

PETER SANGER STANDS IN MY doorway, holding a tote bag. There is something ursine about his build and bearing, a slight scholar's stoop in his broad shoulders, a little shamble in his step. Some months ago I got a letter from him in broadstroke fountain pen calligraphy on custom laid stationery. He'd heard I was working on an essay about him and would I mind if he came by my house to deliver some material on one of his regular trips into Halifax from his home in South Maitland. I called him back and we arranged a time.

We spread the contents of his tote bag over my dining room table. It pretty well covers the entire area. He has brought me everything from old copies of *The Antigonish Review* (containing essays written by him), to books, chapbooks and broadsides, to photocopies of various documents (including all 300-plus pages of *Her Kindled Shadow*, his self-published, out-of-print monograph on Richard Outram), to a slip-cased copy of *Arborealis*, his latest collaboration with photographer and publisher Thaddeus Holownia. Peter talks animatedly, telling me the story behind various documents, explaining the allusive properties of certain poems. And then, quite suddenly, he becomes visibly uncomfortable and makes a precipitously awkward departure. It's as if he felt he was saying too much, getting carried off in his enthusiasm, giving too much away. He has left me with a great deal of reading, but also with a task—a responsibility—far greater than I had imagined.

*

My next contact with Peter was in the form of a letter he sent me after my brief review of his collection *Aiken Drum* appeared in the May 2006 issue of *Quill & Quire*. It was a mixed review, reflecting my ambivalence about the book. Peter was disappointed with the review and extended his sympathies to me for having to spend so much time with a book I didn't like. The review, he felt, did not bode well for the longer essay I was supposed to be writing. He went on to suggest readings of the book that might account for my qualms, explained to me the logic of its structure, the concatenations linking one poem to another. The implication was that if I didn't love *Aiken Drum*, it was because I didn't get it.

*

Peter Sanger has been something of a stranger in the cantons of Canadian poetry. Despite the quality, quantity and vigour of his various literary activities as writer, teacher, critic and editor, he has not developed the kind of following that some of his contemporaries, with similar thematic preoccupations and arguably less talent, intellectual rigour and artistic commitment (McKay, Zwicky, Lilburn), have. This is in part a function of the geopolitics of Canadian poetry and publishing. Ever faithful to the local, all of Sanger's books and chapbooks have been published in Nova Scotia or New Brunswick. He spent his academic career in the unlikely setting of the Nova Scotia Agricultural College in Truro. He has been the Poetry Editor for *The Antigonish Review*, a magazine run by St. Francis Xavier University,[41] since 1985.

---

41 It became apparent in 2005 that *The Antigonish Review* does not swim in the mainstream of Canadian literary culture when its Canada Council funding was suspended, after 35 years of operation, 32 of which were funded by the Council. When Peter talks about this episode, he becomes visibly indignant.

People involved in poetry like to pretend that it transcends the crass vulgarity of market economies. Although it is true that most poetry will never be a mass-market commodity, it is no secret that quiet artistry and commitment to culture are insufficient on their own for a poet to attract a critical mass of readers and critics. Where one travels, teaches and publishes, which organizations one joins, what other poets one edits and publishes, what connections one makes along the way, are at least as important for a thriving poetic career as the actual work one has done and the words one has published. In his resolute regionalism and in his quiet rejection of the trappings of institutionalized culture,[42] Sanger has been to a great extent the author of his own obscurity.

But it's hard to imagine him becoming a more popular poet even if he was paid more critical attention. For Sanger, the idea of "resistance" is central to his poetics. Some people get labelled as a "poet's poet," but Sanger suggests himself that he has been something more rarefied yet; "most other poets that I've come across in my life," he tells Anne Compton, "don't really catch onto what I'm doing." Whereas McKay's poetry might be described as garrulous, Lilburn's as vatic and Zwicky's as epiphanic, it strikes me that Compton's characterization of Sanger's poems as "gnomic" is as good a one-word summary as there could be.[43] There is a sparse, ascetic monasticism to Sanger's work; "uncompromising" is a key term of approbation in his criticism, and one sees it in the strictures of his compressed lines and stanzas, packed with literary and philosophical allusions. Here, from *Earth Moth*, is "Silver Poplar" in its entirety:

---

42   Aside from repeated sideswipes in his prose, most of this resistance has been more or less passive, but Sanger was also involved in John Metcalf and William Hoffer's quixotic "Tanks Campaign" against the Canada Council.

43   Prior to reading Compton's description, I had used this term in reference to Sanger's poetry in a conversation with Wayne Clifford. Wayne responded that he thought "gnostic" more the *mot juste*. He has a point, though the distinction might seem hair-splittingly fine.

So is isn't is. It is: a
negative game, apophatic,
turning to rights inside out.

I'd rather watch riddles
of leaves duck when the wind
hits like a flock of, you know

the kind, black on the back,
white as they veer away. I
wish you'd remember their name.

If he writes riddling verse, Sanger is also the canniest unriddler of poetic difficulties in Canada. He has established himself as the Perfect Reader for such tough nuts as John Thompson and Richard Outram and his own poetry is clearly in quest of a reader like him. It is tempting to describe his poetry as cold. It isn't. But it is so frequently severe in its control and intellection that its emotional temperature can be very hard for an imperfect reader to take.

For Sanger, whose poems keep to themselves, privacy is a positive artistic virtue. In her review of *Ironworks*, Amanda Jernigan says that Sanger has described the work as a "private book." He has also spoken highly of the private aspects of Richard Outram's art, both as poet and as proprietor of a private press. His final statement in the Compton interview, which he reiterates for emphasis as well as for inclusiveness, is that the poet "is the secret sharer," a lone stowaway in a reader's cabin. If Sanger has an audience in mind for his work, it is patently an audience of one-at-a-time, rather than a crowd.

Collaboration is a touchstone concept for Sanger. The partnership he has enjoyed with Holownia is one model for such a relationship, as is the collaborative marriage of Outram and visual artist Barbara Howard, but collaboration also extends to the colloquy between Sanger and the subjects of his poetry and criticism. "The Crooked Knife" is the product of collaboration between

Sanger and his collection of knives (and, through them, collaboration with their anonymous makers), just as *Her Kindled Shadow* is the product of collaboration between Sanger and the poetry of Outram. Sanger expects readers of his poems to play a similarly active role in making them mean—in both senses of that word as "signify" and "have importance." And you can bet that he is not blind to the etymological presence of "labor" embedded in the heart of "collaborate." The size of Sanger's readership will necessarily always be small: one must be very smart to read Sanger, one must be very well-read and one must be ready for heavy digging.

But moreover, one must have an appetite for the work and one must accept Sanger's credos as valid. As Jernigan puts it: "My respect for Sanger as a poet was enough to take me through this maze [the poems of *Ironworks*], but I have sometimes doubted whether another reader, one unfamiliar with Sanger's work, would plunge in so willingly." If I have been unwontedly slow in writing this essay—at the time of writing, it is a year and a half since I was asked to do it—it is in part because my desire to "get" Sanger, for all my admiration of his best work, has been taxed by the process of reading his oeuvre and by the poet's own expectations of how one should write and how one should read. He has at times acknowledged "that poetry is a conversation between poets and readers of many kinds which it is our job [as scholars and critics] to help sustain, not interrupt by overly-insistent deflections into some secondary world of our own." But more often, Sanger's actions and truculent pronouncements have been those of a poetic monotheist, privileging one sort of poet (a *poeta doctus* who writes uncompromisingly dense and allusive verse) and one sort of reader (a cryptographer scarcely distinguishable from the poet she reads) from the heights of his academic silo—and woe betide he or she who begs to differ.

An essay on Eric Ormsby is a particularly revealing instance of Sanger's aesthetic dogmatism. It isn't his distaste for Ormsby's poetry, but the bizarrely strict censure of "cliché" in it that leaves me scratching my head (cliché intended). Sanger makes a list of "ways of saying in [Ormsby's "Gazing at Waves"] which have been used too many times before." This list includes some phrases which one could arguably label clichéd, but also many combinations which, while not startlingly original, are a far cry from "my heart aches with loss." The list includes, for example, "out there," "this gives back" and "at other times." This seems to me completely unreasonable. As Don Paterson has said, "for a reader to be astonished by the original phrase *it must already be partly familiar to them*, if they are to register the transformation." (Emphasis in original.) And no less forceful a critic than Tom Paulin—writing of Yeats!—observes that "Just as acrobats will sometimes appear to make a mistake, so poets know that poems are performances which must now and then seem to put a foot wrong in order to make the words dance perfectly the next moment." For Sanger, "uncompromising" is almost always a term of praise, but there is also a sense in which this word means "mulish." If one is going to be so elastic as to define a cliché as any combination of words one has heard somewhere else, then yes, one will find them, ahem, lurking in every corner. I'm sure Sanger would be dismayed at the results if someone played a similar trick on his own work.[44]

Poetry, even a great deal of apparently accessible work, will always require a degree of active readerly engagement more intense than is necessary for other kinds of writing. But non-scholarly readers not willing to spelunk the deepest caves of etymology and allusion should not be dismissed as dilettantes. It would be irresponsible of *me*, however, to suggest that this is what Sanger always does. As with everything else in Sanger's oeuvre, there is far too much conflict, contradiction and ambiguity in the public ethics of his poetics to reductively portray him as a snobby elitist or aesthetic solipsist. For one thing, he has, like George Johnston, been a regular writer of occasional verse, a kind of poetry despised and dismissed by far less rigorous wordsmiths than they. In his contribution to a feature on occasional poetry in *The New Quarterly*, Sanger argues eloquently

---

44　I have to admit that I was up to just such a game—I couldn't resist—when I pointed out repeated phrasal formulas in Aiken Drum in my review of the book.

that poets should turn back towards the public: "Why should greet-ing card poets be the public's almost sole resource?" he queries, and then asserts that "To dismiss occasional verse is to collaborate in severing poetry from life, the life of others." And while it can be said of almost none of his verse that it is conversational or colloquial, it is true that, at least in his best work, Sanger is, as he says himself, "working for the speaking voice." The sonic and semantic qualities of poems such as "The Fountain," from *Aiken Drum*, testify to this:

Remember the year by a story,
how after a summer
of buckets and jugs, they simply
gave up the old well,
an eighteen-foot barrel
of rocks wedged together,
a church without steeple or people
which plumbed at last dry.

Trying to drill a new well
can seem hopeless
as prayer. He guessed that she prayed while
the rig lifted square on flat feet
and bit the first hole in their purse
then mealed through red clay,
grey shale, sluiced by a shot
of pneumatics to spray

wet muck from the bore. But he
wasn't there when a wave
of new water leaped waist high
heaving sand and gravel
prismatic with brilliants of quartz
and following silvery
fountain falling shared grace
in her lyrical voice.

Glossing this episode now,
distant songs of creation.
Or should he depose it as so
unlikely complacent glissando
where death and sublime resurrection
feast at the sign of the circle?
Pity such choice,
and sacrifice.

"Fountain" is a poem of ordinary human troubles and pleasures, a poem—and there are many others of this sort scattered throughout his books—in which a non-specialist reader can collaborate, not through hard slogging and study, but through shared experience and feeling—through participation in a "community of imaginable words," as Sanger puts it in an essay on Bishop. If he has let down his lexical guard in this poem, and allowed a homeliness of diction and figure (that lovely metaphor of the well as an "eighteen-foot barrel / of rocks wedged together"; the simple but paradoxical simile "hopeless / as prayer"; the auger that not only drills through soil and rock but bites a hole in the couple's purse as well) to sneak in, it is to the benefit of the poem's communicability and at no cost to its integrity. The compromises Sanger makes in the opening stanzas—and his willingness throughout the poem to court what he might call in another poet cliché ("glossing this episode," for instance, or "lyrical voice") in order to better approximate actual speech—go a long way towards licensing and clarifying syntax and symbolism at the poem's end which might otherwise seem hermetically abstract ("should he depose it as so / unlikely complacent glissando / where death and sublime resurrection / feast at the sign of the circle?").

Collaboration entails sometimes meeting readers on their own ground rather than insisting they come to yours. Not pandering to readers is one thing; actively repelling them another. In all fairness, not much of Sanger's poetry or prose is egregiously reader-hostile, but he does come within spitting distance at times of the theory-driven opacity he despises so heartily, and the peculiarity of his passions can be a very private affair indeed.

*

Part of that peculiarity involves a commitment, both as a poet and a critic, to objective detachment. Indeed, Sanger has displayed a marked distaste for the biographical in criticism and for the confessional in poetry. Against the "egotism" of Lowell, Berryman, Plath and Sexton, he champions the guarded restraint of Elizabeth Bishop. For many years the editor of a newsletter published by the Elizabeth Bishop Society of Nova Scotia, he laments, "There are times when one wishes we knew less about Bishop's life." I haven't heard Sanger's opinion on the publication of Bishop's "uncollected poems, drafts and fragments" in *Edgar Allan Poe and the Jukebox*, but it's hard to imagine him approving of the backstage pass it offers.

I can, however, easily imagine him reading it nevertheless—and reading it greedily, if somewhat guiltily. Spend enough time with Sanger's writing and you'll discover a highly ambivalent—if not equivocal—relationship with biography and autobiography. In the case of Bishop, he warns readers about the lures of speculative recreations: "There is enough of the artist in most of us to tempt us into creating 'real' worlds for the writers we admire. … we often, however, construct projected, fictive lives which are really ones we intend to live ourselves (if we are young), or ones we could have lived (given luck and the right chances)." But in another essay on Bishop, Sanger throws down a remarkable sequence of hunches:

> … *A Child's Garden of Verses* and *When We Were Young* were **perhaps** primary books in Bishop's poetic education. **It is possible** to trace their influence upon Bishop's juvenilia … From Stevenson and Milne, **she must have** learned some of the exactitudes and subtle possibilities of poetry. The pure, simple diction of Stevenson's poems and the kind of narrative economy and neatness he had developed as a novelist and carried over into his poems **strikingly resemble** Bishop's. So also

does the frequent ingenuity of his stanzaic variations which are, nevertheless, based upon ballad quatrains and always elegantly accommodate the rhythms of normal speech. From Milne's poetry, Bishop **could have** learned the use of an undercutting irony which is directed both at the poem's protagonist and at the reader who usually so persistently wishes to identify with both the poem's protagonist and the poet. And, like Stevenson, Milne was adept at creating eccentric but colloquial stanzaic patterns which **perhaps served as partial models, no doubt forgotten by Bishop**, for "Songs for a Colored Singer" and "Roosters." **One further possible speculation** is that Bishop's enthusiastic response to samba words and rhythms, which led to "The Burglar of Babylon," might also have been exercised early in her life by some of the poems in *When We Were Very Young*... Finally, in Stevenson's and Milne's books, there are accidental depths not always calculated, **one suspects**, by their authors that become apparent if a reader shifts perspectives from a state of childish innocence to one of adult experience. Bishop **may well have learned from these accidental depths and very consciously emulated them**. [Emphases added.]

Sanger is too conscientious a scholar ("responsibility" is a leitmotif of his criticism) to misrepresent these pet theories as facts, but too enthusiastic about his dubious discoveries not to give them a good airing.

Sanger's criticism has been likened, aptly, to literary detective work. He is preoccupied with sources, with allusions, with influence, with intertextuality. While there is no question that Sanger is a master sleuth, who, as Carmine Starnino has said, lets "no riddling reverberation pass unnoticed," he is prone to indulging a romantic affinity for mere coincidence. In an interview about his collaborations with Thaddeus Holownia, Sanger has said that certain trivial coincidences[45] "indicate[d]" that he and Holownia "were bound to meet." More likely, they were bound to meet

---

45   After they had already become acquainted, Sanger discovered a desk at the Nova Scotia Agricultural College—where he taught and where, briefly, Holownia had been a student—into which Holownia had carved his name.

because they were both artists, with similar interests and common acquaintances, living in the same small region. In his introduction to Thompson's *Collected Poems*, Sanger indulges in an odd digression on certain similitudes of style and biography between Thompson and the English poet John Riley, even after admitting that these resemblances between contemporaries unknown to each other and working on opposite sides of the Atlantic were "only a coincidence."

This might have made for an interesting stand-alone essay, but it's a puzzling thing to encounter, as a half-paragraph red herring, in the critical context in which it appears. Until, that is, you realize just how important Dickensian accidents of fate are for Sanger. *White Salt Mountain* is a book built on a foundation of coincidence. In its opening section he writes: "I have never been able to detach the accident of meeting certain copies of certain books, with their records of particular use and ownership and gifting, from the patterns of feeling and intuition, of thinking and sensation, which make up human fate." It is such a happy *trouvaille* that sends him on his quest for Florence Ayscough's story. Ayscough is the mysterious woman who walks into his office one muggy afternoon with a case he just can't refuse. He feels an "obligation" to find out more about her after coming across an inscribed copy of her translation of Chinese poems, *Fir-Flower Tablets*, the English versions of which were written by the once-eminent American imagist Amy Lowell.

A reader uninitiated into the universe of Peter Sanger should be forgiven for wondering why he should become obsessed with so clearly minor a literary figure as Florence Ayscough. Even he can't, ultimately, rouse himself to a stirring defense of her abilities:

> **Almost anyone** who reads Ayscough's Tu Fu volumes **with some sympathy for their method** will gather a **small anthology** of poems and **fragments of poems** unlike any other translations from Chinese poetry, and as close to the originals in spirit as is ever likely possible. [Emphases added.]

All questions are answered by the revelation that the entire essay is, effectively, a footnote on one line of Thompson's, a virtuoso extension of Sanger's work in *Sea Run*. Even then, his phrasing betrays the impossibility of defending his bet-hedging:

> The subtitle to Ghazal XII **allows the inference** that in the autumn of 1973, when Thompson composed the first thirteen ghazals of *Stilt Jack*, he **might have been reading** Ayscough's translation of Tu Fu. ... There is also the shared couplet form. Thompson's ghazal couplets were intended to be a reworking ... of the Persian ghazal, but no one can read Thompson's ghazals **alongside Ayscough's couplet versions** ... without **sensing an underplay of connection**. Lastly, from Ayscough's Tu Fu, Thompson **could have** obtained the example of that obstinate delight in small things, in wild and country matters, and of that unillusioned, obdurate resignation glinting with irony, which appear so often in *Stilt Jack* and make the exercise of reading it far from a narcissistic enterprise.
>
> **None of these parallels and similarities prove** that Thompson used Ayscough's translation, any more than does the curious happenstance that Acadia University's set of Ayscough's Tu Fu consists of the first volume [an original] ... and the second volume, a facsimile edition which **must have been** acquired ... which, like the first volume, would have been Ayscough's gift. ... **It is tempting to suggest** that Thompson borrowed the original second volume, given by Ayscough, from Acadia as an interlibrary loan, and that the book was destroyed in the fire which consumed Thompson's farmhouse ... [Emphases added.]

Never mind that the fire happened approximately a year after Thompson wrote the supposedly Ayscough-influenced ghazals. These are all interesting speculations,[46] to be sure, but do they

---

46 I suppose it could be answered that all forms of literary criticism are, to one degree or another, indefensible speculations. But it is an entirely different matter to make conjectures about the meanings of a text than to speculate about extratextual biographical events.

really warrant a ninety-page essay? Why *should* we read Thompson alongside Ayscough's patchy Tu Fu? Isn't *Stilt Jack* a powerful enough legacy on its own, without knowing every possible source for its poems? Why would reading it, or anything else for that matter, be a "narcissistic enterprise"? Unless of course one is reading it only because of its affinities with one's own work or because it affords one an opportunity to indulge private whims.

One suspects that another persuasive coincidence in this instance—what attracts the detective to the enigmatic woman—is Ayscough's resemblance to Sanger, at least in his own mind. Like her biographer, though to a more thoroughgoing extent, Ayscough was enamoured of Oriental aesthetics. But moreover, "Ayscough had a characteristically nineteenth-century sense of the need for a screen between the private and the public, and was correspondingly deeply aware of her obligations to others. She believed in manners." When prompted by her husband to write her autobiography, she tells him she is "'far more interested in Tu Fu's Autobiography than [she is] in [her] own.'" Which is so perfectly succinct an encapsulation of Sanger's own literary enterprise, it's no wonder he quotes it.

Sanger observes that Thompson's thesis on René Char is "filled with statements which are as much about the kind of poetry Thompson wished to write and would write as they are about Char." Such an observation could as easily be made of Sanger's writings on other poets. In case a sleuthing reader should be in any doubt about this, Sanger drops hints himself:

> Starting in the 1970s, I tried to express in prose my sense of various kinships wherever I thought I knew enough to say something worth listening to: So there are essays or pamphlets on [Geoffrey] Hill, David Jones, [Paul-Emile] Borduas, Thompson, Saint-Denys Garneau, [Robert] Bringhurst, Outram, Bishop, and others. In many cases, these essays or pamphlets or books are parallel commentary upon poems I've published.

Aha! There is a sense of course in which everything a poet writes is oblique autobiography. And there is a sense in which any poet's criticism can be read as exegetical treatments of his or her own poems. But Sanger's awareness of this facet of his work makes it seem more self-conscious, more intentional—one is tempted to say more preening, having encountered it in so many places—than it is for most. Reading his verse and prose (including interviews) can come to be something of a very literary game of Where's Waldo. If it seems trivial to regard literature as a hunt for hidden pictures of the author, it is a triviality which Sanger has done little to discourage outside of his obligatory grumblings against the fatuousness of contemporary literature and criticism; he has, in fact, sanctified the legitimacy of such tacks with his own bio-critical praxis.

What is important for Sanger—and it is a crucial distinction—is not that a poem eschew autobiography, but that it be something more than mere biography. For Sanger, art "masks to reveal." Consider "Plagiarist," from *Earth Moth*:

He's that best friend you'll never quite have,
the confessional double who shares
every secret and has to forgive
as if you're above betrayal.

Sympathize with his difficult life,
its whirligig jig of feculent
snouts he knows how to cherish,
impossible now to keep going

as time passes by and he'll become
the back number, unless he has found you,
cloaked in transcendent cliché, alone,
half-coherent, and utterly no-one.

"Plagiarist" is the second of a trio of satirical poems, all with identical three-quatrain structures. On either side are "Solipsist"

and "Simoner." They are sinners in Dante's hell (in the case of
"Simoner," Sanger makes this explicit): one is self-absorbed to the
exclusion of all others, one steals words,[47] the third renders the
sacred profane by selling it. This unholy trinity is followed by a
"Lapidary," not by title a sinner, but nonetheless "A man of con-
ventional vices / fraudulent, proud, a false witness, / he often sells
lies considered / quite finished." The lapidary, a maker of fine bev-
elled things, combines the flawed qualities of the preceding three
sinners and makes something of them:

> His hand in that spring had gripped
> hidden displacements, shutters which slid
> thickened translucence concealing
> whatever was there, prismatic, plutonic,
>
> a speck of evading refraction
> which held nothing back and almost
> something he'd seen. *Quartz*, he said later,
> and learned how one usually means.

There are key phrases in these two quatrains—"hidden displace-
ments"; "thickened translucence"; "evading refraction"—that read
like pithy descriptions of the Sanger aesthetic.

It was poet Wayne Clifford—like Sanger, a correspondent
and admirer of Richard Outram's—who first suggested to me
that "Plagiarist," in particular, had an autobiographical aspect.
It hadn't occurred to me at the time—perhaps because I hadn't
yet sunk myself into Sanger's oeuvre, and perhaps because I
took at face value his professed distaste for the solipsism of
confessional verse—but it struck me as intriguing. And accu-
rate; it is no coincidence that the secret sharing Sanger would
later emphasize in the Compton interview first appears here.

---

47 Which for Sanger, as for Dante, would be more significant a theft than a sim-
ple appropriation of "intellectual property." The word, as in "I give you my word" is
significant of troth and obligation, so to steal it is, in effect, to sunder a sacred contract.

Sanger himself has removed this idea from the realm of textual speculation:

> Modern poetry basically has an egocentric basis. Once you cut away all the levels of cosmos we've been talking about, what's left is ego. Under those circumstances, solipsism is easy to slip into, and it's something that I have to fight against in myself. As I said earlier, those poems ["Solipsist" to "Lapidary"] are about other poets, but they're also about me. The irony is directed outward and inward at the same time.

Much of Sanger's poetry can be read as the working out of an ongoing inner struggle. The self- and outward-directed satirical poems are not merely ambiguous,[48] as much of his work is, but deeply ambivalent. It is as though Sanger, who often makes very strong statements of value, has serious doubts that he is living up to those values; doubts that he is doing justice, and not damage, to that which he loves; that his commitment to art is perfect and not ruined by ego and personal ambition. This kind of oblique self-recrimination surfaces again in *Aiken Drum*, especially in one of its most unsettling poems, "Medicine Bundle":

> If I could get one, it might look like this,
>   bound in white cotton and big
> as a book held in bed.
>
> If I could have one, the woman who'd had it
>   might guess my sickness
> and sign with her chokecherried hands:
>
> You mustn't undo this, or sell it, or give it.
>   Hold this on your heart and be well.
> While crickets were twittering so-long September

---

48   For Sanger, this term is every bit as complex as it is for Empson and reflects in language the inherent complexity of the universe. Sanger therefore prefers to think of his poems as "realistic," rather than "ambiguous."

from miles of sunstruck grass, layer by layer
    I'd slowly undo it, peel
cotton and canvas off wool and blank denim,

lift cloths out of pattern, break plaids on their weave
    until I'd uncovered
a cylinder centre of birchbark plugged

neatly by twists of red flannel and tipped
    the piece gently to find
how there's nothing inside.

There is a note explaining the source of this poem at the back of the book: "The poem is based upon a chapter in John Douglas Leechman's *Indian Summer*... Leechman is the anthropologist who purchases the bundles. He was the first Director of Western Canadiana at the Glenbow Foundation in Calgary." Informative, but not nearly as fascinating as Sanger's preamble to his reading of the poem at Gaspereau Press's 2006 Wayzgoose in Kentville, Nova Scotia. Sanger informed the audience that when he read the episode in Leechman's book his "blood ran cold." As a scholar himself, he was appalled that another man of learning could be so disrespectful of the culture he studied. He then explained that he wrote the poem in the first person as though he were such a scholar as Leechman— then he said, in an undertone, "maybe I am." I came to Kentville from Halifax for the weekend in no small part to hear Peter read from *Aiken Drum*, and I came hoping that he would read "Medicine Bundle" and say something like what he did indeed say, confirming for me that at the heart of his monastically committed ethos there is a self-doubt that amounts very nearly to horror.

*

Something of the curatorial clings to Peter Sanger's body of work. Again, Sanger himself has pointed out this facet of his art and related it to his own life story. He tells Matthew Holmes that as a child he "attempted to construct [his] own human and natural history museums." From his earliest publications on, collection, selection and critical framing have been integral elements of his poetry.

One of his chapbooks, *The Third Hand*, is actually a suite of riddle poems written "to accompany an exhibit of hand tools and implements"—a kind of verse catalogue. This preoccupation is extended in *Ironworks*, a suite of poems accompanying Holownia's photographs of rusted tools found and salvaged by Sanger. Like Don McKay, Sanger is particularly interested in the relationship of technology to nature, how the one is not simply separate from the other, as we have come to assume too readily and destructively, but how technology comes from natural products and processes and how it returns to nature when abandoned—how, as he puts it, "The last voice of iron is rust." One of his finest essays, "The Crooked Knife," lays out his views on organic manufacture:

> Using words to describe crooked knives accurately is difficult because the knives are nearly unclassifiable. At first glance, each knife appears simple: blade, haft, and one of four or five methods of binding blade and haft together. But blades, hafts, and bindings occur in regional, private, and natural variations. Bindings, for example, are made of cord, sinew, leather, roots, or snare wire. More elusively, the haft shape of the best knives is largely determined by the natural pattern of the grain in the wood from which it was carved. This shape follows the way root or bough met trunk or tree limb. Their intersection gives the haft its crook, one which is usually deliberately chosen to match the size and structure of the user's master hand. With yet a further turn, the crook's natural and matched-up variations are often used to inspire many theriomorphic and abstract designs. Finally, also making generalization imprecise, are misunderstandings created by English itself. *Haft, knife, blade* evoke an artifact only roughly similar in shape and largely different in use to the crooked knife.

In Sanger's eco-poetics, technology is most responsible, most in tune with natural rhythms, when it is most individual and least mass-produced—when it partakes least in the mentality of seeing the universe in terms of what Heidegger called standing reserve. Reverence, respect, responsibility are the three R's of Sanger's ethics. Not surprisingly, this concern extends for him to the question of language as technology, especially as it relates to poetry: "a good crooked knife in the hand, like a word in a well-made poem, works with its weight so balanced and shaped that it finds individual patterns of rhythm and use, intuition, invention and knowledge."

Both Sanger's poetry and prose are sharpest and most beautiful as they hew to the grit and grain of their subjects. Consider another passage from *Spar*, this one from the essay "Biorachan Road":

> There are plumes of goldenrod looking brittle and dry, but soft to touch as the bloom on a plum. Everlasting plants are here in clumps, dry, not lasting, blurring in fuzz, mottled like a spring rabbit's fur. There are raspberry sprays, arching in wide curves, studded by tough five-armed stars that once clamped fruit, and by the tight, pointed cowls in which next year's leaves are growing. Coarse but pliant ravels of greyish green lichen hang from tree trunks and branches. Beeches are cataracted with scales of fungi, but give back the winter light as if it emanated from their bark rather than from the sky and snow. Where one spruce tree has been struck and opened by a falling limb, it looks as if a door had been built to enter the heartwood.

This is virtuoso description, gorgeously assonantal and perfectly paced, but it is much more than merely ornamental. Sanger's way of seeing things, and of translating that seeing into saying, rivals such naturalist poets as Hopkins and Clare, and has something of Bishop's gift for, as Heaney puts it, "rais[ing] the actual to a new linguistic power." Sight, sound and sense are all accounted for and Sanger's subtle figures make connections not only between aspects of the physical world (the paradoxically transient everlasting plants "mottled like a spring rabbit's fur") but open up portholes to the metaphysical, particularly in the last two sentences quoted. This is territory in which so many poets and essayists go astray into pseudo-mystical fog, but the sheer precision of Sanger's diction and phrasing, which reminds me in passages such as this one of no one so much as Annie Dillard, keeps his mysticism in the realm of the credible.

The hazard of such writing, and of the collector's cataloguing impulse generally, is that of rendering the live and moving life-like but fixed, like a lepidopterist's specimens or Audubon's birds. In salvaging rusted tools from the earth on which they were abandoned, polishing them up and making fetish objects of them, the cycles of creation, adaptation, use and decay are arrested. By removing a horseshoe from the earth, the "last speech" of iron is denied, or least delayed. In putting something in a museum's display case, one abstracts and protects it from the world and its "patterns of rhythm and use." Several of Sanger's studies are like resin beads in which a plant or an insect is in the process of being ambered. Once a crane fly is brilliantly punned into "a filament gantry," it is hard to see one ever again the same way. The play of motion and stillness, silence and sound—the way things are frozen in a poem—is clearly a concern for Sanger. "Fossil Fern" is the first poem in *Aiken Drum*:

> This is the gift of a laminar stain,
> an etching of carbon whose
> black turns back into green
>
> if you taste it, pinnae
> uncoiling, pinnules unfurling
> as if they might fly
>
> and flight were one frond away
> from this throatful of fern
> still growing. A slate of grey

clay is its ground, an earth
you can hold for colour,
shape, speech, all life

in your hands, where spores once
appeared to manipulate silence.

Like Seamus Heaney, Sanger is fascinated by nature's transformative processes of preservation, mummification, fossilization—except for Sanger, the interest is not as anthropocentric. And he is drawn to analogies between such natural processes and artistic ones, which Sanger would argue are arbitrarily and falsely—irresponsibly—seen as distinct. As he says in an essay on Holownia, "all the arts frequently attempt as one of their impossibilities the contradiction of their own physical happenstance." Thus, the fixity of words on a page strives for the impression of motion—and often, in Sanger's hands, succeeds quite beautifully. "Fossil Fern" is an indirect statement of poetics. Even as nature's artistic transmutations have arrested its growth into geological stasis, poetry reanimates the fossilized plant from black, "back into green." Herein lies another pivotal and unresolvable contradiction. Like the Leechman figure in "Medicine Bundle," who destroys something to know it, Sanger sometimes mummifies the living even while trying to animate the dead.

*

There is something profoundly nostalgic in Sanger's urge to collect, restore and conserve old relics. While one sympathizes with his antipathy for the fads, ephemera and destructive practices of our era, Sanger is prone to romanticizing the past as a greener time, even while he insists he is doing no such thing. On returning to the town in which he used to live, Sanger

... kept trying to hear the sounds I remembered as clear, sharp, separate: the steady spool of water passing through the old mill-chute where the rocks let loose and Cameron Lake fell as a river into Sturgeon Lake; the echoing slap of boards being stacked by hand at the lumberyard beyond this river; and the echoless, flat, metallic tric-trac of the blacksmith, whose shop stood opposite the old wheel-worked lock-gates, as he beat out some improvised repair for a rickety, rusted piece of farm machinery. Twenty years later, the blacksmith's shop had gone; the mill-chute no longer dropped through a sequence of rock ledges but flowed smoothly, soundlessly; the lumberyard had expanded to cover several acres, but all stacking of boards was done by forklift. Instead of the sounds I remembered, there was the generalizing suckle of gasoline and diesel engines. Thwitel and usaunt were gone. The fleecy crowns had fallen.

If this elegiac moment moves you, it is in part because it is well-written. But it is also because it taps into a feeling shared by most people; in Joseph Conrad's phrasing, it has "the strong, effective and respectable bond of a sentimental lie." To put this in perspective, I can tell you that, having operated diesel forklifts for five years in my late teens and early twenties, whenever I hear that "generalizing suckle,"[49] smell diesel fuel and exhaust and see drivers nimbly manoeuvring their bulky yet graceful machines in the tight aisles between stacks in a warehouse or yard, I get a little misty. But, if I'm being honest, I also have to admit that those were difficult years full of long hours, lousy working conditions, personal turmoil and not-infrequent injuries. Sanger's normally acute gaze, at moments like this, goes soft-focus. Modern changes are bad to him because they are changes, as much because they are intrinsically bad.

At times it's hard not to see him as a stubbornly anachronistic curmudgeon carrying on about how things ain't what they used to be. Recall his admiration for Florence Ayscough's 19th Century

---

49 How on earth Sanger can conflate the sounds of a gasoline and a diesel engine I'll never understand—and a greater mechanical enthusiast than I am could, with the same kind of rapt, reverent attention Sanger pays to his crooked knives, tell you exactly the differences in the sounds produced by different engines.

belief in "manners" and ask yourself if people today of Ayscough's social class, learning and disposition are really as crass as all that. His paean to Ayscough's gentility echoes an earlier essay on Elizabeth Bishop, in which he analyzes Bishop's poem "Manners." In that poem old ways (manners and simple, handcrafted technologies like a wagon) and new ways (disconnection and modern manufactured technologies like the automobile) meet and clash. Sanger astutely observes that Bishop's chronological framing of the poem "properly compromises any attempt to read [it] either nostalgically or as a fragment of self-solacing autobiography." But in the same essay, Sanger also discusses Bishop's use and description of a peculiar aural form of the word "yes" in "The Moose":

> As Bishop spends a whole stanza saying, it is a *yes* said with indrawn breath, a breath that drags back up against the current of "yes's" denotative affirmation, qualifying it into the connotations of *half groan, half acceptance*, a sounding ground, the base of life's music (*also death*), placed by the speaker's breath between impeding, ineluctable brackets.
>
> *Yes*, spoken as Bishop describes, used like a refrain throughout conversations as her stanzas enact, is another sign that a speaker comes from central Nova Scotia. ... It is now mainly used by country people of at least late middle age. ... the central Nova Scotia "yes" implies a whole culture shaping its use, one which is continuous, reflective, patient and realistic. One which perhaps was.

At the time of writing, I am thirty years old. I was approximately sixteen years old when Sanger published this essay in *The Antigonish Review*. I was then spending school years in Ottawa, but returning to the home in which I grew up, in central Prince Edward Island, during holidays and summers. The "yes" of Bishop's poem, which Sanger here appears to discuss very knowledgeably, is a mannerism I grew up hearing my father—not a central Nova Scotian, but a western Islander, who was schooled in Ottawa from an early age—speak. It is a mannerism of my own speech, one I usually employ unconsciously, even after spending half my life outside of the rural place

I first acquired the trait. I was not aware of it until it escaped my lips once in conversation and my interlocutor demanded instantly to know where I came from. It is a mannerism I have heard in the speech of people of all ages from all over the Maritimes, as well as Newfoundland and some parts of Ontario, particularly the Ottawa Valley. In other words, it is not nearly as peculiar, nor as endangered by the mass media-induced homogenization of Canadian speech patterns, as Sanger seems to want it to be.[50] He is just, it turns out, listening to the wrong people. His anthropological enthusiasms and hyper-valuation of obsolete technologies seem to lead him to embalm quite lively bodies; Bishop's "yes," like the old tools in *Ironworks* and the mill-chute in Fenelon Falls, seem to be of more value to him defunct—or at least dying—than alive.

*

50　That Bishop's "yes" is not so rare, so threatened or so local—if anything, its tenacity and spread indicate that it's a contagious meme, more colonizing than colonized—Sanger appears to acknowledge later, almost grudgingly, in *White Salt Mountain*, when he writes of the affirmative as belonging to "Atlantic Canadian, especially Nova Scotian speech." Why "especially" I don't know; nor does he—he just wants it to be so. This kind of willful, or wishful, misrepresentation is captured beautifully and ironically in a sonnet by Nova Scotian expat poet Geoffrey Cook, an adaptation of Rilke's "Die Insel":

The next tide wipes away the muddy shoal,
and everything's the same on every side;
but the little island out there's shut its eyes;
the labyrinthine dykelands have enclosed
the locals, who were born into a sleep
where they mix up many worlds in silence:
for they seldom speak,
their every sentence
an epitaph for flotsam, the unknown
that somehow comes ashore and stays.
And so it is with everything their gaze
takes in from childhood on:
　　unrelated, unrelenting, and too huge—
　　a come-from-away exaggerating their solitude.

Sanger's relationship with the culture and landscape of Nova Scotia is a problematic one. Since his earliest publications, he has been not only an observer of Nature, but also an avid collector of lore. Jeffery Donaldson has described him as "the go-to guy for maritime cultural history." In *The America Reel*, Sanger's first trade collection of poems, his passion is manifested most plainly in trawls through source material drawn from Maritime history and legend. This area of interest resurfaces in *Aiken Drum*, especially in "Abatos," a 240-line poem that serves as a flawed, but fascinating, center-piece, a biographical narrative focused on a notorious and elusive thief known as Henry Frederick Moon, as well as by a handful of aliases. In Moon, several of Sanger's obsessions intersect. A protean character, not pinnable to a fixed identity, one who bridges myth and reality, Moon is a sinner, a thief and a liar, recalling the char-acter sketches in *Earth Moth* discussed above. If there is something magical about Moon, he is also ruthlessly pragmatic. "Abatos" is, in short, Sanger's most ambitious piece of oblique self-portraiture.

Another exhibit piece culled from regional history is "Jerome" from *The America Reel*. Jerome is a legless sailor found bobbing in the ocean, rescued and brought back to the French Shore of southern Nova Scotia, "where he lived for fifty / eight years and spoke only twice with anyone / near to report it." Like Moon, he is a mysterious stranger with a past that is checkered, probably crim-inal. Another enigmatic traveller appears in *Arborealis*, in the form of the sailor who speaks the poems. Several key subjects of Sanger's critical work (Bishop, Thompson and Ayscough), are rootless voy-agers with strong connections to the Maritimes. It should come as no surprise that Sanger is drawn to such figures: outsiders not entirely welcome, whose presence and activities, to one degree or another, disrupt stable continuities in the fabric of communities, but who become integrated into local mythology.

For one thing, such a paradigm is of fundamental significance to the mythology of Atlantic native peoples—which is almost as important to Sanger as the myths of west-coast natives are to Robert Bringhurst. Glooscap, a central figure in Wabanaki creation stories, is the archetype of the disruptive but creative come-from-away. But more immediately, it seems clear to me that Sanger sees himself as such a figure. Born in Bewdley, Worcestershire, England, in 1943, he moved to Canada with his family ten years later. He did not settle in Nova Scotia until 1970. Had it been in Toronto and not Earlstown that Sanger had come to rest, he might have been able to naturalize himself fairly seamlessly. But the culturally homogeneous rural communities of the Maritimes, for all their vaunted hospitality, are not typically quick to welcome strangers who decide to stay.[51] Sanger, no matter that he probably knows more about Maritime history, geology, flora and fauna than 99% of the region's population, will be ever and always "from away."

Bad enough that he's a foreigner raised in Upper Canada—a geopolitical anachronism still very much a part of everyday speech in the Maritimes—his scholarly vocation, living on a farm without doing any farming himself, would, in fact, make him a doubly suspicious character. Alden Nowlan's poem "The Unhappy People," in which a professor (probably a sociologist or anthropologist) is derided for his clinical analyses of the behaviour of the speaker's cousins, is an excellent illustration of this kind of muted hostility to alien "experts." Sanger is not so cold as Nowlan's professor; his love for his adopted homeland—and, to a lesser extent, its people—is palpable in his work, but it should surprise no one that Sanger sees something pathological not only in his own impulses to collect, dissect, name and categorize, but also in Maritime culture itself.[52]

*

---

51 An amusing and illustrative story was told to me by a co-worker from Cape Breton. Two old-timers, Bill and John, are arguing about current events, but can't agree on anything. Bill turns to a third old-timer and says, "What do you think, Charley, you're from away?" Charley, though born in Ontario, has lived in the same Cape Breton town since he was five.

52 Sanger told Anne Compton that "all the historical poems in the second part of The America Reel have [a] twist of irony in them. Those poems have been often read as rural idylls, or pieces of nostalgia, but I wrote them very carefully to be that and something quite different, something symptomatic, within a pathology."

At its best, Peter Sanger's poetry is as well-made and individual as anything else I've come across in contemporary verse. But his repressive drive to extinguish the egotistical leaves the work on the whole starkly impersonal. One does get a picture of a person behind the poems, but it is a person very reticent, very restrained, very shy, for all his passion—a hard person to know. And I don't have the same problem with such Sanger exemplars as Thompson—whose personality permeates every line of *Stilt Jack*, for all its allusiveness—or Outram—whose humour and pathos make his best poems humanely attractive—or even Bishop, for all her famed restraint. There is nothing so viscerally moving in Sanger's poetry as "One Art," nothing so obliquely revealing of personal trauma as "Sestina" or "The Bight," *Stilt Jack* or Outram's "Grief Tree."

His prose, particularly the essays of *Sp* ·· is another matter. Sanger expands in prose in a way his severe aesthetics don't allow in his verse. One gets to know him better, his motivations, his emotions, and one comes to appreciate the poems better as a result. *Spar* is probably the best point of entry for readers new to Sanger. While I can't claim to *love* Sanger's poetry, for all its manifold felicities, *Spar* is a book I treasure, one of very few contemporary books that I have gone back to, more than once, for my own enjoyment.

*

I am more than a little worried that I have not done justice to the man and his writing.[53] This misgiving is not much modulated by the warm letter I have just received from Peter, this time across the expanse of mainland Canada, from South Maitland to Vancouver. He wishes me well in my move and says that I will be missed on the East Coast, even though we "may not agree at times." He has enclosed the catalogue for an exhibition of Holownia's

---

53   If you ask Sanger, I have cause for concern. I said hello to him at a book launch in early 2012. He responded angrily: "You have to stop telling lies about me." When I expressed my befuddlement, he made it clear that he meant this essay, which had been published five years earlier.

photographs, curated by Peter. The catalogue includes an essay he has written in which he hopes there "may be something [I] can use—something unguarded and symptomatic perhaps." There are indeed such things in it, and I will have to retrace my steps once more.

Peter Sanger is one of a very small number of bar-setters for artistic integrity and commitment in this country. The obscurity which has been his chief reward, while all too explicable, is nonetheless regrettable. You don't have to meet Peter in person to know how important poetry is for him and to know that in his belief system poetry is not something that can be set apart from nature, technology, philosophy, society—from the ethics of a life lived in intense engagement with the self and the world around it. Whatever the particular flaws of intent and execution in Sanger's oeuvre—flaws, it should be said, common to most human beings, but showing up more starkly in Sanger's case when juxtaposed with his stated ideals—the reverence he brings to his work, and which speaks through that work, is exemplary. As he says in the above-mentioned essay on Holownia:

> To the scientific mind, metaphorical connection is accidental, arbitrary, and without factual significance. To the artist, on the other hand, metaphorical connection, the movement and exchange of similitudes between and among entities is a proof of unity. That unity makes any distinction between the process of art ... and the subject of that art only a matter for verbal equivocation played out at best as only preliminary feint in a game whose real victory or loss is whether life is to be held in reverence or not.

NAILING DOWN THE HARD PARTS

Pino Coluccio
First Comes Love

Suzanne Buffam
Past Imperfect

CANADIAN POETRY LOVES A GOOD debutante ball. Since the 1930s, we have heralded the arrival of new generations of poets in anthologies which are the textual equivalent of coming out parties: momentous to the participants and their families, but of very little long-term interest to serious readers (and only erratically predictive of future success in the field). Like the bad hairdos immortalized in grad-class pictures, they more often than not cause embarrassment later in life.

The latest coming of age yearbooks are *Breathing Fire* and its imaginatively titled sequel *Breathing Fire 2*, edited by the surrogate parental duo of Patrick Lane and Lorna Crozier. It cannot be disputed that their efforts serve a purpose: in the wake of the most recent matriculation has come a bevy of book deals for the graduands. But the reason these anthologies are consistently disappointing is that poetry, fickle bugger that it is, manifests not in generational collectives and period styles, but in scattered individuals of eccentric talent. Generations are epitomized by shared characteristics, poetry by exceptionality, oddness, iconoclasm. And the generations presented in these books, having been carefully chosen by their elders and mentors, tend towards the reproduction of both the virtues and the flaws of preceding generations.

But if one sets out to be different without an apprenticeship to past masters, one is apt to come off more freak than unique.

"Woe to him," as Lao Tze said, "who willfully innovates while ignorant of the constant." Following in the shadow of poetry's greats can of course be discomfiting. Harold Bloom's *Anxiety of Influence* deals with the psychological upheaval poets—even great ones—undergo trying to escape the orbit of their mentors and precursors. Small wonder some poets prefer to pretend that they have little to learn from the distant poetic past: it makes their jobs a hell of a lot easier.

Most of the contemporary poets I admire have developed a dialectical knack for folding lessons learned from their ancestors into the batter of contemporary settings and idioms. When baked, these experimental mixtures can create surprising and sponta-neously fresh conceits, structures and turns of phrase. When there is no new thing under the sun (Ecclesiastes 1:9), the key to origi-nality is in the choice of antecedents as they combine with the par-ticularity of the individual poet's experience (including his or her heritage and present cultural milieu), thought and speech patterns. To borrow Auden's distinction, these poets aren't concerned so much with "originality" as they are with "authenticity." They know that if they're going to write the poems that are theirs to write, they must pick and choose those techniques others have used that best suit their own predilections and limits. Such poets don't so much find a voice as they forge a style. Respectful deference is rejected in favour of a bold blend of promiscuous intertextual fraternizing and thievery.

Over the past decade, while we've been showered with volumes of the soon-forgotten same-old, we've also been blessed with an improbably large number of remarkable debuts. Consider the fol-lowing (by no means exhaustive) list:

Ken Babstock, *Mean*
David O'Meara, *Storm Still*
John MacKenzie, *Sledgehammer*
Karen Solie, *Short Haul Engine*
Alice Burdick, *Simple Master*

Elise Partridge, *Fielder's Choice*
Geoffrey Cook, *Postscript*
Souvankham Thammavongsa, *Small Arguments*
Joe Denham, *Flux*
Steven Price, *Anatomy of Keys*
Anita Lahey, *Out to Dry in Cape Breton*
Elizabeth Bachinsky, *Home of Sudden Service*
David Hickey, *In the Lights of a Midnight Plow*
Christopher Patton, *Ox*
Gillian Wigmore, *Soft Geography*
Sachiko Murakami, *The Invisibility Exhibit*
Jeramy Dodds, *Crabwise to the Hounds*

We like to pretend that poetry is not a competitive sport, that rivalry somehow cheapens the transcendent, ineffable beauties of the art. But the facts are that poets are many, readers are few and work of lasting merit is very rare. The competition, like it or not, is fierce. Each of the books listed above stakes a pre-emptive claim on posterity; each says in its own way, be it subtle or bold: "Of all the poets and all the books, you'll be reading me twenty years hence." Their best poems are not merely solidly crafted, but authentic emanations of individual style. Each poet raises the bar for their peers—and for their own future works. Even so, most, if not all, will be forgotten; predicting what will last is a fool's errand, as any perusal of old anthologies makes depressingly obvious.

Two recent debut collections with a fighting chance are Pino Coluccio's *First Comes Love* and Suzanne Buffam's *Past Imperfect*. Neither book much resembles the other, nor do they sound like their peers; both provide pictures of a young poet hacking out their own path through the bush. And in both we see the flowering of an individual style, as well as the blight of strong influence and stylistic habit.

You don't have to read very far in *First Comes Love* before a couple of surface qualities in Coluccio's writing set it apart from the crowd.

The first is his reliance on tightly rhyming metrical and stanzaic struc-tures. In *Breathing Fire 2*, for instance, only one poet's work, Steven Price's, exhibits a similar predilection for patterned stress and sound. To pinch again from Ecclesiastes 1:9: "That thing that hath been, it is that which shall be; and that which is done is that which shall be done." It would be easy to dismiss Coluccio's prosody as anachronistic sport, but with free verse's reign on the wane, it seems to me far more avant-garde than old guard to rhyme as much as he does.

The second thing that sets Coluccio apart is the whimsical and often mordantly ironic humour of his poems, which deliver their punchlines with perfect timing. One of Canada's greatest exports is comedy and we are not without our funny men and women of verse (Jeanette Lynes, David McGimpsey, Stuart Ross, Bruce Taylor, David McFadden and, going back a bit further, George Johnston), but by and large we're a pretty lugubrious crowd. Coluccio provides a possible answer to why this might be so in his first poem, "The CEO of Heaven":

> Our first production schedule gave us
> thirteen days, not six,
> to roll the earth and heavens out.
> But when the moon and lakes
>
> and mountains led to overruns
> I had to change the mix
> and scrap a lot of the bells and whistles—
> why swaths of sun and sex
>
> were clipped clean out of Canada
> and Niger's on the rocks,
> and way more women buy their bras
> at Walmart than at Saks.

Light verse—nonsense, invective, satire—has been given short shrift in recent decades. Relying as it does on formally overdoing it (look at how Coluccio continues to play the "x" sound at the end of the even-numbered lines, a strategy he follows into the poem's fourth stanza as well), *vers de société* was bound to be a casualty of the plain speech revolution in North American verse. "Light" has come to mean "insignificant," "formal" equated with "fussy." It is our good fortune that Coluccio gives fashion the finger.

But Coluccio's choices should not be seen as mere rebellion. The subjects of his poems, his themes of urban and suburban absurdity, family drama, sex and death require a light touch. These topics of course can and have been dealt with more gravely, but Coluccio seems to say there's not much we can do about it all, so why not laugh? There is a growing contingent of critics and writers who wonder why more poems aren't written about the urban lives the majority of our citizens lead. The answer might be that the forms we've habitually cultivated are ill-suited to them because they are the opposite of urbane. Consider the second half of Coluccio's "Our Town":

> Money's what they're here for,
> a merciless amount.
> Dollars can be counted.
> What can't be doesn't count.

> Our many multiplexes
> are lit up from L.A.
> and KFC, the Gap—
> our moods are made away.

> The people here who like it
> aren't from Amsterdam,
> or Prague or Honolulu,
> but Orangeville. To them

there's grit and grandeur here,
they like the hum and glitz.
But they go home for Christmas.
Their mothers knit them mitts.

For households in our city
home is somewhere else—
Pakistan or Portugal.
Their village pride is false

(since after all they left)
but makes them damn Toronto—
"I live here cuz I have to,
not because I want to."

No one really lives here.
It's only where I work.
I don't like it either
but can't afford New York.

This is brilliantly funny stuff, but like all good jokes, it works especially well because just beneath the bluff of its punchlines and rhymes are some incisive observations about our culture. If Coluccio were to paraphrase this content in po-faced free verse, the result would be unbearably didactic opinionating. The form he has chosen, however, has all the right muscles for this particular work. The conclusions he draws are at once axiomatic and delightful.

Other topics Coluccio tackles verge on the hackneyed: immigrant coming of age; the death of family members; tough luck in love: open invitations to bathos and preciousness if the poet's quill is ill-trimmed, if she proceeds more from habit than hard work. But Coluccio's lines are too tight to let sentimentalism slacken them and his ear is near impeccable. Just listen to this sausage-making scene with "ma," a poem reminiscent of Heaney's piece about peeling potatoes with his mother, but unmistakably Coluccio in its diction and sounds:

Nothing is grosser than bowels.
You lift them out in fists
with ma from the sink
and set them out on towels.
They slither down your wrists
oozing mucous, and stink
and feel like worms and snails,
dense slobber in strands
the snipping scissors squish
through. Tacky trails
remain on straining hands.
Slippy and flippy as fish,
they glisten, slick socks,
the ends of them like lips,
once you've cut them up;
and each one gawks
when flexing fingertips
stretch them wide as a cup
around a stump of meat.

The sounds, dense as the meat stuffed in sausage skins, suck you
in from line one, with its grossed out triple modulation of "o,"
to the relentless ugly sibilance ("dense slobber in strands / the
snipping scissors squish") and onomatopoeic play with *ih* sounds.
Everything is so tightly packaged and skillfully enjambed—such
a perfect formal match for the subject matter—that you scarcely
notice the abcabc defdef skin of rhyme that cases it all together.
Prosy free verse simply can't accommodate such effects because,
paradoxically, it is too inflexible. Coluccio's language is simulta-
neously demotic ("Nothing is grosser"), spontaneously inventive
("slippy and flippy") and highly wrought. The subject matter is
the occasion for this poem, but the writing itself is the main event.

When Coluccio pits his wit and verbal audacity against his
own particular circumstances, the results are almost always fun,

often dazzling and disarmingly moving. His poems are chock-full of phrases and experiences that you could only get from a child of Italian immigrants working joe-jobs in present-day Toronto. But in several of the poems in *First Comes Love*, the persona and technique Coluccio employs feel more borrowed than stolen, more imitation or appropriation than authentic utterance. On the back cover, Carmine Starnino says that "even Larkin would be shocked by some of these poems." With all due respect to Starnino, it doesn't take a terribly discerning ear to draw the line between Philip and Pino.

Take a look at the book's title poem, a tight, slightly cynical little zinger:

> There comes a time when sitting home alone
> looking at your life—"I'm such a knob"—
> gets to be a drag. You hate your job,
> your car's a piece of crap, and what you eat
> is fatty, fried and salty. But then you meet
> a girl; the life you've made a mess of pulses.
> And not content to mess up just your own,
> you settle down and mess up someone else's.

I laughed aloud when I read this poem the first time. It has most of the elements in it that make Coluccio's poems work. But it's awfully familiar. This is Larkin's famous take on family life:

> They fuck you up, your mum and dad.
> They may not mean to, but they do.
> They fill you with the faults they had
> And add some extra, just for you.
>
> But they were fucked up in their turn
> By fools in old-style hats and coats,
> Who half the time were soppy-stern
> And half at one another's throats.

Man hands on misery to man.
It deepens like a coastal shelf.
Get out as early as you can,
And don't have any kids yourself.

A lot of Coluccio's poems click shut with similar Larkinesque summaries; a lot of them are pervaded by Larkin's brand of bah humbug misanthropy. It's no mean feat to catch another poet's rhythms and mannerisms so faithfully, but it's not the sort of thing a poet should publish much of, unless it's an intentional parody. Ironically, Coluccio displays an awareness of this in "Cover Band" when he writes that

Nailing down the hard parts
of other people's hits
is all the fame their tiny
talent fits.

If Coluccio's own talent were as tiny as the cover band's, we could leave him to his re-issues of Larkin poems and move on. But someone with his ability should be pushing himself to bigger and better things.

There is a surprising number of poems in this book dedicated to the theme of "aging men" who "lose ... their dreams"—poems that feel especially put on when written by an obviously young poet. Far more effective and affecting—and far more credible as being his own work—than these tossed-off imitations are poems like "Nonno," which blends off-colour jokes with unexpected moments of pure pathos. "Dimensions," another poem that confronts what Irving Layton called "the inescapable lousiness of growing old" with unflinching clarity, is similarly powerful. It's hard to credit that the same poet could have written these poems as wrote "Aging Men." Probably because the same poet didn't write them.

Coluccio must exorcise Larkin's influence—much as Larkin had to banish the ghost of Yeatsian cadences from his own lines—if he is to fulfill the promise of this collection. There are signs already that he will. In "The Wedding Charter," one of the best and most moving poems of the book, there are scattered bursts of the catchy rhyming that predominates elsewhere, but it drifts in and out. It is a poem in which the speaker is caught off his emotional guard by an unexpected event, and it is almost as though, while trying gamely, he can't quite muster his usual defence of jingling joke and gets choked up, carried away. The subtle sophistication of the technique in this poem and the emotional intensity it kindles are things that tell me that Pino Coluccio is far more than a skilled craftsman with a sharp wit and good ear—rare enough things in themselves—but a poet with a significant contribution to make.

Suzanne Buffam appeared in the first *Breathing Fire* anthology in 1995 and in *Breaking the Surface*, another elder-generation-intro-ducing-younger-generation anthology, in 2000; she won the CBC Literary Award for poetry in 1998. Buffam has been a rising star in Canadian literature, in other words, for a good decade. She could easily have published a first book long before now; many have with less impressive c.v.'s. It says a great deal about her dedication to the private art of poetry, I think, that she has not rushed her work headlong into book form. It is noteworthy, for instance, that none of her *Breathing Fire* poems is included in *Past Imperfect*, nor are her CBC award winners, which says to me that she isn't satisfied with the endorsement of others as proof of achievement.

There are parallels to be drawn between the poems of Buffam and Coluccio. Buffam, too, has a terrific sense of humour, but it tends to manifest more in understated wry lines than in the stagey jokes Coluccio favours. "Please take back the sparrows," she pleads, "They are bothersome and cute." Elsewhere: "My hair has grown well past my shoulders, / a feat I achieved by not cutting it."

In "Meanwhile," a sonnet reminiscent of E.E. Cummings in the unparaphrasability of its semantic and grammatical twists and of Hopkins in its dense clusters of stress and internal rhyme, Buffam shows she is no slouch with traditional prosodic tools. Here's the octave:

But could not keep so let seep in the wind.
So rolled the windows down and let it roar.
So felt the fingerbones inside me find
the fingered thing inside this foreign core.

So thickened by the inches, minutes, and the miles,
it hurled us into onwards and so through
the wet blue rolling landscape meanwhile's
made of where we're quickened and most true.

Throughout the book, Buffam plays very close attention to the way things sound, but this degree of strict patterning—along with one other poem in linked tercets, "Stones," a tricky nonce form in which the terminal word in the third line of each stanza is also the terminal word in the second line of the next stanza—is the exception. Several of the poems, in fact, are typeset in prose. As with Coluccio's choice of stanza forms for his comedy and satire, Buffam's formal decisions are appropriate to her concerns. Her poems tend to be intellectual and metaphysical meditations which pair well with the pensive pace and synthetic rhythms of a prose line. The subtle craft she employs, including generally simple, unremarkable diction, complements the subtlety of her psycho-spiritual investigations.

Not that Buffam privileges head over heart. In her restrained fashion, the poems are deeply felt. In one of her best, "Sir Gromore Somyr Joure," the speaker starts off reminiscing about a "happy station, full of sunshine and cabbage," and proceeds through a quirky, loosely connected series of images, remembrances and impressions, concluding:

Wherefore was the question on everyone's lips
though none spoke it, nor plucked it away
but let it hang there like an overripe pear
left out for the gleaners to dispute in the fall.

Had the poem ended here, it would have most of the signature ingredients of a Buffam poem, but it would not be much on the whole. But the poem does not end here, it turns, like the volta in a sonnet, and Buffam's meandering eye comes into sharp focus, as if shaken out of a reverie:

> Every horse had three different names, each one
> more purple than the last. Sir Gromore Somyr Joure
> took the day every day until the very day
> he retired. Did I love that dark horse?
> I did not. His breath stank of cabbage.
> He bit the hands that fed him. He would stand
> in bad weather and refuse the boxwood gate.
> But I was there in the fray and the fanfare,
> I was there in the dooryard, and I was there
> when they laid him down cold to the earth.

There is nothing directly stated here about the speaker's feelings, beyond her perfectly unsentimental denial of love for the horse. But the pathos in the lines meant to demonstrate that lack of love show that the speaker actually identifies with the balky horse, and make the concluding line, with its unheralded triple meter, extremely moving.

While Buffam's poems are not as immediately accessible as Coluccio's, they don't shut out the reader. They exist in a kind of liminal space. The speaker often finds herself between one place and another (which then turns out to be not such a different place at all), between waking and dreaming, between "cosmic dust" and terrestrial dirt, between togetherness with and separation from a lover. Buffam's speaker is relentlessly restless, and constantly caught between the facts of the world and the facts of her own emotions. She is ever in search of something ineffable, or perhaps constantly fleeing the definite, but "Even standing very still like this is a kind of white lie. There is how I feel, and there is this hurtling surface. It is impossible to say something true for all time about either."

This has ever been the poet's dilemma: the finite human in the midst not only of an infinite universe, but also of a world of mostly unknowable finite fellows. Buffam does not shy away from it, as many do, by satisfying herself with pat conclusions and trite pseudo-wisdom. If her poems are sometimes difficult, they are no more difficult than life's ongoing negotiations.

Like Coluccio, Buffam displays a marked distrust for the standard literary manoeuvres. Her opening poem is "Another Bildungsroman," a title clearly out to pick a fight with CanLit formulae. The poem ends not with the speaker older and wiser, or with any one of a number of standard epiphanies, but with "gaps in the sky the sky fills in with sky." That skyward glance is a leitmotif of *Past Imperfect*. Whereas Coluccio's poems are filled with the particular concrete details of his surroundings, Buffam's inhabit the ether and cannot be placed in space and time. This is because their geography is interior—spiritual, broadly speaking; Space and Time, and the individual subject's shifting place in the continuum, are her chief preoccupations. Buffam's business is to "Look more closely from farther away," as she puts it in the book's second poem, in which a Japanese airforce pilot cum "amateur astronomer" "serve[s] the night sky from below, which, he believes, is like searching for yourself."

Tropes of rapprochement and retreat recur frequently and the book as a whole is laced with archetypal motifs: wind, windows (and other glassy frames through which we either see or in which we see ourselves: mirrors, seas, lakes, ponds), doors, stars, moon, light, shadows, the future. The cycling of such stock tropes, in a lesser poet's hands, could result—often has resulted, as in recent work by Lorna Crozier—in a kind of soft-focus mystical haze. Buffam's control of her materials, however, her unflinchingly unsentimental gaze and the variety of her formal approaches, keep the repetitions from being unconscious tics; they feel more like intentional stitches binding the work together.

That said, tightness is not an entirely positive thing, partic-ularly for a first collection. There is something to be said for a book like Coluccio's that shows the young poet trying out different voices, blundering occasionally. When I read a book like Buffam's, I find myself wondering what the poet has withheld, what she has left out, and what she has denied herself in terms of expressive possibilities. *Past Imperfect* is almost too tidy, especially in contrast with the uncertainty and insecurity of its speaker—as though the speaker has figured out a great deal more than she pretends; as though the poet has "found her voice."

Some of Buffam's influences can be gleaned from her work. Stephanie Bolster highlights Hopkins and Dickinson, to which I would add Avison, Stevens and Bishop, but, unlike Coluccio's affinity for Larkin's cadences and moods, none of her poems too closely resembles any one of that august group of metaphysical questers. If anything, Buffam's poems too often resemble Buffam's poems. The less remarkable pieces in the collection drift close to self-parody (particularly in her tendency to end poems with a paradox) or paraphrase of the more impressive achievements—or, as she puts it herself in the book's concluding poem, "My voice has been described as nondescript, yet I continue to use it." Future work will demonstrate whether reservations on these grounds are justified. If Buffam's next book is much like this one, it will likely be a strong book, but it will be disappointing because it will mean that a very talented poet is treading familiar water—or scanning familiar skies. But given the patience and perseverance she's displayed to-date, and given the obvious restlessness of her intelligence, don't be surprised if Buffam turns out something completely different. Or perhaps she'll find a way "to change things by staying the same."

GOING BACK DOWN THE MULGRAVE ROAD
Charles Bruce
The Mulgrave Road

THE COVER BOARDS, which must have once been Granny Smith green, are faded now, slightly browned around the edges, and there's a bit of damage to the top right corner, where the cardboard pokes through the cloth. On the front cover, the title and the author's name, in brown Roman caps, are centred in a simple frame made of three thin wavy lines of the same brown as the text. Nothing flashy about this book, but it is solid, built to last.

The same is true of the poems it holds. Charles Bruce (1906–1971) was not only a journalist, but he literally wrote the book on journalistic prose, the original *Canadian Press Stylebook*. Conventional wisdom makes journalism and poetry strange bedfellows, but Bruce actually manages to enrich his poetry with the no-nonsense ethos of the professional writer. For one, he employs diction that is simple and beautifully clear in poems with the economy of design of a well-built drystone wall. Consider *The Mulgrave Road*'s first stanza, from the poem "Nova Scotia Fish Hut":

> Rain, and blown sand, and southwest wind
> Have rubbed these shingles crisp and paper-thin.
> Come in:
> Something has stripped these studding-posts and pinned
> Time to the rafters. Where the woodworm ticked
> Shick shick shick shick
> Steady and secretive, his track is plain:
> The fallen bark is dust; the beams are bare.

Bruce's poems have the authentic ring of the spoken voice, with every comma and conjunction contributing deliberately to that effect. The frequency with which Bruce uses "and" in this and several other poems—a figure of speech known as "polysyndeton"—would no doubt raise alarms in a workshop discussion of his poetry. But try taking one or both out of the first line of the stanza above and see the damage it does to rhythm, and hence to the meaning. Try taking the commas out; same problem. Neither the conjunctions nor the punctuation are grammatically necessary, particularly not together, but they are important structural elements, like shim stones in that drystone wall.

Many of Bruce's poems are metrically regular, but this sample gives a good idea of the pragmatic flexibility of his approach to metre and rhyme. The base metre framing this passage is iambic pentameter, but the timing is phrasal, not metronomic; the third and sixth lines are obviously curtailed, but so too is the eight-syllable opening line, which doesn't scan anything like regular iambic, at least not the first half of the line, with three stresses falling on four syllables (a trochee and a spondee).

If condensation is one thing Bruce imported from journalism into poetry, concreteness is another. Bruce does not eschew abstraction altogether—note that "Time" is pinned to the rafters of the fish hut—but the fact that it is fastened to a solid beam is significant: Bruce always brings the abstract back to earth with particular imagery. Another example is in the sestet of his sonnet "Disapproving Woman," one of several deft character sketches in *The Mulgrave Road*:

> The years have given her all the years require:
> Birch in the woodbox, credit at the store,
> Comfort and friendship, work and food and fire;
> But life has endless grief to answer for—
> Death, and the sins of men and the blood's desire,
> And muddy footprints on the kitchen floor.

It's those muddy footprints that bring into focus, and justify by ironic contrast, the inventory of abstractions and generalizations that precedes it. One expects that the woman's disapproval will be exonerated, but this poem is too honest to eulogize mawkishly. But neither does Bruce indulge in caricature; there is the very real sense that this woman, whatever her flaws, deserves our respect. Like her, Bruce is "Never unkind and never wholly kind" in his treatment of his fellow Nova Scotians; he pays respect without being reverential.

The pastoral mode from which his poems originate is prone to sentimental fudging, but Bruce the journalist and expatriate—like many Easterners, he had to leave home to get work—sees things with a canny, often moving, blend of a local's devotion and a stranger's detachment. As he puts it matter-of-factly in the book's title poem:

> If they stay they stay, if they go they go;
> On the Mulgrave Road it's a choice you make.
> There's an axe in the stump and a fork in the row
> Or a bag to pack and a train to take.

Bruce's economy is also on display in the book's unpadded table of contents, which lists only twenty-eight poems, four of which were reprinted from the poet's previous collection, *Grey Ship Moving*. The last poem of the book falls on page thirty-nine, by which point we are scarcely halfway through most contemporary collections. Oddly, although poetry is a notoriously tough commodity to sell and is in no danger of becoming a commercial blockbuster, publishers and poets have embraced a showbiz ethos in recent decades, with flashy graphics, author photos and biographies, blurbs, lengthy acknowledgments and inflated page counts—in bindings often so shoddily assembled they promise to disintegrate within the author's lifespan. This book is free of embellishment and contains very little text apart from the poems. This is probably more a question of publishing conventions than authorial preference, but it's easy to imagine what a poet of Bruce's sensibilities would make of our present literary culture. And it's easy to agree with him.

The Mulgrave Road won the Governor General's Award in 1951 and a selection of Bruce's poetry, also entitled *The Mulgrave Road*, was published in 1985, but posterity has thus far not been wholly kind to him. None of his books is in print and until the recently published *In Fine Form*, none of his poems appeared in anthologies with a national scope. The understated Bruce, distrustful of trends and faithful to the local, has been overshadowed by more forceful poetic personalities, nationalist visionaries, and postmodern suspicions of traditional poetic forms. But with recent essays by Sandy Shreve, who included Bruce's work in *In Fine Form*, and Carmine Starnino, and with the awakening of many younger (and a few older) poets to the formal potential of metrics and rhyme, Charles Bruce's work, which is still crisp and bright apple-green, may soon be reanimated by new generations of readers.[54]

---

54   This piece netted Bruce at least one new reader. Shortly after its publication in *Canadian Notes & Queries,* I got an email from the cartoonist, and *CNQ* designer, Seth, who had ordered a second-hand copy of *The Mulgrave Road* after reading my review. I suppose it's not surprising that someone as enamoured with the 1940s as Seth is would respond warmly to Bruce's poetry; they also have a shared affinity for quiet grace. Seth had a particularly fine observation about his favourite poem, "Orchard in the Woods": "Like an excellent old black and white photograph, or the rarest sort of steel engravings, it gave me that sharp, distinct sense of *being there.*"

MR. IN-BETWEEN
Patrick Warner

By the time I began writing seriously, I had already been rewarded for putting my non-whiteness, and the performance of my racialized subject position in relation to national identity, front and centre in my work. The aesthetic tradition of my university instructors was such that the entry of a non-Caucasian identity position into the space of art would always have an exoticized flavour, a kind of freshness and a kind of foreignness, that, as long as it occurred within a recognizably Eurocentric tradition, guaranteed a certain kind of approval.

–Sonnet L'Abbé, "On Beauty"

SONNET L'ABBÉ'S CANDID INSIGHTS into her own cultural capital—in the context of an academy hungry for internal, hyphenated others to be slotted into various matrices of identity politics and post-colonial theory—reveal a great deal about what is hot in the world of contemporary poetry. They also, indirectly, shine a beam on a more obscure, less intellectually sexy, immigrant experience in our poetry—an immigrant experience that could well be more polyvalent in its nuances than your standard accounts of displacement and disjunction.

We tend to take it for granted that non-whites will find themselves more strange, and their predicaments therefore more poignant than their pale-skinned counterparts, on arrival in Canada. But such a belief depends on the benignly racist idea that white people are more-or-less alike—that beige is bland—as well as on the false assumption that there is such a thing as generic Canada. Imagine instead a boy born and raised in a small town in County Mayo, Ireland, a nation famed for its schisms, but also for the greatness of its poets, past and present. Imagine him moving to Canada as a young man in the early '80s, "at a time when [he was] not sure what [his] talents might be, or if [he] had any," to improve his economic prospects. But he doesn't come to one of the usual places; not to Ottawa, Montreal, Toronto, Vancouver. No, imagine instead he finds himself in St. John's, Newfoundland, a province—barely—whose long-established white populace is itself a minority on the margins and is notoriously suspicious of outsiders; a province whose geography, culture and history locate our man, almost literally, in a limbo space between the country of his birth and the country of his adoption. Now imagine he comes relatively late to poetry, perhaps a decade or more after first setting foot on Terra Nova, and not long before entering a realm of middle class security by becoming a librarian. If you're intrigued by this scenario and by the sort of poems its tensions might engender, you can stop imagining and turn instead to the books of Patrick Warner.

Some of us have been reading Warner with delight for years—his first book came out in 2001—but I have never had the sense that we are legion. Certainly, the cover bumph from Warner's 2009 collection, *Mole*, pushes the limits of factual accuracy in claiming that he is "one of our most celebrated and deserving poets." Deserving, yea, but even while Warner has twice won the E.J. Pratt Prize for best book of poetry by a Newfoundlander, he has never been shortlisted for a major national award and if you compare his currency with that of contemporaries such as Bowling, Babstock, Solie, Clarke, Heighton, McGimpsey or Robertson, to name a few, it becomes disingenuous to keep pretending that Warner is some manner of come-from-away national treasure. Perhaps the publisher of his latest book of poems, *Perfection*, wished to dial down the rhetoric a half-notch by calling him "one of the most respected voices in Canadian poetry," respect being a form of faint praise difficult to gainsay and impossible to quantify.

Then again, if Warner had a hand in the composition of his cover copy, as poets often do, we might read *Mole*'s grandiose blurbage as a piece of canny, winking self-invention, intentionally at odd angles to the titular underground critter, and the later, more modest praise—again, clashing with the apparent braggadocio of *Perfection*—as a half-defeated admission that the Canadian poetry establishment didn't take the bait in '09. (If it's true that he "refuses to rest on his laurels," it could be because those scanty boughs don't make for the comfiest couch.) As he puts it rhetorically in "The Ravine," "If how we see the world is largely imagined, / can we not break and remake associations, reorder?"

One of the reasons, I suspect, that Warner has not received as much love as some of his peers is that he is very hard to peg. As Mark Callanan has observed, "Warner's poetry is a slippery thing." Whereas some poets take pains to cultivate a signature style, Warner has been an incorrigible experimenter, with great formal and tonal range. In his oeuvre, we find political commentary; satire; elegy; irony; earnestness; pure wordplay; plain speech; narrative; virtuosic description; intense inner self-examination; all manner of poetic forms, prescribed and nonce; dramatic monologues; romantic ruminations; long sequences and aphoristic zingers. Given any randomly chosen dozen of Tim Bowling's poems, a reader previously unfamiliar with him would have little difficulty determining that they are the work of one man, because his voice has been so consistent. I rather suspect that a dozen Warner poems would be assigned by the same reader to six—or eight, or twelve— authors, not all of them male.

I would call the former category the poetry of persona—poems emanating from the special self of the poet who is in charge when it is time to write—and the latter the poetry of personality, because, like a personality, it is a poetry prone to mercurial shifts; it presents different facets of itself in different situations; it resists tidy encapsulation and it is only occasionally internally consistent—except at its core, where its true integrity becomes manifest. The capacity to write good poems of persona is a rare enough gift and not to be denigrated, but it takes an extraordinary talent and a bold, brave vision to successfully undertake the poetry of personality.

Such a talent is Patrick Warner's. But before we accord him too much credit, we need to go back to the peculiar soils in which that talent took root. Introducing a short essay on his expat status in the Irish journal *Metre*, Warner says that "[p]oetry … is nothing if not personality." He goes on to acknowledge that his own identity has been shaped by his bifurcated life:

> The diaspora, then, is a mental state. It is nothing, or nowhere, an in-between. It is as much suspicion as it is possibility. To live in it is to be preoccupied with the idea of fidelity. How can you write with depth and comprehension about the place where you live when your primary images, metaphors and language still arise from a place you have been away from half your life? How do you speak with any degree of confidence about the culture you still call home when its present incarnation is only an echo of what you remember? And how might this tension be reflected in poetry? Perhaps, this tension produces a poetry which works, successfully or unsuccessfully, to blend images which have no obvious association; perhaps, recognising that immigrants already play a subversive role in the culture, the primary movement of their poetry will be towards harmony and the middle ground.

The middle ground might sound like a compromise, but Warner's best poems, to steal a phrase from PEI poet Brent MacLaine, have a way of making the middle be. In-betweenness—or liminality, if you prefer the *en vogue* jargon term—is everywhere in his work, which, to repurpose his own phrasing, we most often find "caught in the middle / between ironical disbelief and pious devotion." Mid-points, turns, hinges, limbos and reference points such as "here" and "there" recur as leitmotifs in his poems; the middle is where things start, the zone from which excursions might be launched to any cardinal point.

We see the obsession with "in-betweenie status" nowhere more explicitly portrayed than in Warner's novel, *Double Talk,* an uneven work that nonetheless sheds light on its author's more accomplished poetry. The book is largely concerned with fictions of identity. Warner's female protagonist is Violet Budd, an upper-middle class kid who moves across the country to St. John's from Vancouver Island and reinvents herself as a rough-edged punk. At one point, he has her recall an essay she wrote for a Creative Writing class, a piece that "was supposed to [be] a faux memoir. No one in her class knew that she was writing the real thing."

Brian "Baby" Power, Warner's male protagonist and Violet's beau-cum-husband, is not a thinly veiled cipher for his creator, but there are too many intentional and overt parallels to ignore. Like Warner, Brian comes to St. John's from Ireland as a teen in the early '80s and although he does not actually write poetry, his wealthy lawyer father-in-law derisively refers to him as "the poet." Brian and Warner also, not surprisingly, share an anxiety about their status in Newfoundland. Brian, after effortlessly employing a local expression, is "delighted to feel that b'y slip off my tongue as if I had been saying it all my life." Warner is similarly "chuffed" in the poem "Augur" to be taken for "a local man," briefly removing him from

> ... the labyrinth
> of ever more complex exclusions,
>
> beginning and ending with
> that porthole view on the self,
> claimed as objective, third-party,
> dispassionate, removed.

Rather than a faithful facsimile of himself, Warner has fashioned Brian as a literary doppelganger, both Warner and not-Warner, a feckless alternative self who occasionally has insights that sound like the poet ventriloquizing his own poetics:

Doubleness, the Disease of Life, how do I describe it? It's an inability to let things go. It's a tendency to second-guess, to think twice, to double-take, to correct. There is no ordinary world anymore, no ordinary things. And all of that signalling points towards something new. It's the flux of the worn-out as it disperses, before being baptized into a new form. It's a disease of old people and those who live firmly in the past/present. It's a foggy window on the future. But the future of all old people is death. Goodbye, we whisper. Goodbye! And we wave our handkerchiefs: some wet with tears, some damp from mopping up our relief, some bone dry and snapping like flags of independence. But for those who have known "Doubleness, the Disease of Life," death can never be seen as an end. The death it brings about is birth by another name.

Ya, right.

For Warner, being in-between, and thus perpetually apart, has helped to make him an especially keen observer, one who "enter[s] and inhabit[s] an action, a sight, a process so completely as to make it immediate," as Ruth Roach Pierson has said. Pierson was writing about *There, there*, Warner's second book, but we see such a Schopenhaurean fusion of contemplator and contemplated already in "Less Grave than Gravy," a poem from his first collection, *All Manner of Misunderstanding*:

> I was watching the sea between the wings
> of my elbows and looking down over my chest,
> when I was seized by a lifting sensation,
>
> a drawing-up, as though a blunted hook,
> or the wing of an anchor was about to burst
> out through the middle of my chest.

The speaker in a Warner poem is often to be found watching, looking, staring, listening, smelling, absorbing and recording his surroundings obsessively. Like Brian, he "gather[s] ... textures"

and there is an eidetic, often synaesthetic, quality to his recall of
sensations experienced long ago in Wordsworthian spots of time.
Consider part V of "Bears":

> Strange how things build on top of one another—
> the details of that small back yard before
> the builders built on the kitchen extension.
> Those seat-covers, for instance, draped to air
> remind my back of the shape of those seats,
> the rub of synthetic fur against my skin,
> like the hiss of wet cement in a mixer,
> softer and beyond the engine's hard sound,
> like the sound of the curry-comb I used
> to lift clumps of moulting hair from the dog,
> fist-fulls of which I stuffed in the hedges
> and discovered later, woven in birds' nests—
> all details I found a way to record before
> the whole became too small for my attention,
> which, little by little, was showing symptoms
> of something incurable—a disease perhaps
> like the one that withered the dog to bones.

Or take a sniff of this olfactory bonanza from "The Pews," in which
we can't help hearing *pee-yew!*:

> And if that hardwood spoke of elevation,
> it was in the cursive free-hand grain,
> and in the peppery raw-wood smell
> that oils and varnish could not conceal,
>
> that coaxed my nostril's shy snail foot
> to creep along the pew-back's rail,
> until its wax and spice ignited sneezes,
> great earth-shaking bugle blasts

that cleared the way for other scents:
soaps and Right Guard antiperspirant,
tidal waves of Old Spice aftershave,
hairsprays that hacked bronchial tubes,

mints melting on the heights of halitosis,
lavender tucked into beds of cold cream,
and above it all, the whiskey-like whiff
and heavy musk of expensive perfumes.

Whenever I think of hardwood pews
I think of these olfactory disguises
that sanctified but could not hide the news
from the most angelic of our senses.

By way of contrast, in a new poem set in a dance bar, the speaker ironically celebrates "the body's honest smells: / pit stink, crotch funk, butt whiff." Warner studied anthropology as an undergrad, and so often his observations of phenomena expand into broader commentaries on the human condition, individual and collective, in all its vanities, vagaries and contradictions. He has, as the speaker of "The Mole" puts it, a "penchant for darkness and filth, / [a] penchant for sticking [his] nose in."

The act of observation is fraught and something we'd rather, in many instances, not be caught doing. As Warner acknowledges, echoing Seamus Heaney's self-reproach of "artistic voyeur," "Some say to watch is to be a voyeur / and that watching is somehow perverted." But he understands that watching is fundamental to how we conceive of and invent ourselves. He has a preternaturally strong intuitive grasp of the neuropsychological insight that self-consciousness is a recursive awareness of other people's awareness of us—a feedback loop enabled largely by what neuroscientists have identified as "mirror neurons."

Not surprisingly, the mirror is another key leitmotif in his oeuvre, and Warner has commented that

Other people are both windows and mirrors. We see them, we see through them, we see ourselves in them, and the view never stops changing. Whether we are conscious of it or not, we never stop asking Who are you? Who am I? Paradoxically, the answers to those questions can only be found in relation to the "other."

We see this idea enacted dramatically in *Double Talk* and in a few of Warner's poems, to say nothing of how we, as readers, are drawn into participating in the cycle, as we are often watching him watch someone or something else. In "Bloom," an early sequence craftily narrated in the second person, the speaker says:

> standing before the oval of the mirror,
> your eye searches, seeking to behold
> some image of itself that is personal,
> and finds itself, unaccountably, beheld.
> Now balanced on the rim of this negative,
> you see a life that is without limit,
> something both natural and unnatural,
> where what is most personal is alien[.]

And "Snowbirds" gives us this tense, ironic little drama:

> I will enjoy the beautiful girls on the beach,
> all locals, and not one afraid of being topless,
> especially this one who sticks out her tongue
> when she catches me watching her watching him,
> that surfer turtling seaward through the swell.

Because Warner occupies what he has called a nowhere, he can put himself anywhere and can even watch himself. On more than one occasion, he narrates an out-of-body experience, as in "Turkey," where the imperative command to the reader explicitly involves us in the watching game:

watch how I peel away from myself
like one layer of semi-translucent onion,

to watch how that ghostly self hovers over
my sleeping self like a proud father, ready
to dart back at the first sign that I'm waking,
worried in case it does not make it back in time,
and, waking bereft, I set about ransacking

the world for something I can never find.

In "Premature," the speaker, an as-yet-unborn version of the poet, narrates a scene in which he exists as nothing more integral than unmatched gametes, "[f]rom somewhere high in the air in a corner":

I watched her watching him watching her undress
in the dresser mirror. Then she turned, and he
swept back the covers, and they collapsed together,
eight months and two weeks before I was born.

The interplay of self and other can, of course, become pathological. In "Frigidaire," a terse dramatic monologue in the voice of a refrigerator, there is a hint of this when the speaker concludes "that you will always find in me / something you long ago depleted, / something you have not replenished." Warner picks up this notion again, to devastating effect, in the new poem "Anorexia":

The less there is of you the more of me.
The doctors refer to me as he.
He is not you, they say to her.
She takes a shaky breath, she runs around
and I run with her underground.

I play my hostess like a violin,
my minimalist concerto for torso and limbs.
That's you in the loo, your woodwind guts,
the cymbal splash of watery vomit,
the kettledrum of bowels in the bowl.

I am the heart of these stick figures,
don't bother asking where I come from.
Look to the weak strain in your code.
Look to notions of perfection,
to where you fall short in execution.

If the reader twigs to something familiar in the prosody, tone and shockingly gruesome images of these lines, Warner confirms it later in the poem when he, in the voice of the disease, confesses to having "plucked" two lines "from Fred Seidel." It's a brilliant, daring manoeuvre in a poem about a parasitic force that invades, dominates and, left unchecked, extinguishes a personality.

Not only are people always watching people, but the inanimate also has its eyes on us in Warner's world. In "Bloom," we find "the pupil-like O of the well"; in "Coronation," "the barren's many-coloured eyes"; and in "Stone" the titular object is a "glad eye from the Pleistocene." Warner sees the self as a set of shifting coordinates within ever-wider concentric circles: body/mind, relationship, family, town, nation/race, planet and finally as the product and plaything of insuperable forces (genetics, physics, geology) beyond our ken. As he puts it in "Ossicle," "leaving oneself behind / happens in geologic time." We are never far in Warner's work from the Conradian sense that primeval violence could erupt through the veneered sheen of civilization at any point, as in "The Bacon Company of Ireland," in which the horrors of the slaughterhouse slide discomfitingly into a domestic breakfast scene.

Tropes of time—personal, historical and geologic—recur throughout Warner's books. Time and the individual personality, he understands, are intertwined where they meet: in memory. As

Brian Power puts it, "Who was to say which aspect of a person was the real person, and who was to say which version of the past was the true one? ... a different past could mean a different future, one in which a hidden aspect of personality might be revealed." In "Precious," the identities of the speaker and his siblings are confused when souvenir packets containing locks of childhood hair are mixed up by one of the mother's "darling children— / she couldn't remember which child exactly." Or so, at least, she says.

It takes a personality like Patrick Warner's, a personality distilled in the alembic of liminal otherness, to recognize identity as a place of possibility and play, even while it remains an arena of anxiety and atavism. The humble "perhaps" is one of the most important words in his poetic vocabulary, a word, when spoken by the mother in "Precious," he thinks he might have misheard as "the sound of a Yes when it's / slurred through a mouth full of pins." The tension between potential and doubt, between accident and intention, embodied by "perhaps" has animated his writing from the beginning. "Tradition," the boldly titled first poem of Warner's debut collection, commemorates a night of mushroom- and booze-fuelled intoxication and ends with an epiphanic scene that sets the tone for his oeuvre to come:

> I came to a stop by the Garda Station,
> and there, in amazement, I listened
> as an unseen hand strummed
> cowboy ballads on the overhead wires,
> while a few yards away, my thoughts,
> alien and precise as engines,
> assembled and disassembled
> in Pat Joe Connolly's window,
> assembled and disassembled until
> I was certain only of my doubts.
> I wish I could say it was then
> a voice came whispering to my mind,
> but it didn't. I stood in the dark,

half-choking on my own spit,
giggling like a fool as the world
stamped the ages on my ruined brain,
wondering how all the marvels I had
witnessed could be considered
no more than self deluding visions,
illegitimate keyholes to the divine.

I don't know if anyone in contemporary poetry is bearing more eloquent, precisely strange witness to the certainty of their doubts than Warner.

GO LEAVING STRONG
Go Leaving Strange
Patrick Lane

SOME PEOPLE JUST DON'T KNOW when to quit. Whether it's George Foreman dragging his overweight, overage self back into the ring for one more doomed-to-failure comeback, or Pete Rose batting .219 at age 45, or Gordie Howe returning to the NHL at 51 to score 41 points, there's something pathetic about a one-time champion trying to recapture glory in his golden years.

In poets the correlation between advancing age and diminishing performance is not as inevitable nor as pronounced as it is with athletes. Some poets continue to write well long past the age at which many people can no longer write a cheque, and show almost no sign of attenuation, Yeats being the preeminent example. Most poets, however, seem to have a heyday of ten to twenty years in which they compose their best poems, before and after which they are subpar. But poets, because their skill set is not strictly physical and the means of evaluating performance are to some degree subjective, tend more often than athletes to outlive themselves. Irving Layton is a perfect example of this. At his peak, from around 1945–1960, Layton wrote arguably the greatest poems of any Canadian at any time. From the '60s through the '80s, however, Layton reads like a blustery imitation of himself, convinced of his own unflagging genius.

Patrick Lane has long been one of Canada's most highly regarded poets. If you believe his own press, as he seems to, he is "the best poet of his generation."[55] He has staked his reputation on themes of sex, death, violence and the hard lives of the rural and urban poor, writing mostly in a quiet, reflective, meditative mode. His best work, whether or not it is the best work produced by *any* poet, is distinguished by poignant candour and spare elegance.

The narrow tonal and formal range of that best work, however, renders its exaltation as second-to-none wishful thinking. In 1976, Al Purdy, in a letter to Lane, nailed the younger poet's predilections:

> I'd like to see at least a poem or two from you in which you wake up in the morning … and feel good, and the poem reflects it. You know? The grisly side of your nature is amply demonstrated, but I'm saying that all of us laugh once in a while, all of us feel good—even John Newlove … It's just that real life is not quite so one-sided.

Purdy's critique appears to have made little impact on Lane, to judge by the lugubrious body of work that followed it.

In *Go Leaving Strange*, Lane returns to his customary themes. The book is divvied into two sections, "After" and "The Addiction Poems." The former contains mainly longer rambling pieces written in likewise long and rambling lines. There's a rhythmic persuasiveness to Lane's methods here, which include run-on sentences whose clauses are all connected by the conjunction "and," and refrain-like iterations of natural inventories:

---

55   Lane has been known to insist that this line, which appears on his personal website, be attached to promotional materials for his public appearances. A couple of years after I wrote this review, I had the opportunity to attend the awards ceremony for the BC Book Prizes at the Lt. Governor's residence in Victoria. That year, Lane was given a lifetime achievement award. In his acceptance speech, he made the outrageous claim, straight-faced, that the interior of British Columbia "didn't exist" before he started writing about it, a statement that made many people in the room cringe, but probably no one so much as the First Nations writers present, to say nothing of Katherine Gordon, the author of *Made to Measure: A History of Land Surveying in British Columbia*, which took home the Roderick Haig-Brown Regional Prize that night.

And the woolly burdock blooms in the yard and beside the grey
    boards of the fence
and in the wasted fields beyond and the absinthe and the nodding
    thistle
also bloom there with pigweed and tumbling mustard and prickly
    lettuce
and they are weeds and the poor live among them
and believe them flowers just as they believe the quack grass and
    the wild oats,
the downy brome and foxtail barley, and the witch grass are lawns,
and the children of the poor pick the tall buttercup and the low
    larkspur,
water hemlock and wild carrot, death camas and yellow locoweed,
and bring them home to their mothers as bouquets
and their mothers place the blooms in milk bottles
and the children look upon the blossoms there in the kitchen and
    laugh
as children do when they have made their mothers happy
and then they go back out into the wasteland and play their
    games,
for it is summer, and it is good to be a child there on the beaten
    clay
among the glacial stones and broken branches of poplars and
    aspens
and I can see them there and part of me is made glad by their
    fierce joy,
and part of me is not, for I know what it was to endure there and
    that happiness
was rare in that world and not to be imagined or wished for.

The looseness of this kind of lope-along line, however, is prone to
slack in the form of banal repetition and prolixity, as with "water
glasses / beaded from the sweat of air when the cold meets it."
One wants to scream at such wordiness: "CONDENSATION!"
Similarly, one wonders why egregious redundancies like "vitrified

glass" weren't caught and excised. The long lines can obscure these flaws, but do not excuse them. Also, Lane goes to the well far too often in "After," so that what starts off as incantatory becomes, after several poems composed in like manner, hypnotically dull.

Consider the first section of "Weeds": the poem is 463 words long; 62 of those words are "and"—and, and, and it is followed by five sections employing similar syntactic strategies. But the most significant problem with these poems is that the technique and style aren't so much Lane's as they are cribbed from Ernest Hemingway. Let's compare:

> and in the fall when the rains came the leaves all fell
> from the chestnut trees and the branches were bare and the trunks
>   black with rain.
> The vineyards were thin and bare-branched too and all the country
> wet and brown and dead with the autumn. There were mists over
>   the river
> and clouds on the mountains and the trucks splashed mud on the
>   road
> and the troops were muddy and wet in their capes

vs.:

> And when I was a child in that world, the wasteland of barren
>   fields,
> the deserted shacks and burned-out houses, and the creeks
> with the rusting bodies of Fords and Packards drowned among the
>   cattails
> and milfoil, the clasping-leaf pondweed and marsh horsetail, and
>   mosquito larvae
> in the broken bottles jutting their jagged necks from the mud,
> and pieces of machinery, transmissions and oil pans, gas tanks and
>   differentials,
> bled their oil and gasoline into the puddles

One quotation is from *A Farewell to Arms*, with line breaks added for camouflage, the other from *Go Leaving Strange*. Can you see the difference? I'll give it away: the only real difference is that Hemingway is good enough to give the reader respite with the odd period.

I didn't have to look long and hard to find these nuggets, as Lane's book is chock-a-block with signature Hemingway elements. He even has the gall to use a quote from Hemingway as the epigraph to one of his poems! In another, he paraphrases Hemingway's "iceberg" theory of fiction: "A story is what you require, a plot, / where what you leave out is more important than what you tell." One wonders if the section wasn't originally entitled "After … Hemingway." This goes far beyond influence into the realm of pure imitation, which may be the sincerest form of flattery, but is pretty bad form for a senior poet. As Eliot said, "Immature poets imitate; mature poets steal; bad poets deface what they take, and good poets make it into something better, or at least something different."

"The Addiction Poems" are wholly different in style, though not, unfortunately, for the better. If "After" mimics Hemingway's prose, "The Addiction Poems" borrows his public persona. In a much earlier poem, Lane wrote: "That whole life / was violent but it didn't seem so at the time. / We were just living, you see." The kind of restraint embodied by these lines is what makes the best of Lane's earlier poetry successful. And it is precisely that restraint which the failing older poet jettisons in "The Addiction Poems," trying to shock his readers where he can no longer sway them with greater subtlety:

> Babies died back then and no one said a word
> though you could tell by the missing eyes
> what daddy kept his girl too close to him.

This section has all the bathos of bad Country 'n' Western songs, right down to titles like "Crying Time Again" and "Hurting Song," in which latter we receive the instruction to "Go break your heart and then with crazy glue / spend your hours healing what is broke." I'm pretty sure the instructions on the tube don't recommend this. In one poem, we are treated to the singular observation that "Pity is hard. So is shame. … Pity or shame, they're both hard." Yuh-huh, pretty much. Just before this flat declamation, the speaker experiences an earth-shaking epiphany: "I knew looking at her I wasn't Jesus and never would be." Don't you hate it when that happens?

Most of these poems have the feel of one-offs and draft notes; despite their brevity, they manage to occupy even more useless space than the longer poems of the first section. But in the midst of the refuse-strewn and weed-choked fields of the first section, the knife fights, coke binges and beatings of the second, there is the odd glimmering indication that Lane's muse has not yet abandoned him completely, such as this arresting passage from "My Father's Watch":

> So white, so white her dance
> in that room of fluttered light.
>
> Dark earth, a staghorn's prance
> among the fallen leaves at night.
>
> How small her gentle feet, her glance,
> wet willow leaves, her hands, their slight.

One wonders if such formal constraints, otherwise not much in evidence in the book and exceedingly rare in Lane's body of work, might be the key to an eventual return to form for him. The book's title poem also stands out from the rest of the drek:

> Hounds run silent till they catch the spoor.
> It's why you close the door
> and when your woman asks what's wrong, say
> nothing, the sky inventing clouds
> where no clouds are, the light in the thin pines
> turning pale and the hounds lost in their steady run.

Again, here Lane gets away from singing the sadsack song of his self-image and manages to get some serious, stubborn poetry written. If he has more such poems in him, I wish he'd save them up before rushing his next book into print. Otherwise, he should think about retiring from active duty to devote more time to minor-league coaching.[56]

---

56 Lane, as it happens, published another collection, *Last Water Song*, three years after *Go Leaving Strange*. Much of the book is prose, but one of the stichic poems bears the ungainly title, "He Answers the Young Critic Who Demands that His Poems Change, Offering the Boy Blood and Tomatoes in Hope They Will Be Enough." The poem, far from a direct response to my review, is a narrative piece in which the poet stitches up a wounded boy, but it contains the following digression:

> All things proceed from such
> attention and it is hard to be as hard as the young
> when they admonish their elders. How difficult
> it must be to ask the rust on the iron knife
> to go back to the beauty of the blade in
> its first fire? Surely dust is its own beauty.
> It is the same as picking up a stone
> from among the many myriad stones
> by the river and holding it out to see
> the lichens growing there. One white.
> One red. They are eating each other.
> It will take another five hundred years.
> That is what the young critic wants,
> I think, but what do I know
> of such abstract wishes? Imagine
> the loneliness of just being a man.

Besides pointing out that it is impossible, according to the rules of grammar, to tell what precisely Lane is referring to when he says "That is what the young critic wants," and that "many myriad" is redundant, all I can say is that if the knife is rusty, it might not be made gleaming new again, but with oil, steel wool and whetstone, it can be cleaned and made just as sharp as before. And the beauty of dust depends entirely on how thickly layered and grimy it is.

Attention Paid, Taylor-Made

Bruce Taylor
No End in Strangeness: New and Selected Poems

I MET BRUCE TAYLOR ONCE, briefly. It was in 2005, at the Montreal launch of Carmine Starnino's anthology *The New Canon*. Carmine, knowing that I admired Taylor's book *Facts*, introduced me to him. It had been seven years since *Facts* was published, so I asked Bruce if he'd been doing much writing. "No," he said thoughtfully, "not much. Every now and then when someone asks me to write something I do, but mostly I'm building boats these days." At the time, I was disappointed. I read into Bruce's statement something about how popular and critical neglect had turned him off poetry and driven him in the direction of less-public pastimes.

The publication of *No End in Strangeness* proves my assumptions wrong, in more than one way. First, it contains a full book's worth of previously uncollected poems, thirty in all, many of them among the best he has produced. Not a huge tally, spread over thirteen years, but hardly evidence of someone who has abandoned the game. But more importantly, the poems themselves—both new and previously published—affirm something crucial about Taylor's work that I hadn't properly appreciated when we met: that when he is building boats—or making guitars, or creating darkfield photographs and charming jazz videos starring the microorganisms he has filmed through the lens of his microscope—Taylor is in fact hard at poetic work.

That these "hobbies" furnish fodder for poems is not the point, though there are excellent poems on all of these topics to be found in *No End*. More fundamentally than that, it is now clear to me that when Taylor is not writing poems, he is practising the same sort of deeply engaged idleness—a secular monastic ideal he identifies in a poem about microscopy as "wasteful curiosity"—that makes his best work both sprightly and wise. The slow, deliberate, meditative activities on which he expends his energy don't simply help to pass the time, but to reify it, as in "Rebuilding the Guitar" in which the instrument is "the hours of your life in solid form, / the liquid shapelessness of your days / grown into a kind of crystal." There is also the "would-be / boat-restorer" who, in purchasing a half-finished vessel, acquires "a new supply / of fresh, unsampled days."

The undertakings into which Taylor pours his "liquid hours" are quintessentially poetic, insofar as they involve the unschooled amateur striving towards expertise, the child seeking out new wonders to marvel at, the philosopher uncovering fresh puzzles to ponder, all at his own pace, unhurried by the exigencies of the social and economic world. The hustle and bustle of *homo economicus*, by contrast, along with the artist's relative sloth, are sent up in the satire "Getting Started":

> … it's time to start behaving
> like Information Officers and Third Trombone,
> and salesmen, psychotherapists and thieves,
> retailing products nobody should own
> by saying things that nobody believes,
> to service our absurd, collective yearning
> to keep these engines of enchantment turning,
> mile on clattering mile on awful mile.
> It can't be stopped, so what the heck.
> Seize the day and wring its skinny neck
> and toss it with the others on the pile.

In this Horatian reversal, killed time acquires the decidedly less appealing solid form of a corpse.

Taylor, who makes time instead of "killing [it] without mercy," is always alert, looking closely at things and "enlarg[ing] / inconsequential items," as we find him doing in a short poem actually called "Idleness":

Drawing a treble clef
on the wall with my eye,

squinting at a chandelier
till each bulb in its red fez sprouts
vibrating bristles,

counting flies in a museum cafeteria
next to a table
where two lovers are coming apart
with a long talk and whole minutes
of horrified silence:
they are doing this terrible thing,
unwrapping their sadness
and showing it
to one another.
It is so awful how their voices
tremble,
but notice
the idleness of their hands
stacking coins,
pushing crumbs with a bank card,
breaking chunks from the rim
of a disposable cup
and placing these inside the cup until
there isn't a cup to contain them,
just a small pile of styrofoam chips.

It's easy to imagine a well-meaning editor's advice: "Listen, Bruce, you need to cut those first seven lines, they have nothing to do with the central drama of this poem." But it is precisely the acts of purposeless, distracted attention that prepare the poet to see how these people are "unwrapping their sadness." That line itself—a textbook violation of the show-don't-tell principle—is a lovely example of a technique Taylor often exploits to magnificent effect. A lesser poet might end the poem on such a line, emphasising her own wisdom cloyingly, but from its vague abstractness, as if saying "that won't do," Taylor veers into a second triad of precisely observed idle activities, culminating in an image—a devastating twist on Frost's lines about "the ... pains you use to fill a cup / Up to the brim, and even above the brim"—that gives the earlier abstraction its objective correlative.

In the context of this poem and of Taylor's oeuvre as a whole, it's worth revisiting Eliot's definition of that term as "a set of objects, a situation, a chain of events which shall be the formula of [a] particular emotion; such that when the external facts, which must terminate in sensory experience, are given, the emotion is immediately evoked." In Taylor's poems, "external facts" abound. Indeed, the very word "fact," besides supplying the title for his second book, crops up no fewer than a dozen times in his published poems.

David Godkin has observed that "Taylor does not describe things so much as allow them to grow on the page, without the abstract intrusions that so often infect contemporary poetry." This is well put and generally accurate, but not perfectly true. There is something in Taylor that loves the big capital letter themes and eternal verities—a poem entitled "Nature" has pride of place as first in *No End*, nor does he eschew such things as "time" and "that bold Viking, Truth"—but that doesn't quite trust them. "If God were alive," Taylor writes wryly, "I'd tell him where to go." More than he loves ideas and theories, Taylor is enamoured of facts, "stuff" and "our things" in all their teeming, decaying, entropic glory. Any time he invokes an abstract concept, he can be counted on to zoom from it towards the concrete, the specific, the dynamic and three-dimensional. And so a poem that begins "The past is lovely, it lasts forever," resolves in an image of beetles "struggling down into the leaf mulch, / kicking frantically."

Consider the tension between the accumulation of prosaic particulars and grandiose abstractions in Taylor's Seussian masterpiece, "The Slough," which might have just as aptly been titled "The Slew":

Off in the aftermath, what's up there?
A million metric tons of air.
Peacocks in the weeping figs
amble through a land of twigs
and flocks of phosphorescent, screaming
crook-nosed parrots copulate
upside down inside the gleaming
spirals of an iron gate.
Plying the trackless, gassy skies,
the wild cranes have crazy eyes
and jagged claws and skinny necks.
The natural world is quite complex.
Praising nature, one suspects
the Lombardy poplars pitch and sway
because these trees are having sex
with other trees three miles away.

. . .

Where is the love that spins the gears,
that honks the goose and flaps the crane
and cranks the sun and other stars
across the crinkled diaphane?
Where is the foot that pumps the treadle?
Whose the hand that tracks the moth?
Who scales the wooden frame of evening
tacking bolts of yellow cloth?

> Who ignores this? When is ever?
> Why am I stupid? What is true?
> None of that transmutes to answers
> anywhere next to, beneath, or on top of,
> over or under the slough.

In this, as in so many Taylor poems, it's hard to quote concisely because so much of the poem's subject is the movement from thing to thing and thought to thought. (It is with no small reluctance that I forgo transcribing the final seventy-six lines of "Fortune's Algorithm," which consist of a single, syntactically dazzling sentence; few poets as much as Taylor make me want to give up critical analysis and just say, "Listen to this!") The swerving enjambments and scattershot rhymes contribute to the spontaneity of the poem's effect and to the overall impression, as Michael Lista has observed, that Taylor's "form supplies a good deal of his meaning."

It is that alacrity of mental movement that makes what should by rights be dud lines sound like lightning strikes of counterintuitive genius. It's hard to imagine a *pensée* more banal than "The natural world is quite complex." But poised—paused—between a vivid inventory of those very complexities and the speaker's own bewilderment, the line couldn't be better—until the speaker asks "Why am I stupid?" as his penultimate rhetorical gambit, providing for that complexity its perfect foil. This strategy brings to mind Al Purdy's famous poem "Trees at the Arctic Circle," in which he writes:

> I have been stupid in a poem
> I will not alter the poem
> but let the stupidity remain permanent
> as the trees are
> in a poem
> the dwarf trees of Baffin Island

Compared with Taylor, however, Purdy's *mea culpa* moment comes off rote, flat-footedly prosy, almost precious, in its self-consciousness.

Which is not to say that Taylor lacks self-consciousness. In "To My Body," for example, we find a sly take on Cartesian dualism and in "Dead Metaphor," he says "I have spent my whole life in myself." But he consistently resists the impulse of drawing attention to himself as the central concern of his poems, as in "Fortune's Algorithm":

> ... oh the dazzlements
> and distractions, finding
> myself wherever I look,
> as if each thing should have
> hands and feet and be a sort
> of small me, my selves
> all around, diminutive
> and large, but those go too,
> as we burrow down to our
> fusiform truth, purer
> than Brancusi's polished steel
> plantain or larval snail or
> whatever it was supposed to be,
> for even that has edges
> and makes a shape
> against its background,
> and what we are after
> is less than a faint dusting
> of blue light in a dark
> and quiet room, a pulsing
> hum from a faraway machine.
> Or something hard perhaps
> but elemental, clean
> and penetrating like a quill,
> the song cut down to one note,
> the poem reduced to its one
> good word, the word
> that says it all.

Taylor's swerve from self-consciousness into a Hopkinsesque apprehension of inscape is nowhere articulated better than in his tour-de-force *ars poetica* "Doodle":

> It happens quietly, without commotion.
> Your mind is elsewhere. Something interferes
> with empty paper and a thing appears
> …
> And that is what my poem wants as well,
> to make things happen, but without exertion—
> baffling arabesques unfurled
> like faxes from the underworld
> in one authoritative motion.
>
> It needs the fluency and expertise
> of the ingenious, brainless world,
> which doodles on itself incessantly,
> scribbling meanders on the parched plateaus,
> black veins in the pliations of a rose,
> medieval riddles in a woodworm's track.
> The world is lavish, never at a loss.
> It puts a caterpillar in a ball of string,
> then dresses it in oriental cloth—
> batik for the monarch's wing,
> paisley for the moth.

Taylor's focus might drift towards himself and the human world more broadly, but always sheers outward. The speaker in a Taylor poem, like John Clare, is most often found enraptured: staring, observing, listening, listing, recording, reporting. He is frequently distracted, but always on high alert, embodying the maxim of theatre director Declan Donnellan that "the actor must make a distinction between concentration and attention. People think that they can concentrate on things and pay attention to them at the same time—they can't. Concentration destroys attention."

For Taylor, it is as much a matter of looking *through* as looking *at,* as with the marbles of his boyhood, recalled as "lens[es] through which to enlarge / whatever was scarce and untouchable, / treasure, the future, the body of a girl." Cannily placed near the beginning of *No End,* these lines from a new poem anticipate the book's terminal sentence, from "Moontown":

> And it has been strange,
> but one thing has never changed, I still
> look into the future
> closely inspecting the days left,
> staring at them until they grow transparent,
> like the blades of a fan.

Again, we see time given solid, albeit see-through, form.

It isn't just the "natural world" of objective reality that Taylor stares through, nor the metaphysical phenomenon of time, but also the domains of social anthropology and myth. Striking parallels between the previously cited "Nature" and one of the older—and best—poems in the book, "Social Studies," show that Taylor does not dichotomize when it comes to humanity and the non-human world. Both poems have classroom settings. In "Nature," the speaker and his classmates are growing mould on bread, while in "Social Studies," students are being presented a dodgy, but all too commonly taught, version of Canadian history. On a map of Canada we find "the names of towns, / Manigotagan, Flin Flon, Churchill Downs, / stuck like mayflies in a web of red / roads and rails," while in "Nature," Taylor's zoom lens contracts and the micro-macro metaphor flips so that "all these heedless, headless, / nerveless, needy / greedy intertwingled beings / would compete / to own a piece of food you didn't eat / and turn it into one continuous / thatch of felt, / a little Manitoba in a jar." Like van Leeuwenhoek, "the first Microscopist" hero of the brilliant sequence "Little Animals," Taylor is "a man who look[s] / at pieces of his world and [finds] / more worlds inside them."

Taylor plays many such games with perspective and scale, finding the macro in the micro as often as he does the small in the large. In one poem, a paramecium is "serene as a basking shark"; in the next people are like microbes "under the stars, newly revealed / on the dark field." These are tropes that aren't merely clever or decorative, but, as they should be, ripe with formal meaning. Taylor unerringly puts the human in its place, celebrating our exceptional abilities and accomplishments, but reminding us also of our relationships with "lower" life forms. He does this no more memorably than in "Life Science," in which he points out that "we are all / *deuterostomes*, that is, / 'beings whose mouths come second,' meaning / that in our embryonic phase the anus / unfurls first, a trait we share with starfish / and the spiked echinoderms." Working out the metaphysical ramifications of this fact, Taylor muses that

> ... if we are not just food for worms
> as poets and smirking churchmen say,
> but worms ourselves,
> then what unfurls behind me on my way
> through life, as I go slithering
> forth through it,
> can only be, forgive me, shit.

If I have complaints about *No End*, it isn't that there's too much shit, but that there are a few things missing from the castings. Bill Coyle and Michael Lista, in otherwise praiseful reviews, have both identified weaknesses in the book and I don't disagree. In particular, I wish that "Ephemeroptera," a three-page gimmick poem produced in conjunction with CBC's *Canada Reads* game show (it contains the titles of all five novels in the 2005 competition), had remained ephemera. Any volume of this sort is bound to contain the odd dud, but what really disappoints me, given the slimness of Taylor's oeuvre, is the omission of several very strong poems. Most notably, I miss "What the Magdalen Islands Are Like" from *Cold Rubber Feet*—a poem Starnino liked well enough to include in *The New Canon*—and the mesmerizing oneiric narrative "The Facts," the title poem of Taylor's second collection, a piece I never tire of re-reading. There's a case to be made for the inclusion of several minor gems, as well; given that the book clocks in at under 120 pages, I almost wish Taylor and editor Robyn Sarah had erred on the side of inclusiveness and made it a "New and Collected" edition.

Perhaps, given the newly kindled interest in Taylor's work, such a book will appear next, a decade or so down the line. Before I sat down to write this review, I thought I would spend a paragraph lamenting the fact that Taylor is so grossly under-appreciated, while poets who tread similar ground with far less distinction (e.g., Don McKay, a poet whom Taylor has said he admires) are routinely heralded as our finest makers. We ardent fans of Taylor have been few and far between. But the appearance, since its publication, of several substantial appreciations of *No End* suggests that Taylor's eschewal of the scene and of a career in poetry has not been terminal, and that perhaps the scene has finally caught up to Taylor—or at least that it's no longer eating his dust.

What effect will this new wave of appreciation have on Taylor? Fortunately, probably none. There is a wry passage in one of his new poems, "Pacific Coho," in which a poet is about to hang himself, "But as he teeters on the kitchen chair / he glances at the mail, and what is there? / a late reprieve, a laudatory note, / a handsome cheque for something that he wrote!" The conceit of the poem is that this scene happens in the film version of a poem; the original poem on which the movie is based is free of such melodrama. Clearly, Taylor is not oblivious or immune to the outward signs of success, nor to the effects of "abandonment and neglect," but neither does he take them too seriously.

Taylor is, among other things, one of the funniest poets writing today. So when Bill Coyle calls *No End* "[a] book about entropy and failure," he overstates the case. These tropes are indeed leitmotifs in Taylor's oeuvre, but they are not his prime preoccupation and the bleak is ever "intertwingled" and "embrangled" with the ludic. If life, as Taylor writes in "Tomato Hornworm," is "something you can fail at," it is also, manifestly, an opportunity for success, however unconventional. When Taylor's speaker, in the middle of the night, steps on a guitar he has painstakingly constructed, his response is to "rebuild" the instrument verbally, to "search through the wreckage / looking for poetry." Although Taylor ventures into the apophatic wilderness made familiar to Canadian poetry readers by Tim Lilburn and others, in which we "fail / to have a use for words" and "the facts collapse / upon themselves," he does not dwell on the *via negativa*, but affirms the imperfect efficacy of language:

> It turns out you do
> need words for that,
> or somehow none of it is
> really there.

Some dozen years before I met Taylor, my cousin, Ker Wells, made his acquaintance in Montreal, where they were both living at the time. Ker, a theatre actor/director/writer, shared his impressions of Taylor with me in an email: "The thing I remember most distinctly about him was an air of unruffled but attentive calm. When he talked about making a guitar—I think he had just begun to make them—he gave the impression that it was something anyone could do." His poetry radiates the same kind of unperturbed ease. In their dynamic balance and range, artfulness and conversational flow, expert confidence and amateur enthusiasm, humility and boldness, Taylor's poems—among the most accomplished and exciting being written today—exude the signature of their maker's singular personality at every turn.

Looking for Trouble
Carmine Starnino
A Lover's Quarrel: Essays and Reviews

A COMMON REBUTTAL to hard-nosed reviewers is that they are "self-serving" in slapping down other poets. That line of argument is difficult to sustain—"Give me a break," says Carmine Starnino in his first collection of critical prose—given that self-interest in our cultural climate is far better served by celebration, collusion or silence than by blunt criticism, as Starnino knows well:

> Moreover, and especially in this country, negative reviews, given the reprisals they invite, invariably bite the reviewer back, specifically in terms of whatever grants, prizes and publications the outraged poet (or sympathetic associates) will one day be in a position to dispense. These days, in other words, poets who write reviews are looking for trouble.

Starnino has found what he's looking for, to the detriment of conversation about his book. *A Lover's Quarrel* has been the victim of gross critical mishandling to-date, from reviewers who have oversimplified his tastes and intentions, and I hope that this review will help correct the course of the debate.

Starnino is transparent about the "partisan" nature of his tastes and he makes his points with vigour. This has led some reviewers to respond to the tenor and tone of his book more than to the substance of his often nuanced arguments. Harry Vandervlist, writing in *Quill & Quire*, said that "Starnino overplay[s] contrasts and tr[ies] to spook readers into choosing between false dichotomies." He goes on to call Starnino an "upholder of a narrow range of poetic values"—which statement prompted a terse retort from Starnino in *Q&Q's* letters page. In *The Globe and Mail*, Fraser Sutherland condescendingly opined that "Starnino resembles nothing so much as an impressionable youth bedazzled by formalist filigree and Parnassian self-importance." These readings do much to reinforce Starnino's complaint that Canadian critics are often guilty of reading "crudely." While some of the reviews Starnino includes in his book are unambiguously negative in their appraisals and a few unreservedly celebratory, they more often strike an ambivalent equipoise.

Sutherland tells us that Starnino praises A.M. Klein and that he "treasures the philosophically rich Tim Lilburn." This is not altogether inaccurate, but betrays a cursory reading of the essays on these two poets. Though Starnino finds much to admire in Klein, he also makes the clear-eyed statement that, with only two significant exceptions, "there seems to be no signature note, no inimitable inner speech that surfaces in Klein's accomplished utterances." And the crux of the review of Lilburn's GG Award-winning *Kill-site* is that the gifts of the poet, after his first three books, decline steadily and that his "voice stops being a voice and becomes the recurring sum of its previous effects." In a review of David McGimpsey's *Lard Cake*—a book that stereotyped notions of "formalist filigree and Parnassian self-importance" would insist he despise—Starnino finds much to praise. Likewise, in his now-infamous review of Christian Bök's *Eunoia*, he gives Bök his due, saying that his lipograms possess "immense diversionary charm, and only a tin-eared fool would deny them that." And he puts the lie to Sutherland's completely unfounded assumption that "he treasures ... virtually the entire backlist of Signal Editions, the poetry imprint he edits," with a skeptical review of John Reibetanz's *Morning Watch*, which Starnino says is marred by "a self-conscious lyricism that, although sophisticated in its effects, strikes me as being mechanical and lifeless."

Impressionable youth, indeed. The "false dichotomies" with which we've become enamoured in this country are those of "formal poetry vs. free verse" and "experimental vs. traditional." Far from encouraging this kind of simple bipartisan approach, Starnino, at his best, seeks to explode meaningless Manichean thinking to take a closer look at the *particular* flaws and virtues of our poets. That said, Starnino's rhetoric, while it enlivens his prose, is often at odds with the sophistication of his knowledge and aesthetic sensibilities. To carp on this is to get caught up in quibbles; however, I'd be remiss in not pointing out a couple of significant chinks in Starnino's armour. One of these is a predilection for dropping names, often in lists, as though the names alone constitute an argument. On the penultimate page of the title essay, for instance, no fewer than twenty-three contemporary Canadian poets are roll called. Most of the names receive little or no substantive treatment—sometimes not even a second mention—elsewhere in the book. The catalogue thus becomes a sort of critical shortcut, an argument from authority effectively excluding the reader unfamiliar with the work of these poets and giving the impression of precisely the sort of garrison that Starnino deplores, adding fuel to the fire of critics like Sutherland and Vandervlist who see him as enamoured with a certain type of poetry, published by certain presses. (By my rough estimate, of the twenty-three named in the above-mentioned list, fourteen have published books with Signal Editions, seven with the Porcupine's Quill and four with McGill-Queen's, all presses with which Starnino is affiliated. And yes, that does add up to more than twenty-three.) I must make it clear that I don't think these poets are all of a type (I haven't even read all of them), but in the absence of substantive analysis of their work by Starnino, it's impossible for the uninitiated reader to tell otherwise.

Another problem is Starnino's failure to quarrel with certain poets, most notably Michael Harris, Eric Ormsby and David Solway, all three of whom have been friends and mentors to Starnino. He does his most painstaking and sensitive close reading on poems by each of these three, and his admiration for their work is plainly sincere. But I can't help wondering if friendship hides their flaws in Starnino's blind spot, precluding the kind of sensible balance to be found in his evaluations of Outram, Bök, Lilburn, Layton, Dudek, Klein, McGimpsey and Reibetanz. A generous assessment would conclude that the imbalance is meant to correct the neglect this trio has suffered. But a dispassionate view says he's stacking the deck.

In a review of Solway's *Chess Pieces*, Starnino excuses some weak writing in one poem as a clever setup for a later change of tone; he makes a convincing argument for the strategic value of the lame opening gambit, but I wonder if such strategies might exhaust his patience in other writers, especially given that he's "a huge fan of the maxim that a poet's identifying presence should be awake in the smallest sample pruned from their oeuvre." Of the line "lithe scintillas of exuberance" in Ormsby's poem "Garter Snake," Starnino says that it's a "ravishing" phrase "pieced together by an ear that refuses to dim language to its lowest common denominator." Yes, this is no dollar-store description, but it strikes my ear as more gaudy than ravishing—vacuous blurb-word, that—and vaguely imprecise in its evocation. As Pound said of such abstract-concrete-abstract phrasal formulae, Ormsby has dulled the image. Worse, he is speaking sonorous nonsense. Try to picture a scintilla of an abstract noun like exuberance. Now try to picture a lithe one. If you see something other than words, you've got a far more active imagination than I do. And in Harris's poem "The Dolphin," Starnino makes much of the fact that the poet's use of a simile in the final stanza "creates enough of an opening to allow the ending's sprezzatura to whistle out." The actual simile ("the flat tail-flukes / like the wings of a solitary angel") drifts dangerously close to spiritual kitsch. I mean, not just an angel, but a solitary one! We're in Lorna Crozier land here, folks.

Although Starnino comes down squarely against the glorification of ancestors and the colonial special pleading that has helped preserve mediocre works by the Confederation Poets, it seems to me that in calling Pratt the "dominant Canadian poet of the twentieth century," he is indulging in his own strained quest for important antecedents. I've never been a fan of Pratt, but for the sake of this review I revisited two long poems, "The Witches' Brew" and "The Cachalot," both of which Starnino singles out for praise. These are fun verse thumpers alright, with some unquestionably virtuoso technique at the helm, but I can't help thinking that they feel, as Starnino says of Klein's verse, "uninhabited." I tend to agree with Al Purdy's assessment that "the lack of a single personal human face behind E.J. Pratt's epics ... leaves me indifferent to him and them."

Starnino would probably dismiss Purdy's view as the thought of "a poet who'd rather adjourn to the ease of his persona than launch into the vexations of style." Which raises another sticking point for me. Purdy's name crops up in *A Lover's Quarrel* from time to time (five times by my count, three of which occur on a single page), but never for anything more than a brusque dismissal. Starnino maintains that "a poet should be judged by his best poems (not convicted by his worst)" and he extends the benefit of the doubt to the abundantly gifted but grossly overproductive Irving Layton as well as to poets like Milton Acorn and Alden Nowlan, who were also wildly uneven and undiscriminating in their output. But he seems all too ready to accept the stereotype of Purdy (purveyed by both his fans and his foes) as the aw-shucks all-Canuck avatar of slack craft, rather than engage sincerely with his oeuvre, which, though at times perfectly compatible with his critics' worst opinions, is far more subtle and various than writers like Starnino and Solway care to admit. Like him or not, Purdy's a figure that any serious critic of Canadian poetry—as Starnino unquestionably is—needs to deal with. His failure to do this properly is one of the biggest holes in this book.

I suppose I'm giving the impression that I don't think much of *A Lover's Quarrel* and that I'm not much of a friend to its author. But really, by taking issue with some primary elements, I think I'm honouring the book's spirit. As Starnino says at one point, his goal is "never to prevail, but to participate." I happen to agree with his judgments more often than not, but saying "yes, yes, that's wonderful, how true" is not much fun, now is it?

A Lover's Quarrel is a book that should be read. It is both good and good *for* Canadian literature, which suffers a surfeit of love and a shortage of quarrel. I'm keen to see what direction Starnino takes in his criticism now that he's passed this stage in his "discipleship in the discipline of prose." Here's what I'm looking forward to: more essays on significant non-Canadian poets to complement his yeoman's work on verse within our borders. Starnino has a lot to tell us about poetry and it would be a shame for a critic with such skill and insight to remain a provincial specialist.

THE TRIBE OF AL?
Yours, Al: The Collected Letters of Al Purdy
Ed. Sam Solecki

Breathing Fire 2: Canada's New Poets
Eds. Lorna Crozier & Patrick Lane

IN A REVIEW OF AL PURDY'S so-called collected letters,[57] Jeremy Lalonde concludes with the hope that the book "will impose a corrective on [the] disappointing trend" of Purdy's neglect in recent years. This stands in sharp contrast to David Solway's surly observation, in a past number of *Canadian Notes & Queries*, of "a unanimous threnody among the poets of this country who profess to have been profoundly influenced by [Purdy's] dedication to poetry, his iconic presence and his originality." This gulf is but the latest instalment of an ongoing critical debate in which each side regards Purdy more as symbolic avatar than as a practising poet.

Champions of Purdy—as Solway says, "even those who have not read him"—have for decades made the mistake of casting him in the role of the Canadian common man, his idiom that of Canadian common speech. Critics of Purdy have, by and large, made the mistake of taking Purdy's fans at their word. Both sides beg the question; Purdy's cheerleaders, taking his greatness for granted, find value in everything he wrote, while his detractors, as a reflex reaction to Purdy's reputation, find value in nothing he wrote. Both sides are

---

57 The subtitle is misleading, if not an outright misnomer. What editor Sam Solecki has provided is not so much a "Collected Letters" as a selected correspondence, including a clutch of epistles from Purdy's correspondents. Readers should beware of assuming that this is anything near an objective portrait; to be sure, Solecki provides enough material to paint a well-rounded picture, but this book is still a carefully manipulated work of image-building.

blinded by the poet's "iconic presence" (something of which Purdy was well aware, as he wrote in 1980 to George Johnston: "Long ago I realized that, that people, the media in particular, are going to seize on a few things they think they see in you and emphasize them."). The fundamental disagreement, then, is not over whether Purdy is the epitome of *homo Canadensis*, but whether that status is praiseworthy or damnable. This volume of correspondence will not likely put an end to misplaced paeans and polemics, since articles of faith held by lazy readers are rarely disturbed by empirical evidence, but it does help complicate the picture for anyone willing to assess Purdy and his legacy with more even-handedness than is typical.

For one thing, there is Purdy's vehement rejection of the label "common man." In response to a favourable review by Dennis Lee in *Saturday Night*, Purdy wrote to Robert Fulford, then the magazine's editor, "I certainly deny that I am the 'common man'—I think that's shit! ... you go into a pub and talk to the habitués, they don't talk either your language or mine." In an earlier letter to Charles Bukowski, another poet whose reputation is plagued by iconicity, Purdy brags:

> ... I have no one style, I have a dozen: have got to be virtuoso enough I can shift gears like a hot rod kid—So I doubt that my exact combo ever came along before. Unlike some, I have no ideas on being a specific sort of poet ... And don't think it's very important to make definitions, like some of the culture bugs in Canada who want a lit and a culture etc. Couldn't care less.

Perhaps Purdy protests too much on the one hand and exaggerates his own versatility on the other. There is much in his oeuvre that is indeed too loose and colloquial; sometimes his tranny downshifts into a throwaway joke, as Solway complains, and certainly some of his poems, particularly in later collections, have the feel of laureate hymns to Canadiana. But there is also plenty to contradict these elements. Purdy's detractors, if they wish to be heeded by someone other than the Purdyphobic choir, should ditch the bad habit of reading perennial vaudevillian crowd-pleasers ("At the Quinte

Hotel," "Homemade Beer," "He Sits Down to Play the Piano") as quintessential. This lite fare is the broad side of a Prince Edward County barn; striking it says little for one's marksmanship.

In his excoriation of Purdy's "Standard Average Canadian," Solway quotes Borges' dictum that "in the long run, to break the rules, you must know *about* the rules." There has always been evidence, both biographical and poetic, that Purdy's apprenticeship was a long vexed process and that his eventual style was informed by reading of, and practice in, formal verse craft. There is compelling evidence of Purdy's formal education in his early poems, such as "Invocation," a draft of which, sent to Earle Birney in 1947, features distinctly un-Purdyesque slant-rhymed lines:

> The horse-clopping, the bell-ringing time of earth,
> The cloud-beaten, wind-bullied hammers of blood
> Bursting in noiseless thunder—no sound heard—
> Only the sky emissaries slow going to bed.

These verses, almost parodically Yeatsian in their overuse of hyphenated compounds, display a certain technical savvy and sophistication, even if the diction is forced and the metre padded. Most of Purdy's prolonged negotiation with his influences—including an unfortunate early affinity for Bliss Carman's verse—has been obscured by his own understandable decision to suppress almost all of his early efforts, which became to him "rather embarrassing to read." This is probably for the best, but it creates a false sense of Purdy's apparently sudden efflorescence in the early '60s. The poem drafts included by Solecki do much to bridge the gap.

Equally revealing is Purdy's correspondence with George Johnston, a poet with aesthetic sensibilities very different from his own. Johnston—unlike many of his admirers who regard poetry and poetics like his as the antithesis of Purdy's—saw that Purdy had "developed a style without rhyme that is recognizably all of a piece." In a later letter, Johnston expresses admiration for Purdy's "rangy style which carries so much with so little seeming effort, it can only be the achievement of much hard work." For his part, Purdy responds, "I quite often use rhyme myself, and metre as well, trying to vary and conceal it within poems where it isn't expected and seems accidental if you do notice it. ... Perhaps it's not quite as artless as you seem to think?" The two have spirited arguments about the relative merits of various techniques, but it is more a discussion between artists implicated in the same tradition than a clash of ideological opponents.

The poets that Purdy most often cites as influential in these letters, besides D.H. Lawrence, are Chesterton, Kipling, Thomas, Layton, Yeats and Auden. Later in life, he develops an affinity for Rilke and Akhmatova. Whitman, Pound, Williams and the Black Mountain/TISH schools (and even Dorothy Livesay and Raymond Souster), on the other hand, he has little patience for. These letters demonstrate that Purdy's outlook is more akin to that of his harshest present-day critics than they would care to admit.

Purdy has had a significant influence on the shape of Canadian verse, but if his example has indeed led to the proliferation of Standard Average Canadian poetic diction, it is due to fundamental misreadings of his life and work. That said, we cannot let Purdy off the hook entirely. Though the letters show him to be generally frank in his criticism of the efforts of younger poets (as when he tells Bryan McCarthy to "get your mind off yourself and your own opinions"), he played no small role in transforming Canadian poetry into the industry it is today. One of the ways he did this was the editing of anthologies, such as *Storm Warning* (1971) and *Storm Warning 2* (1976), two books showcasing the poetry of a generation of emerging writers. In a deeply ambivalent 1967 review of Souster's *New Wave Canada* anthology (a forerunner of the *Storm Warning* books), Purdy says that few of the poets "will hold you enraptured (unless you badly want to feel enraptured), or lure you away from stock quotations or the hockey game" and concludes that he'd "like to see young poets start to be themselves, find out themselves what they are, using techniques of any kind selectively, judiciously, for whatever their purpose may be." But a few years later, Purdy embraced the role of midwife to the birth of new, often premature, poets.

Patrick Lane (one of the poets in the first *Storm Warning*) and Lorna Crozier picked up Purdy's guttering torch in 1995 with *Breathing Fire* and have now followed up with *Breathing Fire 2*. The editors recruited Purdy for an endorsement of the first book and the by-then-venerable and much-mellowed poet complied effusively, gushing that "These are excellent poems, much better than the work of my own earlier generation. They are here by an act of magic, ripened and full blown, youthful yet experienced, a gift we have given ourselves." Given the persistence of these anthologies, Crozier and Lane clearly have grounds for optimism in their hope that "[t]he tradition begun by Al Purdy and continued by us has … a life of its own."

Whatever the flaws of Purdy's anthologies, he at least didn't pretend that all the poets he included were of equal merit. Some poets are given several pages, some only one. In spite of Jack McClelland's pressure to include more women in the second book, and John Newlove's opinion that there are "not enough Western poets" in the first, the books don't come across as politically or geographically correct compromises. The poetry is not great, but the poems have been sifted by a sensibility and the books feel like they have undergone an editorial process.

The same cannot be said for *Breathing Fire 2*. Crozier and Lane claim that the almost perfect male/female split of 17/16 is "an accidental balance we didn't strive for. We refused to pay attention to gender just as we refused to pay attention to geography, race, colour or sexual orientation." This simply does not ring true; clearly, they are self-conscious enough about the matter to mention the double-barrelled refusal in their introduction. What they mean, surely, is that they did not exclude anyone on the basis of such factors, but inclusivity must have been a goal for editors who believe "that there is room for every kind of poetry regardless of taste, attitude or concern." If one does not base decisions at least partly on "taste," then how does one decide? Purdy at least had the good sense to stand up for his choices on the basis of his "personal belief that certain poems and poets are good." Crozier and Lane also claim to have a bias only for "the good poem finely wrought." How, then, account for the fact that every single poet in *Breathing Fire 2* is allocated no fewer than five and no more than six pages? They must all be equally good! What an astonishing culture we have to produce thirty-three such uniformly talented young versifiers!

And yet, the text of the anthology *is* remarkably uniform; not much of the poetry drifts into the realm of the outright terrible and even less of it flirts with the very good. Assuredly, some poets do come off better than others (particularly Shane Book, Mark Callanan—whose "Divination" is, I think, the only genuine show-stopper in the book—Joe Denham, Adam Getty, George Murray—though I would have selected other poems to represent both Getty and Murray—and Steven Price) but the medium-length samples have a way of obscuring the merits of the better poets and exaggerating those of the less talented. Ray Hsu, for example, is represented by four sections of an integral nine-part suite of poems on Walter Benjamin. Anthologies are notoriously hard on poets who work in longer forms, but Crozier and Lane's lack of editorial backbone is inexcusable when it comes to butchery like this.

Perhaps if the publishers hadn't decided to eat up seventeen-odd pages with large author photos and bio notes (yet more evidence that the focus is on poets, not poems), more justice could have been done to work like Hsu's, but really all it would have taken, without even deleting any of the anointed, would be to pare back the selections of some of the less accomplished inductees. Steve McOrmond and Matt Rader, for instance, each have one good poem, but the balance of their selections is filler. Lane and Crozier have been eminently "fair" in their allocations of space, but unfortunately, *pace* the mythology that keeps creative-writing programmes churning out mild poetic sausage, the distribution of poetic talent is manifestly *un*fair. No doubt they are earnest in their desire to include "fifty instead of thirty-three writers," and perhaps some deserving writers who didn't make the cut would have got a hearing in that case, but the result would have to be, given the editors' predilections, a long mediocre book instead of a short one.

Another levelling factor can be gleaned from the poets' bio notes. In thirty-three bios, attendance at specific universities is cited no fewer than thirty-five times. Particularly frequent are references to the University of New Brunswick, University of British Columbia and University of Victoria. By my count, ten of the poets (nearly one third!) have attended UVic; I'm sure it's only a coincidence that both Crozier and Lane teach at that august institution. There are also numerous references to participation in Banff writing studios; significant publications and awards are dutifully recorded. If nothing else, it's curious that these young poets should be so professional and conservative in laying out their c.v.'s, something that the editors praise as evidence that "[t]his generation seems to be savvier than those in the past about how to get by in a world that doesn't reward such an esoteric endeavour." Rather, it would seem that they have developed strategies for advancement in a world, created by those past generations, that *does* reward the production and reproduction of poems—a secret world accessible only by a magic train where esoteric practices and "act[s] of magic" are par for the course. This book is material evidence that the institutionalization of poetry instruction—far more than the nefarious influence of one Alfred Wellington Purdy—has led to a homogenization of the craft. The vast majority of these poets, at least as they are represented here, write in the by now very familiar unadorned, earnest free verse anecdotal/lyric mode that has predominated in Canadian poetry for the last forty-odd years. With a few exceptions, the generic rhythms, diction and syntax (not to mention the predictable subject matter drawn from the daily round) they employ are scarcely distinguishable from prose and fail to cohere in anything resembling a signature style.

This is where Crozier and Lane show themselves to be most out of touch with the work of today's younger poets and where today's younger poets, as selected for this anthology, are farthest from following the true example of Purdy and other diligent autodidacts of CanLit past. Poetry refreshes itself by writing *away* from its immediate predecessors, not by following the groove worn out for them. Much of the really exciting work published in recent years has been produced by poets who have embraced the challenges of metre and rhyme and have fused traditional prosodic elements with colloquial speech, poets who have—like Purdy in his day, but in their own individual ways—diverged from norms. This includes some of the poets in *Breathing Fire 2*, but with the exception of the densely-textured rhyming poems of Steven Price (who is both an alumnus and faculty member at UVic) and the heavily stressed alliteration and assonance of former UVic student Joe Denham's fishing poems, very few of Crozier and Lane's selections reflect such hybrid traits.

I have to wonder about the exclusion of Shane Neilson, whose chapbook *The Beaten-Down Elegies* contains some of the most powerful poetry I've read recently from a younger poet. No retreat-going networker, Neilson has no doubt made his fair share of enemies through his book reviewing; in particular, he has criticized Lane's "insta-editing" of various books in recent years. I'd like to think this has nothing to do with Neilson's absence from this book, but perhaps that's naïve. It also amazes me that David Hickey and Elizabeth Bachinsky, both of whom received honourable mentions in the 2004 Bronwen Wallace Award, were passed over. No doubt, with such notable omissions, there were many other poets left out who should have replaced at least the weakest writers included.

If anything, poets excluded from this "groundbreaking" and "influential" book (as it is bound to be labelled by the culture bugs) can take solace from the fact that they are in good company and that their writing has not been conscripted for a dubious publishing industry occasion that has as much to do with the perpetuation of the old as the celebration of the new. As a P.R. kit, the book no doubt does its job admirably and has provided exposure and future bio lines for thirty-three ambitious young writers, who may or may not go on to do great things. It will probably sell far more copies than most books of poetry can ever hope to. But, just like its ancestors, and regardless of what its poets eventually accomplish, its lack of vigour and variety doom it to a short shelf life. I doubt anyone will be reading it by the time the next one is cranked out a decade or so down the road.

THE NEW GARRISON

Todd Swift and Evan Jones, editors
Modern Canadian Poets: An Anthology of Poems in English

ANTHOLOGIES, PARTICULARLY THOSE dedicated to presenting the poetry of a particular stretch of geopolitical space-time, are, by necessity, Procrustean beds. Thousands of poets producing work over many decades get pruned to a mere few dozen names. Each of those lucky versifiers might have produced hundreds of poems in a lifetime of work, but can only be allotted, at most, a few pages in the Big Book of Nation Y's Essential Verse. The situation is further complicated by the fact that anthologists are rarely neutral arbiters, tending to be more prescriptive than descriptive. Their goal is not to offer a photo album of the chaotic muddle that is any place's poetry over any given period of time, but to perform a cinematic edit on all that raw footage, crafting it into something resembling a coherent narrative. Such edits, however, are as likely to distort as to clarify. Often, we find our zealous editors stretching small accomplishments and minor reputations, whilst cutting off the legs of bigger bards in order to make everything fit their version of how things *should* lie. It gets even trickier when the geopolitical entity being represented is a sprawling, sparsely populated, multilingual, amorphous nation plagued by crises of identity, guilt and inferiority complexes, and resentments. Now try framing this anthology for an audience comprised not only of foreigners, but nationals of your former colonial mother country—people, in other words, not just likely to misunderstand you, but to assume, in a negligently passive sort of way, that you're vaguely inferior. The anthologist in such a sticky wicket is burdened not only with the already vexing task of presenting the poetry of his or her country in such a manner that it might be apprehended and appreciated, but also with the anxiety that the poems meet with his readers' *approval*—so that they don't come to the conclusion, as Carcanet Press editor Michael Schmidt once said of Canadian poetry, that the work they are reading is "a short street."

To Schmidt's credit, he was willing to have his mind changed. Legend has it that expat poet and tireless poetry activist Todd Swift, in what he has referred to as his "*Flashdance* moment," stood up at a conference in Norwich and hectored Schmidt about his offhand dismissal of Canadian poetry. Schmidt's response? He gave Swift, along with fellow expat Evan Jones, the chance to edit an anthology of Canadian poems for Schmidt's Manchester-based press.

A cynic might say that Schmidt's gift to Swift and Jones was just enough rope. No matter how well anthologists do their job, the book they produce is bound to please only some of the people some of the time. Anthologies of the canon-constructing sort aren't detailed topographical maps, they're tailored guidebooks. The anthologist has no choice but to leave out far more poets and poems than she can include. It's all the more important, therefore, to figure out ground rules, to establish beforehand a set of ultimately arbitrary but deliberate, rational criteria according to which certain poets and poems will be eligible for inclusion and others will be excluded automatically. The crisper and cleaner the boundaries, the less cause critics will have to cavil over calls made or missed.

With a title like *Modern Canadian Poets*, we're off to a bad start. "Modern" is one of those words that, because it can mean, and has meant, almost anything, needs to be defined if it's going to be of any use. Swift and Jones fail to do so. The word "modernist" gets bandied about a fair bit in their introduction, but this is not an anthology of Canadian modernists, neither in terms of the aesthetics, nor the vintage of its contributors, who were born between

1879 and 1962. This can't even be accurately called an anthology of 20th Century poetry, as the poems included date from the late 19th Century to the first decade of the 21st. Given this breadth, a less era-specific title like *35 Canadian Poets* would have been far more apposite and would have relieved the weight of expectation generated by the gravitas of *Modern Canadian Poets*. Either that, or the editors should have kept the title, but drawn a tighter bead on their target.

As it stands, we have a book with an identity crisis (how Canadian!): part historical anthology and part gathering of contemporary work. No explanation is given for the 1962 end-date; when asked "Why that particular cut-off?" by Maurice Mierau in a recent interview, the editors skirted the issue: "we found that we disagreed more the closer we got to our own ages. This in retrospect is a natural thing: a sign to us that our own generation needs more time to develop, for reputations to cement." Sure, but Swift was born in 1966; are poets born in the late '50s and early '60s not of the same generation? 1962 is such a random year that it's more than a little tempting to speculate that it was chosen, instead of an equally arbitrary but more conventional cutoff like 1960, so that David McGimpsey, a long-time friend of Swift's, could be the anthology's junior contributor. In answering that same interview question, the editors said that they didn't want this book to "cross over ground covered in other anthologies," such as *The New Canon*, which selected work from poets born between 1955-1975. This could have been easily accomplished: set the bar at 1954. Yet 1/7th of the poets in *MCP* were born after 1955, and four of those five poets appeared in *The New Canon* as well. So much for not crossing over.

The exclusion of later-born poets from *MCP* is further problematized by the different rates at which poets develop, and the often erratic trajectories poetic careers follow. Consider Ken Babstock, named in the introduction to *MCP* as a prominent member in "the impressive younger generation of Canadian poets." Babstock was born in 1970, so he didn't make it in. But Babstock's first book was published in 1999, earlier than the debuts of Anne Compton (b. 1947) and Elise Partridge (b. 1958), whose poems do grace the pages of *MCP*. Sina Queyras, Christian Bök, Carmine Starnino and Stephanie Bolster, all of whom are named along with Babstock in the introduction, also had books in print before one or more of the poets included and have each published several volumes since. But they're too new to be modern, apparently.

Conversely, E.J. Pratt appears to have been too old. He otherwise seems to fit the editors' desiderata (cosmopolitan outlook, broad influence, formal brio). Not only is Pratt slightly younger than Emile Nelligan, the oldest poet whose work appears in *MCP*, but Pratt was still writing long after the precociously modernist W.W.E. Ross's (b. 1894) two self-published books came out, which makes him both Ross's senior *and* junior. Swift and Jones don't address the exclusion of Pratt or any other pre-1894-birth Anglo poets, so we're left guessing. Which we really shouldn't be.

The editors' wavering aim extends to their title's second adjective as well. It is commendable that Swift and Jones attempt to present a broad idea of what a Canadian might be by including many immigrants and émigrés, but they fail to follow their own logic. In their introduction, they list several "international poets who have contributed to Canadian poetry in the 20th Century but are not included [...] because of their stronger connections to other, sometimes larger literatures." Yet the very same things could be said of several of the poets they do include. Not only *could* it be said, they actually do say it, when they complain that "Sibum and Kociejowski, as well as many others with connections to larger literatures and traditions that look beyond Canada, are sidelined within the discussion of Canadian poetry, because they look outward." It is baffling to read such baldly contradictory statements in the same essay; it's almost as if the editors took turns writing paragraphs and didn't bother checking for continuity problems. I have no quarrel with calling Joan Murray, Daryl Hine and Eric Ormsby Canadian, but it's perfectly arbitrary to put them inside and Molly Peacock—an American by birth, but one who presently resides in Toronto, publishes with McClelland & Stewart and presides over the *Best Canadian Poems in English* anthology series—out. Ditto Elizabeth Bishop, who called herself ¾ Canadian and whose imagination was attached to no landscape more firmly than Nova Scotia's Parrsboro shore. Ditto Lorna Goodison, who is explicitly excluded by the editors, but is named in the book's front matter as one of the Canadian poets published by Carcanet!

Even the term "Poets" gets prevaricated upon by Swift and Jones. Leonard Cohen, they write, by way of justifying his exclusion, "is second only to Bob Dylan as singer to the world and needs no reintroduction here." Similarly, Atwood and Ondaatje are "no longer poets firstly [sic], but literary figures who have staked their best claims on prose." Perhaps this is just a cagey way of saying that they're not good enough as poets, but if that isn't what's intended—and it's by no means unambiguous—it's absurd to leave poets out because they happen to be more famous as songwriters or novelists. Not least of all because the same could be said of certain poets who *are* in the book. Steven Heighton, like Atwood and Ondaatje, is known more as a novelist than as a poet. John Glassco is best known as a memoirist, Robert Bringhurst as a typographer and ethnologist. Others (Robert Allen, Marius Kociejowski) have arguably "staked their best claims" on prose. Because Swift and Jones have done such a shoddy job establishing rational criteria for inclusion, they must have recourse, repeatedly, to imaginary and easily disputable ones.

Lack of focus plagues the sub-title, too. In "An anthology of poems in English," one has cause to expect, well, poems in English. Indeed, all of the text in the book is English-language (even the franglais macaronics of A.M. Klein's "Montreal" are predominantly Anglo), but not all of it started out that way. Swift and Jones tell us that they decided to include Anne Hébert because they "recognized in the translations of Alan Brown such a significant achievement as to merit her inclusion within the body of Canadian English-language poetry." Be that as it may, Brown's versions were never intended as English-language originals. The decision to include them, without providing the original French *en face*, is a stupefyingly blind act of cultural colonization, made even worse by the fact that it appears in a *British* book. Swift and Jones give themselves a pat on the back for their "spirit of open-ness," blithely unaware that the inclusion of one Francophone poet in the midst of thirty-four Anglophones is not just a bad editorial decision, but an affront to French-Canadian poetry as a whole—a slap in the face that could have been obviated by simply sticking to the stated parameters of their book.

The editors go one worse by including "versions of works by Emile Nelligan, Hector de Saint-Denys Garneau, and Robert Melançon." These versions don't appear under the names of the poems' originators, but under those of their translators. This is a disservice to both the Franco poets and to their Anglo interpreters. Three of John Glassco's five poems are translations of Saint-Denys Garneau. The editors maintain that these translations are "among [Glassco's] greatest accomplishments," but so are original, signature poems such as "The Burden of Junk" and "The Entailed Farm," which get squeezed out by making Glassco's entry do double-duty. The inclusion of Nelligan translations (one by Steven Heighton and two by Anne Carson) is more perplexing yet. Nelligan is fifteen years older than the oldest Anglo poet in the book and produced no poetry in the 20th Century (his poems were first collected in 1903, four years after his career-ending psychotic breakdown). Carson's transla-tions have not yet even been published in book form, so the editors really had to go off the beaten path to include them. They made an even further *hors-piste* excursion to net two Melançon translations by Eric Ormsby, originally published in an online magazine that doesn't seem to have archived them. Both Carson and Ormsby have substantial bodies of published work; it's hard to believe that Swift and Jones actually thought these serially published adaptations made for better anthology pieces than time-tested original work, particu-larly considering that the Ormsby translations are excerpts of a long sequence. And Heighton's translation of "Le vaisseau d'or" is not half as good an English poem as some of his own sonnets.

Considering all the lumps and warps in the book's structure, A.G. Bailey's lines from "The Bumpkin and the Bobcat"—"The frame / buckled in a dozen / places"—take on an unintended resonance. If the haphazard architecture of *MCP* isn't enough to shake your confidence in the acumen of its designers, then the shoddy details should finish the job. This is supposed to be a provocative remix of the Canadian poetry canon, but in the introduction, Jones and Swift seem more intent on demonstrating that they've done their homework than in establishing bona fides as after-school shit-disturbers. The editors provide a canned history of anthologization in Canada in a six-page yawn of an essay, composed in a prose more stodgy than startling, larded with off-the-peg phrasing ("may never have read before, but will soon find unforgettable") and inelegant sentences that signify little. We learn, for instance, that "[b]ecause of the variety of its many strengths, Canadian poetry has always been a challenge to characterise." This statement, a microcosm of the introduction as a whole, is as unintelligent as it is vague and wordy. The poetry of any nation is "a challenge to characterise." This isn't "because of the variety of its many strengths," but because it is composed of work produced by disparate, eccentric individuals over long periods of time. Any writing that is not a challenge to characterize doesn't deserve to be called literature because it is more properly understood as a genre. Canada is in no way exceptional.

The undergraduate awkwardness of the prose carries into the bio notes provided for each of the book's contributors. In the W.W.E. Ross entry, we learn that Ross's work, paradoxically, has "never been popular in Canada" and yet that his "two privately printed collections [...] made an impact few poets of his generation achieved." On whom? one wonders. Alfred Bailey's poetry is out of print, we are told, but it has nevertheless made "a lasting impression." Pun intended? In Bailey's note, the editors also use the adjective "important" twice in one sentence, shortly after telling us about Bailey's improbable "importance." The editors clearly think it important that we believe Bailey should be important, but it is also important to be factually accurate (i.e. the fact that few living poets even know who Bailey is means that he can't be important, strictly speaking) and to vary word choices in a brief text. A thesaurus is an important resource for achieving the latter goal; a dictionary might have helped with the former.

What's missing most in these notes is assistance from a manual of style. Consider the closing sentence of Mary Dalton's introduction: "Her major subject matter is the exploration of feminine desire and the natural world, via the land- and seascapes around her, through which she maintains a tough yet versatile sensibility at once recognisable and distinctly different." This train-wreck of a period wouldn't pass muster in Composition 101; as an attempt at literary criticism, it is, as the kids are saying, an epic fail. Even if one fixed the infelicities of its construction, the statement would still be bereft of substance. What the editors say about Dalton's "sensibility" means precisely nothing, which makes one suspect that they haven't given Dalton's poetry the attention required to make any penetrating observations of its particular qualities. The syntactic disasters and empty statements accumulate throughout the editorial commentary, to the point that one has a very hard time trusting Swift and Jones as arbiters of good writing. The publisher might have saved them from the worst of their blunders, but it appears that Michael Schmidt also thinks of copy editing as a short street.

The proofreading is equally abysmal. After encountering numerous typos—including, ironically, a badly botched stanza in a poem by Robert Bringhurst, a world authority on book design and production—I decided to proofread George Elliott Clarke's entry. It starts badly with the bio note, which features "the historical region of the three maritime provinces." A)This is a geographical region. B)Canada has eight *maritime provinces*—it has three *Maritime Provinces*. The three-and-a-half pages of poetry allotted to Clarke, meanwhile, contain five transcription errors. Whether this is better or worse than other entries I can't say, but the overall sloppiness is far too typical.

None of this is to say that *MCP* isn't worth a read. It is awfully good to see underrated poets like Bailey, Glassco, Anne Wilkinson, George Johnston, Richard Outram and Daryl Hine included in an exclusive anthology; some of the contemporary poets included are indeed among our finest. There are a lot of good poems in this book and a few great ones. The book's failings are so disappointing precisely because it contains several of this country's very best: Klein's "Heirloom"; Irving Layton's "Keine Lazarovitch"; Johnston's "War on the Periphery"; P.K. Page's "Cry Ararat!"; Outram's "Barbed Wire"; Hine's "A Bewilderment at the Entrance of the Fat Boy into Eden"; Bringhurst's "The Beauty of the Weapons"; Robyn Sarah's "Day Visit"; Clarke's "Monologue for Selah Bringing Spring to Whylah Falls." Poems like these—hair-raising, ear-catching, mind-grabbing poems—form the bedrock on which a very credible anthology of 20th Century English Canadian poetry might be built.

Swift and Jones have failed to curate such an anthology, not only because they over-extend the book's timeframe, make ill-advised and tokenist forays into French-Canadian verse and pay insufficient attention to very important details, but because the book betrays their prejudices. In reviews of *MCP*, much has been made of the poets not included: no Atwood, no Purdy, no McKay, no Crozier, etc., etc. Even a non-revisionist book of this length and scope would be bound to leave out a few of the higher-profile poets in the country. Because this is not such an anthology, the gleeful slaughter of sacred cows is to be expected. I have no problem with the exclusion of certain canonical poets; I welcome it, in fact. But the rationalization for the choices—to say nothing of the silence surrounding the exclusions—smells funny.

"Cosmopolitan" is the word that comes up again and again in the editorial apparatus of *MCP*. It isn't surprising that this would be the default preference for two urbanite expatriates, but their insistence on this aesthetic as corrective to the straw figure of a "loud-mouthed, formless Everyman whose verse dominates many Canadian anthologies," reveals a regrettable failure of imagination and sympathy. (Their obsession with cosmopolitanism, more-over, is gauchely provincial, reminding me of nothing so much as Vancouverites neurotically lauding their high-rent hometown as a "world class city.") Jones, in particular, has gone out of his way in the past to present a caricature of Al Purdy as a poet whose "most noteworthy poems are about being drunk in bars," as he put it in a letter to the editors of *Poetry* in 2008. The classist basis for this misrepresentation was evident, as Jones continued, in a highly personal vein: "I remember a friend of mine, an older poet whom I still see as a mentor, asking if I found something exotic in that voice of the drunk at the bar. 'That bar is my family's bar,' I told him, 'and he's been drinking all day and has twice called me a fag because I'm quiet and don't know anything about hockey. He's also been hitting on my mom.'"

Is it unreasonable to see *MCP* as a retributive act against the boors of Canadian verse? John Thompson's bio note is illuminat-ing; as an English-born and American-educated academic who looked to French and Persian poetry for inspiration, Thompson is in many ways the ideal candidate for inclusion in this book of Canadian cosmopolites. In other respects, however, he represents exactly the sort of poet Swift and Jones want to take down a peg. In his bio note, in a bravura display of cognitive dissonance reduc-tion, Thompson's "rough, hard-drinking, and foul-mouthed" per-sona is laughed off by the editors as a satirical "farce." If so, it was one Thompson kept up with incredible self-destructive per-sistence. Usually, when such behaviour traits lead to a person's premature death, as they did with Thompson, we call it a mental illness. Dismissing it as a prank is disgraceful.

The presentation of *MCP* as a gathering of work that "a British audience can understand and relate to" seems to me at best a mealy-mouthed excuse for the editors' own aesthetic biases and at worst an accidental accusation of provincialism on the part of British readers. (It is also a disingenuous statement, because the editors must have known full well that the book would receive far more attention in Canada than abroad.) Does an English-born poetry reader fail to understand and relate to Lorca? Can a Scot not get Neruda? Why would a Londoner who loves Thomas Hardy not be able to wrap his or her head around, say, Peter Trower, a poet with predilections for local speech and elegy akin to Hardy's poetics? Any Mancunian with an appreciation for Robert Frost or Edward Thomas would find much to love in the plain-speech lyrics of Charles Bruce. A Glaswegian able to find room in their imagination for the emotionally raw utterances and pastoral scenes of John Clare might be thrilled by the exposed-nerve candor and rural flavours of Alden Nowlan or the politically-inflected love and anger of Milton Acorn. As one British reviewer has said of *MCP*, there is "a tidiness about the poetry that maybe reveals a distaste with extremes."

The fact is that the British poetry audience is every bit as difficult to characterize as Canadian poetry is and attempting (or pretending) to cater to it is a mug's game. The goal, therefore, should be to present the best possible book of Canadian poems and not one that a stereotyped reader is supposed to be capable of understanding: let the poems convince the readers; don't let the readers dictate the choice of poems. Had they been willing to exercise as much informed judgment in their choices as taste, the editors of *MCP* might have made such oddball inclusions as Joan Murray and Daniel David Moses a bit more credible, but as it stands, it's hard to avoid the conclusion that Swift and Jones don't know the field as well as they pretend to, that they don't know their audience as well as they think they do, and that they are overly enamoured of surprising iconoclastic choices for their own sake, at the expense of appropriate selections.

The problem isn't just that Swift and Jones fail to expand their range, but also that they make very odd omissions within it. Where, one wonders, is Peter Van Toorn, with his magpie eclecticism and formal derring-do? Since the republication of his seminal book *Mountain Tea* in 2003, Van Toorn has had far more influence on contemporary poets than a good many of Swift and Jones's picks.[58] And how was it decided that Earle Birney, a scholar whose influences ranged from Anglo-Saxon verse, to balladry, to concrete poetry, was more loud-mouthed Everyman than erudite cosmopolitan? What was it in the orientally oriented verse of Gwendolyn MacEwen that was deemed too inward-looking? Why are David Solway and Michael Harris left out when their associates Sibum, Kociejowski, Ormsby and Sarah are included? What an opportunity for redress was missed by excluding John Smith's musically dynamic, formally adventurous and intellectually sophisticated sonnets—an omission made doubly perplexing by the fact that Evan Jones, the poetry editor for Fitzhenry & Whiteside, published Smith's most recent book. Maybe if they hadn't strayed so far towards the present, *MCP*'s editors would have found room for more senior poets whose presence would be both unconventional *and* incontrovertibly apt.

As for the poets they do include, the choices of poem are often odd. Where, one wonders, are Page's "Stenographers" and "Photos of a Salt Mine"? All of the Page poems included are fine (although "Planet Earth" has been greatly overrated because of its topicality and because that topicality led to its being adopted by the UN as an anthem), but only "Cry Ararat!" is a bona fide peer of the two I've named, which have been anthology standards for very good reason. As have Margaret Avison's "Snow" and "The Swimmer's Moment," both absent from *MCP*. It could be that because these are two of the most canonical poets in the book, Swift and Jones wished to make their entries fresher, but if so, it's another case of personal preference trumping good judgment. It also runs counter to their premise that this is a book intended primarily for readers with little or no prior knowledge of the poets.

The case of Irving Layton is even more of a head-scratcher. Oddly, in a book supposed to favour quality of poetry over size of reputation, we find the argument that Layton's "work is still respected, but his star has waned somewhat." (Recall, by contrast,

---

58   As Swift should know, since the essay on Van Toorn that appears in this volume was commissioned by Jason Camlot for an anthology co-edited by Swift.

the "impact" and "importance" of Ross and Bailey.) The editors say in the same paragraph that Layton "managed to write a handful of near-perfect lyrics, both formally and rhetorically as strong as any work of the period." Layton's poem selection seems to accord more with the former statement (to say nothing of the editors' aversion to "his swaggering messianic self-directed persona") than with the latter, as his three poems—rather too few to comprise a "handful"—take up only three pages of *MCP*. No poet in the book is accorded less space than this, in spite of the fact that Layton, *pace* Swift and Jones, is still widely regarded as *the* 20th Century Canadian poet. The editors don't hesitate, for instance, to call in Carmine Starnino in support of Klein, but they are notably silent about the fact that Starnino, in his book *A Lover's Quarrel*, rates Layton much more highly than he does Klein. Given that Klein is anointed by Swift and Jones as "the poet who comes closest to being the great Canadian figure of the twentieth century," and that Layton was once a pupil and later a critic of Klein's, it's hard not to read Layton's demotion in *MCP* as the editors' way of stacking the deck. The Layton poems they've chosen, moreover, represent an extraordinarily narrow slice of his vast range. A reader with only this anthology to go by would think that Layton was a poet who wrote about family members (there's a poem for a wife and a poem for a mother) and … produce. The selection of the decidedly minor "Marché Municipale," which wasn't even included in Layton's overly-capacious Selected, is an index of the editors' lack of interest in presenting Layton at his best. In the interview with Mierau, they say in defence of Layton's short-sheeting that "[t]hose three poems sum up Layton, really." No one who has read Layton with any care would concur.

Writing in *The Globe and Mail*, Jacob McArthur Mooney suggested that Swift and Jones' canonical recalibrations were "dishonest." It's hard not to agree with him. The only alternative—which is also tempting, given how slipshod the book is—is to dismiss them as incompetent. But I think we need to be wary of the sort of dichotomies *MCP*'s editors too readily embrace, and come to the conclusion that their book is both mendacious and cack-handed. As a minority report, it isn't without highlights, but it should be read more as an eccentric miscellany than as a well-rounded and -grounded exhibit of the best Modern Canadian Poetry. In attempting to position themselves against the essentialist special pleading of Atwood et al., Swift and Jones, rather than tearing down the walls of the garrison, have erected new ones. Theirs happens to be an urbane stockade, with good cafés, dog bakeries and cocktail parties, but it is a garrison nonetheless, projecting in large measure, by means of obsessive appeals to authority, passive-aggressive exclusions and unsignalled omissions, the shadow portrait of its architects' neuroses.

FROMAGERIES

James McIntyre
Ode on the Mammoth Cheese

Weight over seven thousand pounds.

We have seen thee, queen of cheese,
Lying quietly at your ease,
Gently fanned by evening breeze,
Thy fair form no flies dare seize.

All gaily dressed soon you'll go
To the great Provincial Show,
To be admired by many a beau
In the city of Toronto.

Cows numerous as a swarm of bees,
Or as the leaves upon the trees,
It did require to make thee please,
And stand unrivalled, queen of cheese.

May you not receive a scar as
We have heard that Mr. Harris
Intends to send you off as far as
The great World's show at Paris.

Of the youth beware of these,
For some of them might rudely squeeze
And bite your cheek, then songs or glees
We could not sing, oh! queen of cheese.

We'rt thou suspended from balloon,
You'd cast a shade, even at noon;
Folks would think it was the moon
About to fall and crush them soon.

There are two ways for a poet to achieve immortality: 1) Write at least one, but preferably several, indisputably great poems; or 2) Write at least one, but preferably several, indisputably atrocious poems. The latter might seem easier to do, but to compose verse that isn't just slight, mediocre, disposable, dull—to make truly awful poetry—requires a kind of "inverse talent," as Kathryn and Ross Petras put it in the introduction to their anthology *Very Bad Poetry*:

It also helps to have a wooden ear for words, a penchant for sinking into a mire of sentimentality, a bullheaded inclination to stuff too many syllables or words into a line or a phrase, and an enviable confidence that allows one to write despite absolutely appalling incompetence.

Only three poets in the Petras anthology are allotted more poems than James McIntyre (1827–1906). Thus, although it remains true that Canada has not produced a Yeats, we can say without hyperbole that we have our very own McGonagall.

Great poets have themes, or obsessions, that drive them to write. So too it is with awful poets. For McIntyre, a furniture maker and undertaker in Oxford County, Ontario, that theme was dairy products, and "Ode on the Mammoth Cheese" is the Ingersoll Cheese Poet's masterpiece (though it could be argued that "Prophecy of a Ten Ton Cheese" is superior—which is to say, inferior). The Petrases say rightly that, as is the case with great poetry, "we can't exactly define a very bad poem except to say we know one when we see one." Such is the case with this bathetic *chef-d'oeuvre*, but there are elements in it that deserve highlighting.

First, there is the rhyme scheme and the lengths to which McIntyre goes to sustain it. Terrible poetry is always unintentionally hilarious, and McIntyre's dogged adherence to his metrically challenged AAAA quatrains provides the foundation of this poem's *par hasard* comedy. It's a pity there are no extant recordings of the cheese poet reading his verses; I'd love to hear him emphasize the last syllable of TytonTO and I wonder if—I hope!— he'd try to slur the feminine rhymes of the fourth stanza to make "scar as" and "far as" sound like "Harris" and "Paris."

The requirements of the rhyme scheme, combined with McIntyre's tin ear and absurd subject matter, lead to weird non-sequiturs, badly tortured syntax and awkward turns of phrase—necessary elements of any terrible poem. Particularly outstanding are "Thy fair form no flies dare seize"[59] and "Of the youth, beware of these," the former adorned with the internal rhyme of "thy fair" and "flies dare," the latter marred beyond mere badness by the redundant duplication of "of." The refrain "queen of cheese" creates the formidable challenge of finding nine rhymes for "cheese." This hurdle leads to some memorably bizarre metaphorical touches. My favourite is the comparison of the herd of cows to a swarm of bees or "leaves upon the trees"—not *tree*, mind you, it wouldn't rhyme properly.

But the crowning glory of this *fromagerie* has to be its terminal stanza. This is pure anti-genius, the sort of thing you couldn't think up yourself if you tried. Where on earth did the hypothetical image of this monstrous globe of ripened curd "suspended from balloon" come from? How did McIntyre dream this up? Did he see a hot air balloon whilst composing his poem and—eureka!—realize that it was just the thing he needed to wrap up his cheddarific ode?

---

59   Note how McIntyre randomly flips between the informal mode of address (thee/ thou/thy) and the formal (you/your). It's as if the cheese is simultaneously an object of worship and a dear friend.

The muse only makes such visits to a peculiar kind of visionary in a fit of divine afflatus. The moon as cheese is not at all original, but the cheese as moon?! The deflation that follows could only be accomplished by a perfect poetic bumbler, with an unerring instinct for the wrong phrase at the wrong time. The idea of this lump of lunar lactose falling from the sky to crush the awestruck "folks" below is an incomparably brilliant anticlimax, enough to secure James McIntyre a permanent seat in the Valhalla of poetasters. Oh! McIntyre, King of Cheese!

INTERVIEW

Deep Time, Black Magic and Ugly Stuff

An Interview with Jesse Eckerlin

I CAME ACROSS HALIFAX-BASED writer Zachariah Wells' most recent book of poetry, *Track & Trace*, in what I suppose was a somewhat unorthodox fashion. Last summer I undertook an agricultural apprenticeship in Valleyfield, PEI, Wells' native province, and just happened to be working at the same Charlottetown farmers' market where, among myriad stalls of produce, meat, coffee and assorted foodstuffs, his mother sold her artisanal wares. Amongst piles of toques, mittens, sweaters and other painstakingly crafted handiworks was an unassuming table bearing some of Zachariah's books: *Unsettled, Jailbreaks: 99 Canadian Sonnets, The Essential Kenneth Leslie*, and the book mainly discussed in this interview, *Track & Trace*. I hadn't heard of him; but struck by the handsome design and inimitable illustrations of renowned visual artist Seth, I decided to browse through *Track & Trace*. I bought a copy upon finishing the first poem I flipped to, "He Finds An Acceptable Way to Grieve," the poet's ode to his deceased dog Mutt and an instance of what Wells calls below "the oft-conflicting imperatives of ... money and soul."

For awhile I thought that the clashing sensibilities involved in this experience—buying a poetry book in a farmers' market from the poet's artisan mother in a province all but clichéd into oblivion—were completely antithetical, or at the very least amusing. But upon rereading *Track & Trace* several times and conducting this interview, I realized just how mistaken I was. Nothing was out of place; in fact, a better scenario couldn't have been dreamt up as an invitation to his milieu.

Jesse Eckerlin: First of all, let me you congratulate you on the warm reception of *Track & Trace*. Readers have responded fondly to the distinctiveness of both its printing and design (somewhere between a chapbook and trade collection, but crafted with more care than is usual for either) and the assured, concise, and prescient lyrics within. Although neither a strictly linear nor thematically arranged collection, the book's thirty-four poems, despite their apparent diversity, share unmistakable affinities, and there is a rich emotional and imagistic resonance between them. For one thing, they are almost all preoccupied with the myriad personal and/or cultural legacies both inherited and bequeathed by the speaker, sometimes simultaneously. In this sense *Track & Trace* reads as both a creative rite of passage and a somewhat troubled act of self-preservation. Can you talk about some of the legacies that informed the writing of *Track & Trace* and why you felt it imperative to document them?

Zachariah Wells: This is an interesting question to me, because I'd never really thought of the book in precisely these terms until now, but it's undeniably a big part of its aboutness. I think the most honest answer is that the poems embody things that matter a great deal to me as an individual, as a member of a family, as a citizen and as a writer. So legacy was bound to pop up. We are in large measure composites of the places and people we've come from, so each of us is a legacy. And we are legacy machines, made up, to borrow Richard Dawkins' term, of selfish genes for which we are the medium of transmission.

For a poet, this extends into literary concerns, too (because literary concerns and life concerns can never really be teased apart and memes can be every bit as selfish as genes): any poet is the sum of his or her influences and every poet—or at least any who doesn't take postmodernism and its ideologies too seriously—hopes to write a thing or two that lasts at least a little while after they're gone. I'm afraid I can't answer any more specifically than that, because I didn't set out to "document" legacies per se; I just wrote a bunch of poems over a fairly extended period of time and tried to arrange them, often long after initial composition, in a complementary way. The title came out of the arrangement process (as well as from a short story by Ivan Klíma) really, as I was trying to do something that was simultaneously bold-face (track) and subtle (trace), trying to find a way (the book was published shortly after I turned thirty-three, so Dante's "the right road lost" comes into it), to forge forward but leave something behind. So yeah, legacy, eh...

JE: In the spirit of articulating matters important to both the writer and citizen at large then, part of your task seems to be an attempt to collapse the oft-held distinction between mundane and domestic reality and the so-called traditional 'intellectual objects' of literary pursuit. I'm thinking of "Rhythm" for example, where the metrics of your mother's knitting become an aesthetic yardstick against which lyrical measures are conceived, and knitting becomes a metaphor for the way disparate words are 'stitched' into larger utterances and, ultimately, poems; or "The Poetry in Him," in which, counterintuitively, your father's 'poetic qualities' are seen to reside precisely in "his honest / talk [...] stripped of artifice / and ornament." Why do you think the commonplace yields so many incandescent moments for you?

ZW: I'm glad you brought up those two poems. The book is dedicated to my parents and I think of those as the "mother poem" and the "father poem." I don't think it has a lot to do with "the commonplace," however. My mother was my first role model for actively choosing an unconventional life. A highly educated type-A personality, she chose to quit a well-paid federal civil service job, with all the security that attends such a career, and moved from Ottawa to rural PEI, a place where, at the time, she knew only one person: the man she was marrying. She stayed at home with me and my brother and once the most intensive years of child-rearing were finished, her pastimes of dyeing, spinning, knitting, weaving and designing grew into her principal occupation. The metrics of the knitting are a metonymic figuration of the lessons in rhythm—writ large—that I learned from her example: that you can dedicate your life to creativity as well as productivity; that satisfaction in life can't come from following a groove.

With the other poem, it isn't so much that those poetic qualities "reside in" my father's plainspokenness, as that it's "not hard to miss" the poetry because it's hidden beneath a taciturn exterior and because it inheres more in deeds than in words. (Conversely, it can be easy to mistake empty rhetorical grandiloquence for poetry.) My father's working life was dedicated to politics, that realm in which circumlocution and prevarication are altogether too normal. But he wasn't a politician, he was a civil servant, an advisor, an aide. It was a better setting for someone of my dad's disposition than elected office, where by necessity one has to compromise a great deal more—unless one has no interest in being elected.

We think of "speaking truth to power" as the province of otherwise disenfranchised activists, but my father's life is an example of how it can be done within the structures of power. It cost him in the end. He played a key role in the administrations of Premiers Alex Campbell (who served four terms as Premier) and Joe Ghiz, but a falling out with Ghiz over his dalliances on the federal scene (it was the Meech Lake years) and subsequent lack of favour with Catherine Callbeck and her principal advisors led to his being pushed to the margins (heading up the Housing Corporation and Workers' Compensation Board) and early retirement at an inopportune time. After that happened, he went public with his grievances against governmental mismanagement.

That's why I compare him to *King Lear*'s Kent in the poem. Kent is a loyal servant and he speaks his mind, even when it isn't in his own best interest. And even once he's banished, he still comes back to serve surreptitiously, in disguise. There's a fantastic exchange between Lear and the disguised Kent early in the play, part of which goes:

KING LEAR
What services canst thou do?

KENT
I can keep honest counsel, ride, run, mar a curious tale in telling it, and deliver a plain message bluntly: that which ordinary men are fit for, I am qualified in; and the best of me is diligence.

The other dimension of that poem is that my dad is, like my mom, someone who makes things. He built our house virtually all by himself, teaching himself how to do it as he went, and he's a very fine self-trained woodworker. From both of my parents I've learned the lesson that just because you don't know how to do something doesn't mean you should hold back and that just because something is beautiful doesn't mean it has to be useless. A poem can't be useful in the way that a sweater or a box can, but it can be insofar as it reveals to a reader something they'd never thought about before, perhaps.

I've also learned many things about fidelity, in its broadest sense—or "diligence"to use Kent's word—from both parents. "The Poetry in Him" isn't a statement of poetics along the lines of Plain Speech = Poetry. Too many other poems in the book contradict that. Rather, I think it's crucial to use language that is faithful to the subject matter and diligent in its choices. I think that's where a lot of poets go off the rails; they have a personal style that perhaps fits some subjects, but when they turn to other matters, they stick to that style and it simply isn't appropriate, so you get a slippage between structure and content. Randall Jarrell called it "the real graveyard of poets, My Own Style," the other principal danger of which is writing essentially the same poems over and over again for a lifetime.

To get back to your question, then, I think there's very little commonplace about the subjects of those two poems, so I'm not sure really that the commonplace does yield me incandescent moments. I draw far more on external reality than on pure imagination in my poems, if that's what you mean. I don't tend to think abstractly; I need the concrete world of facts and objects, people and places, as a ground to my imagination. This is perhaps a weakness for an artist who uses language as a medium, but it's one I hope that I alchemically convert into a strength. My favourite poets tend to be those who have their eyes trained on the ground rather than the heavens.

JE: The lone long-poem of the book, "After the Blizzard," seems to me an anomaly in regards to this tendency to emphasize "external reality" over "pure imagination." The physical reality of the blizzard is certainly the backdrop against which the sonnet sequence is framed, but it seems more a dramatic means to yoke a playful musicality and the embellishments of the writer, rather than an imminent threat. Much of the 'action' occurs squarely in the writer's mind, and the poem seems to emphasize this fact more explicitly than others in the collection. What was the strategy behind "After the Blizzard," and why did you include it in a collection of mostly short and self-contained lyrics?

ZW: The stupid answer to your good question is that I mostly write "short and self-contained lyrics," so I'd be unlikely to find somewhere else to put it. As long poems go, it's a pretty short one, just ninety-eight lines, and it's composed of seven sonnets, so it's really more a linked series of short poems, each with its own internal logic, than a long-poem, per se.

And yes, the poem is about an actual blizzard and its aftermath, but as you suggest, the occasion becomes a blank page on which the speaker doodles imaginatively. But he also does a fair bit outside his head. In the first sonnet, it's snowing and the speaker looks out at the blizzard as it happens. Not much else to do during a storm. He shovels his parking spot in the second section of the poem and accidentally sends snow down his own neck, which causes him to look up, where he sees the crows that become the catalyst for the third sonnet, in which the poet character finds himself at the end, bone weary from his physical exertions and writing sonnets (postmodern meta moment alert!) about, we imagine, shovelling snow. He gets tired of concrete images and so goes for a bold declarative statement, which leads to the rhetorical centrepiece of the fourth sonnet, which in turn unfolds into a primarily descriptive sonnet itemizing the state of the sidewalks and the hazards they present to pedestrians. In the sixth sonnet, the poet is himself a pedestrian, out in the world at night, stumbling through a graveyard in a half-drunken state (and coming up with crazy-bad cider-inspired similes) and he is arrested, upon exiting the graveyard like Jonah from the belly of the whale, by the wonderful spectacle of a loader clearing the street. It's a moment similar to when he sees the crows and is very much about how "external reality" engages the artist's imagination. In the seventh, the speaker is back home, "danc[ing] and shiver[ing]" because there's no heat in his flat and the poem ends with him once again contemplating the blank possibilities of the "empty parking lot." So it's a poem with a lot of movements and shifts of perspective and tone, which I think a longer poem not driven by narrative has to be, if it wants to keep a reader's interest.

As to why it's in the book, I think it fits because it is quite literally concerned with tracks and traces—which the corona form itself embodies none too subtly—but also because it has this confrontation of the urban, human world with the non-human hugeness of a once-in-a-lifetime storm, the oft-conflicting imperatives of city and self, money and soul. Standoffs of that sort come up frequently in the book.

JE: As you have just alluded to, one such recurring standoff, explored variously in such poems as "Dream Vision of the Flood" and "Water Works," is the point at which human endeavour and natural catastrophes, sometimes irreparably, collide. A poem like "Orkney Report" for instance, with lines like "The Old Man of Hoy's a peedie boy / compared with what's crumpled about him," seems an inquiry into something similar to what Gary Snyder has called "deep historical time." In previous interviews you've refused to be pigeonholed as a 'nature poet' per se; rather than contenting itself with traditional pastoral subjects, would you say that *Track & Trace* explores certain shifting ecological paradigms?

ZW: It isn't so much that I don't want to be pigeonholed as a nature poet; I just think the term is pretty meaningless. It has more to do with staking out territory in the poetry world than it does with either nature or poetry. I couldn't write traditional pastoral poems if I wanted to, if only because there's no dramatic interest in it. As Ruskin suggested a long time ago, most of what passes for "pastoral" is just sentimental treacle, "poetry written in praise of the country by men who lived in coffee-houses and on the Mall."

I tend to write about things I've seen and places I've been. I grew up in a rural area and I spent years living in some of the most isolated territory on offer in this huge country. Exposure to both bucolic settings and hostile, barren wilderness makes it rather hard for me to idealize either. (The poem of mine that was reprinted in an anthology of nature poetry was about Canada geese getting killed by the downdraft of an Airbus ...) Someone invested in the idea of being a "nature poet" will probably never tell you how boring "nature" is most of the time.

But really, everything is nature. If you write poems about anything, you're a nature poet. I'm as much a nature poet when I'm writing about city traffic—did you know that traffic flows according to the laws of fluid dynamics?—as I am when I'm writing about animals or the ocean. I'm keenly aware, as most people who pay attention to current events are, that, for whatever combination of reasons, the environment is changing fast and that the change often manifests in catastrophic events. And I have no bloody idea how it might all shake down and neither does anyone else, if they're being honest. The only thing that seems clear at this point is that we're not likely to slow down, much less stop or reverse, the temperature trends unless something radical gets invented to do it or something truly cataclysmic happens. Which makes me anxious, occasionally, in the way that living beneath a long-dormant but potentially active volcano must make people nervous as they go about their daily round. So these things show up in poems.

"Orkney Report" has a lot to do with deep time, yes, as do a number of the other poems. I read geologist Richard Fortey's great book *Earth: An Intimate History* a few years back and I think it's probably had more influence on my writing than I've realized. And if any place on earth is going to make you think about deep time, it's Orkney, with its Neolithic sites that are so old in human terms, but nothing compared with the archipelago's geologic past.

JE: In some of the poems with decidedly rural settings though, lack of idealism and sentimentality does not necessarily preclude a sense of wonder. In "Field of Floes," for instance, the speaker dreams of "get[ting] lost in the million acre flow" of ice floes off PEI's northern shore; in "Doe," the tail of the observed creature of the same name is "a beacon." It seems that even in spite of something like PEI's well documented history of agricultural exploitation, and its somewhat fraudulent tourism industry (of which, to say the least, you write unfavourably), certain mediated images retain their power to move. How do you find stable ground from which to frame an authentic emotional gesture in a cultural climate of increasingly rampant and contrived givens?

ZW: Absolutely. Sentimentality (false emotion; wishful thinking) and sentiment (genuine emotion; fraught feeling) shouldn't be confused, as they often are, for example, by some writers who self-identify as avant-garde.

If those two images you cite work—if they succeed in being unsentimental—it's because a) they contain no explicit emotional content and b) the implicit emotional content is mixed. They're both ambivalent moments. Stepping off the land and getting lost on a frozen sea with your lover may have a romantic side, but is also terrifying, life threatening. "We could" do this, but everyone reading the poem, I think, knows it ain't gonna happen. There's something melancholic about it.

Same with the doe's tail. The word "beacon" has the ambivalence built in. It's at once a summons ("beacon" shares a root with "beckon") and a warning to stay away (as with a lighthouse beacon). An earlier draft of that poem actually ended with "a summons, a warning," but it was helpfully pointed out to me by my editor that it would end more effectively on "beacon." He didn't have to tell me why this was so; I saw it right away. It rendered the image instantly more mysterious, less explicit. The mixedness of it was still there, but it was there for the reader to linger and puzzle over, rather than be informed of it and move on.

The problem of emotion in poetry is twofold: 1)Direct statements of feeling, with notable exceptions, generally fail to elicit that feeling in the reader. People who talk about their feelings all the time are tedious and so are poems with similar inclinations. 2) Unalloyed emotions—pure grief, pure terror, pure joy—don't tend to be very interesting when written down. They're pre-verbal, they activate primitive brain regions too far from our language centres. They either write white or purple. The most authentic and the most poignant emotions tend to be mixed ones, and mixed feelings defy articulation because there's more than one thing happening at one time. Which is the same thing language does in a poem. So there's a kind of black magic involved in trying to write something that instills emotion in the reader. Shortcuts are always tempting, but they almost never get you where you want to be. T.S. Eliot's idea of the objective correlative applies here.

So in this way, the ugly stuff you talk about (agricultural exploitation, fraudulent tourist bumph) can actually be an ally; by incorporating that stuff into a poem, the poem resists the sentimental lies of omission on which tourism ads depend, while keeping on board the truth of the place's beauty and the possibility to have authentic, relatively unmediated experiences of beauty there, which is what made it a draw for tourists in the first place. This reminds me of Alden Nowlan's sonnet about the

St. John River, in which he talks about the pollution and the lies of the tourist brochure, but concludes "and yet the real / river is beautiful, as blue as steel." The ambivalence the poem builds up licenses the final couplet. It's one of those rare instances in which the use of the abstract word "beautiful" is justified, I think.

JE: You seem to have a deeply rooted propensity for turning "ugly stuff" into allies: you neither resort to omitting paradoxes for the sake of convenience, nor dismiss them with token ironies. You could choose to focus on surface beauty, but that would mean embracing tourist kitsch, advertisement. There is a great segment in your tribute to Al Purdy, "At the Rebecca Cohn Auditorium," that reads "Jeez, maybe I should write flower poems / But the North I know is not the same /as the place Purdy briefly toured in '65," and then goes on to enumerate the differences. As far as legacies go, Purdy's is a tough one for Canadian poets to tackle, if only because of its near omnipresence.

In an article you wrote about Charles Bruce's *The Mulgrave Road*, "Going Back Down the Mulgrave Road," you say that "the understated Bruce, ever distrustful of trends and ever faithful to the local, has been overshadowed by more forceful poetic personalities, [and] nationalistic visionaries." In addition to fidelity to anachronism, is it some kind of aversion to the potentially nationalistic poetic tropes of an Al Purdy that prevents you from writing "flower poems"?

ZW: Ha! I guess not, because I have indeed written flower poems. The speaker in the Purdy tribute is a younger me, fresh off his first summer in the Arctic, just starting to write poems, just figuring out a few things about being an adult and being a citizen. Purdy was indeed an early influence and one I've moved beyond, as one must, but still a poet I admire at his best—even while I recognize that he has been overrated for pretty dubious reasons. And that reading at the Cohn was a pivotal moment for young me. The place was packed and the reading was amazing. I came away from it recognizing that one could devote a significant portion of one's life to writing poems and yeah, you'd probably wind up old and tired and poor, but if you were lucky and did what you did well, you might just be admired and loved for it. Which can't be said of many other occupations.

The nationalism espoused by writers of Purdy's and Atwood's generations was understandable in its time, but I don't think it's something my generation identifies with. (I didn't go north to get to know my country and write poems about it; I went north to pay for my education. The book I eventually wrote about the place was the product of seven years of actually living and working there, not of a summer excursion. Purdy didn't stay long enough to really get over the north as exotic locale.) Nationalism begets its own form of sentimentality, its own rhetorical claptrap and a lot of what Purdy wrote fell into that claptrap.

Personally, I think what's great about being a Canadian is that you don't have to have an identity. The place is too big, too heterogeneous for that. I've travelled the breadth and height of Canada and I've lived in a lot of different parts of this country—all three coasts and several of its major cities—and most of those places might as well be foreign lands to each other. Someone growing up on PEI probably has more culture in common with a New Englander than with a Vancouver Islander, who in turn would be more at home in Washington State than in Labrador. I think someone aspiring to be the poet of Guysborough County is more likely to meet with success than someone who wants to be the poet of Canada. The local, vividly realized, is more universal than the national, dimly so.

JE: My last question regards the poem "Skunk," which, judging from its placement as the closing poem of the collection, and its supplementary presence on the back cover, is of central thematic importance. The poem seems to explore the mutability of experience and memory: "When you live with a constant / scent in your nostrils, you can't / stand it at first, then come to love it, then / it grows so faint you forget its existence." It also points to a movement from youth to maturity; from the anger of the reactionary child, to the feigned acceptance of the young adult, and finally, to the forbearance of an adult. Is the final stage of this fidelity to a "constant scent" akin to the true love that dare not speak its own name?

ZW: The placement of the poem isn't so much because it's of central importance as because it was a logical poem to put last. (And it's on the cover because I loathe conventional cover copy.) I arranged the poems in a kind of arc and "Skunk," as a quiet, reflective poem, looks back on everything that precedes it. The arc is also, like the corona form of "After the Blizzard," a loop—a closed track, if you will—and I like the way "Skunk" talks to "What He Found Growing in the Woods," the book's first piece, which is very much a forward-looking poem. (Which is itself a trick of perspective, since I had to look backward to write "What He Found" and forward to write "Skunk.") The last sentence fragment of "What He Found" is "His last full head / of hair and the first faint traces of stubble." The last line of "Skunk" is "it grows so faint you forget its existence." I didn't write the poems to echo each other intentionally—they were composed two or three years apart—but the rhyme definitely helped me decide where to put them in the collection. I also really like how the book closes with that line, because poems and books, the ones we live with all our lives, can be like that scent of skunk spray.

As for what that final stage stands for, let's just say that I prefer to leave my metaphors open-ended.

Acknowledgments

Versions of some of these pieces were first published in the following periodicals and anthologies: *Arc Poetry Magazine*; *Bookninja*; *Books in Canada*; *Canadian Notes & Queries*; *Contemporary Poetry Review*; *The Danforth Review*; *The Fiddlehead*; *Language Acts: Anglo-Québec Poetry 1976 to the 21ˢᵗ Century*; *Maisonneuve*; *PoetryReviews.ca*; *The Puritan*; *The Rain Review of Books*; *Richard Outram: Essays on His Works*; *The Vancouver Review*.

"Why I Am Not a People's Poet" was delivered as a talk at the Public Poetics Conference at Mount Allison University, September 21, 2012.

"Attention Paid, Taylor-Made" won *Arc Poetry Magazine*'s Critic's Desk Prize in 2013.

Thanks to Alessandro Porco and Jesse Eckerlin for permission to reprint their interviews.

ABOUT THE AUTHOR

Zachariah Wells is the author of the poetry collections *Unsettled* and *Track & Trace*; co-author, with Rachel Lebowitz, of the children's book *Anything but Hank!*; and editor of *Jailbreaks: 99 Canadian Sonnets* and *The Essential Kenneth Leslie*. Over the past decade, his critical reviews and essays have appeared in numerous periodicals and anthologies in Canada and the US and he has won *Arc Poetry Magazine*'s Critic's Desk Prize four times. Originally from Prince Edward Island, Wells now lives with his family in Halifax, where he works as a passenger train attendant and as a freelance Zach-of-all-trades.